Improvisation for the Theater

IMPROVISATION
for the
THEATER

**A Handbook of Teaching
and Directing Techniques**

By
VIOLA SPOLIN

Originator of
THEATER GAMES

Northwestern University Press

**To Neva Boyd,
Ed Spolin, the Young Actors' Company,
and my sons Paul and Bill Sills**

Publisher's Note

The two decades since the first publication of *Improvisation for the Theater* have brought home the essential power of its problem-solving exercises—now referred to as Spolin Theater Games. They began simply as the author's way of solving directing problems in her Young Actor's Company. One day, while watching a very ordinary group of children—none of them actors—create an unself-conscious, exciting performance on stage after a few weeks of participating in workshops, she realized that such games encompassed an accessible approach to theater for all age groups. Since the publication of the book and the formation of the Compass Players in Chicago by her son, Paul Sills, and others, an entire Improvisational Theater Movement has sprung up, primarily in the form of countless workshops and small theaters all over the country and around the world (the book has been translated into a variety of languages, including Portuguese, Dutch, and German). The hallmark of these theaters is the author's game "Suggestions by the Audience" (p. 222). As a theater text the book has been ranked with the works of Stanislavsky and Artaud, and it has inspired the work of actors, directors, and writers in theater, television, and film.

In addition to its impact on the theater, the book has had wide influence in the fields of education, mental health, psychology, and even ecology, as the games bring the players closer to their individual nature, to their fellow players, and to the world they share. In workshops and seminars at the author's Theater Game Center, elementary and secondary school teachers learned the potential of theater games for solving pedagogical problems.

Since their operational structure has been said to correspond to Jean Piaget's stages of intellectual development in children, it is perhaps not surprising that they have effectively assisted learning in many areas of the curriculum.

In addition to their educational value, the games have therapeutic uses now recognized by psychologists, social workers, and speech therapists. Prisons have used the games in their rehabilitation programs, where their nonverbal approach is useful in breaking down communication barriers and their nonauthoritarian approach helps eliminate self-consciousness.

For her contribution to professional, educational, community, and children's theater, the author has received numerous awards, including the 1974 Founder's Award from the Secondary School Theater Association, and the 1983 Monte Meacham Award of the Children's Theatre Association of America. In 1979 she received the honorary degree of Doctor of Arts from Eastern Michigan University in recognition of her life-long work in enriching the lives of people of all ages from all walks of life.

Acknowledgments

I wish to thank Neva L. Boyd for the inspiration she gave me in the field of creative group play. A pioneer in her field, she founded the Recreational Training School at Chicago's Hull House, and from 1927 until her retirement in 1941 she served as a sociologist on the faculty of Northwestern University. From 1924 to 1927 as her student at her house, I received from her an extraordinary training in the use of games, story-telling, folk dance, and dramatics as tools for stimulating creative expression in both children and adults, through self-discovery and personal experiencing. The effects of her inspiration never left me for a single day.

Subsequently, three years as teacher and supervisor of creative dramatics on the WPA Recreational Project in Chicago—where most of the students had little or no background in theater or teaching—provided the opportunity for my first direct experiments in teaching drama, from which developed a non-verbal, non-psychological approach. This period of growth was most challenging, as I struggled to equip the participating men and women with adequate knowledge and technique to sustain them as teacher-directors in their neighborhood work.

I am also grateful for the insights I have had, at sporadic times throughout my life, into the works of Constantin Stanislavsky.

To my son, Paul Sills—who with David Shepherd founded the first professional improvisational theater in the country, the Compass (1956–1958)—I owe the first use of my material, and I am grateful for his assistance in the writing of the first manuscript a dozen or so years ago and his experimental use of it at the University of Bristol while a Fulbright Scholar. From 1959 to 1964 he applied aspects of this system with actors at the Second City in Chicago. The final revision of this book could only take place after I came to Chicago, observed his work with his company, and sensed his vision of where it could go.

I wish to thank all my California students who nagged me over the years; and my assistant Robert Martin, who was with me during the eleven years of the Young Actors Company in Hollywood where most of the system was developed; and Edward Spolin, whose special genius for set design framed the Young Actors in glory.

My grateful thanks to Helene Koon of Los Angeles, who helped me through the second rewrite of the manuscript, and all my dear Chicago friends and students who helped in every way they could during the arduous task of completing the third and final draft of the manuscript.

Preface

The stimulus to write this handbook can be traced back beyond the author's early work as drama supervisor on the Chicago WPA Recreational Project to childhood memories of delightful spontaneous "operas" that were performed at family gatherings. Here, her uncles and aunts would "dress up" and through song and dialogue poke fun at various members of the family and their trials and predicaments with language and jobs as newcomers to America. Later, during her student days with Neva Boyd, her brothers, sisters, and friends would gather weekly to play charades (used as WORD GAME in this book), literally tearing the house apart from kitchen to living room as pot covers became breastplates for Cleopatra and her handmaidens and drapes from the window became a cloak for Satan.

Using the game structure as a basis for theater training, as a means to free the child and the so-called amateur from mechanical, stilted stage behavior, she wrote an article on her observations. Working primarily with children and neighborhood adults at a settlement-house theater, she was also stimulated by the response of school audiences to her small troupe of child improvisers. In an effort to show how the improvising game worked, her troupe asked the audience for suggestions which the players then made into scene improvisations. A writer friend who was asked to evaluate the article she wrote about these activities exclaimed, "This isn't an article—it's an outline for a book!"

The idea for a book was put aside until 1945, when, after moving to California and establishing the Young Actors Company in Hollywood, the author again began experimenting with theater techniques with boys and girls. The creative group work and game principles learned from Neva Boyd continued to be applied to the theater situation in both workshops and rehearsal of plays. Gradually the word "player" was introduced to replace "actor" and "physicalizing" to replace "feeling." At this time, the problem-solving and point-of-concentration approach was added to the game structure.

The training continued to develop the form that had appeared earlier in the Chicago Experimental Theater—scene improvisation—although the primary goal remained that of training lay actors and children within the formal theater. The players created scenes themselves without benefit of an outside playwright or examples by the teacher-director while they were being freed to receive the stage conventions. Using the uncomplicated guiding structure labeled Where, Who, and What, they were able to put the full range of spontaneity to work as they created scene after scene of fresh material. Involved with the structure and concentrating upon solving a different problem in each exercise, they gradually shed their mechanical behaviorisms, emoting, etc., and they entered into the stage reality freely and naturally, skilled in improvisational techniques and prepared to act difficult roles in written plays.

Although the material has been drafted for publication for many years, its final form was reached after the author observed how improvisation works professionally—at the Second City in Chicago, the improvisational theater of her son, director Paul Sills. His further development of the form in use professionally brought new discoveries and the introduction of many newly invented exercises in her Chicago workshops. The manuscript underwent total revision to include the new material and to present the clearest use of the form for professional as well as community and children's theater.

The handbook is divided into three parts. The first is concerned with the theory and foundations for teaching and directing theater, the second with an outline of workshop exercises, and the third with special comments on children in the theater and directing the formal play for the community theater.

The handbook is equally valuable for professionals, lay actors, and children. For the school and community center it offers a detailed workshop program. For directors of community and professional theater it provides insight into their actors' problems and techniques for solving them. To the aspiring actor or director it brings an awareness of the inherent problems which lie before him.

1963

Preface to the Updated Edition

Over my past twenty years of living with the games/exercises, of working to keep them constantly alive and exciting, several of their key ideas have emerged as essential, and I have tried to stress them as much as possible in this new edition.* (1) The importance of group response, in which players see themselves as an organic part of the whole, becoming one body through which all are directly involved in the outcome of the playing. Being part of the whole generates trust and frees the player for playing, the many then acting as one. (2) The need for players to see themselves and others not as students or teachers but as fellow players, playing on terms of peerage, no matter what their individual ability. Eliminating the roles of teacher and student helps players get beyond the need for approval or disapproval, which distracts them from experiencing themselves and solving the problem. There is no right or wrong way to solve a problem; there is only one way—the seeking—in which one learns by going through the process itself. (3) The need for players to get out of the head and into the space, free of the restricted response of established behavior, which inhibits spontaneity, and to focus on the actual field—SPACE—upon which the playing (energy exchange) takes place between players. Getting out of the head and into the space strengthens the player's ability to perceive and sense the new with the full body. My years of working with the games have shown that this living, organic, non-authoritarian climate can in-

---

*Some of the thinking included in this preface was developed while compiling my *Theater Game File* (Evanston, Ill.: Northwestern University Press, 1989)

form the learning process and, in fact, is the only way in which artistic and intuitive freedom can grow.

When I started this work forty or more years ago, one of my most difficult problems was to capture the nonverbal essence of my approach to drama in words. Words can easily become labels, dead and useless. The word or the subject matter should not take the place of the process; it is the process of solving a problem that releases intelligence, talent, and genius. Just as in my teaching practice I change the focus when a game isn't working, so here, in this edition, I've changed some terms in order to reflect new understanding and workshop practice. Most significantly, I now use "focus" instead of "point of concentration" (although it was not possible to change this term throughout the book). Point of concentration suggests a set object. It can be a blinder, like a magnifying glass held over one object or an absent-minded professor falling off his chair while concentrating on a thought. "Focus," on the other hand, suggests to me a moving energy, like a ball in a constant state of movement, the players all acutely conscious of everything going on around them while keeping their eye on the ball. Similarly, whereas "relationship" is static and implies role playing, "relation" is a moving force—seeing, hearing, perceiving. "Motivation," a commonly used term, I have replaced with "integration." Motivation is limited and subjective; it cuts the players off from ongoing stage life, and it implies that you have to have a reason for everything. I also now even further deemphasize mime and conscious muscular memory, and I no longer recommend visualization or memorization of invisible objects/props. Instead of visualization and memorization, which are in the head (the intellect, the known) and not in the space (the intuitive, the unknown), to make the invisible visible I refer to "space" substance or objects. Space objects are projections of the unknown, the inner self, into the visible world. When one player throws an invisible ball (space object) to another, the activity makes visible the player's sharing and connecting with the player who catches the invisible ball. Here there is no time lag between facing a problem and solving it. There is no time for thinking about playing—the player plays. I use "X-area" to supplement "intuition." "Intuition" is an over-used term which means many things to countless other schools. "X-area" emphasizes the undefined and perhaps undefinable nature of intuition, the hidden well-springs, the unlabeled, beyond intellect, mind, or memory, from which the artist (the player) draws inspiration.

The most significant change in the games themselves is the addition of "Follow the Follower" (p. 61), a variation on the "Mirror" game in which no one initiates and all reflect. This game quiets the mind and frees players to enter a time, a space, a moment intertwined with one another in a non-physical, non-verbal, non-analytical, non-judgmental way. Played daily, this exercise can bring miraculous unity and harmony to a group of players; it is a thread woven through the entire fabric of the theater game process.

The changes in this new edition will, I hope, enable players to be present to the moment they are present to, to directly see and be seen, touch and be touched, know and be known. The games, I hope, will awaken the natural talent within everyone. I would like to thank Carol Sills for her assistance in preparing this edition.

1983

Contents

Contents

Contents

Alphabetical List of Exercises

List of Exercises

List of Exercises

List of Exercises

List of Illustrations

Theory and Foundation

I. Creative Experience

Everyone can act. Everyone can improvise. Anyone who wishes to can play in the theater and learn to become "stage-worthy."

We learn through experience and experiencing, and no one teaches anyone anything. This is as true for the infant moving from kicking to crawling to walking as it is for the scientist with his equations.

If the environment permits it, anyone can learn whatever he chooses to learn; and if the individual permits it, the environment will teach him everything it has to teach. "Talent" or "lack of talent" have little to do with it.

We must reconsider what is meant by "talent." It is highly possible that what is called talented behavior is simply a greater individual capacity for experiencing. From this point of view, it is in the increasing of the individual capacity for experiencing that the untold potentiality of a personality can be evoked.

Experiencing is penetration into the environment, total organic involvement with it. This means involvement on all levels: intellectual, physical, and intuitive. Of the three, the intuitive, most vital to the learning situation, is neglected.

Intuition is often thought to be an endowment or a mystical force enjoyed by the gifted alone. Yet all of us have known moments when the right answer "just came" or we did "exactly the right thing without thinking." Sometimes at such moments, usually precipitated by crises, danger, or shock, the "average" person has been known to transcend the limitation of the familiar, courageously enter the area of the unknown, and release momentary genius within himself. When response to experience takes place at this intuitive level, when a person functions beyond a constricted intellectual plane, his intelligence is freed.

The intuitive can only respond in immediacy—right now. It comes bearing its gifts in the moment of spontaneity, the moment when we are freed to relate and act, involving ourselves in the moving, changing world around us.

Through spontaneity we are re-formed into ourselves. It creates an explosion that for the moment frees us from handed-down frames of reference, memory choked with old facts and information and undigested theories and techniques of other people's findings. Spontaneity is the moment of personal freedom when we are faced with a reality and see it, explore it and act accordingly. In this reality the bits and pieces of ourselves function as an organic whole. It is the time of discovery, of experiencing, of creative expression.

Acting can be taught to the "average" as well as the "talented" if the teaching process is oriented towards making the theater techniques so intuitive that they become the students' own. A way is needed to get to intuitive knowledge. It requires an environment in which experiencing can take place, a person free to experience, and an activity that brings about spontaneity.

The full text is a charted course of such activity. The present chapter attempts to help both teacher and student find personal freedom so far as the theater is concerned. Chapter II is intended to show the teacher how to establish an environment in which the intuitive can emerge and experiencing take place: then teacher and student can embark together upon an inspiring, creative experience.

Seven Aspects of Spontaneity
Games

The game is a natural group form providing the involvement and personal freedom necessary for experiencing. Games develop personal techniques and skills necessary for the game itself, through playing. Skills are developed at the very moment a person is having all the fun and excitement playing a game has

4

to offer—this is the exact time he is truly open to receive them.

Ingenuity and inventiveness appear to meet any crises the game presents, for it is understood during playing that a player is free to reach the game's objective in any style he chooses. As long as he abides by the rules of the game, he may swing, stand on his head, or fly through the air. In fact, any unusual or extraordinary way of playing is loved and applauded by his fellow players.

This makes the form useful not only in formal theater but especially so for actors interested in learning scene improvisation, and it is equally valuable in exposing newcomers to the theater experience, whether adult or child. All the techniques, conventions, etc. that the student-actors have come to find are given to them through playing theater games (acting exercises).

Playing a game is psychologically different in degree but not in kind from dramatic acting. The ability to create a situation imaginatively and to play a role in it is a tremendous experience, a sort of vacation from one's everyday self and the routine of everyday living. We observe that this psychological freedom creates a condition in which *strain* and *conflict* are dissolved and potentialities are released in the spontaneous effort to meet the demands of the situation.[1]

Any game worth playing is highly social and has a problem that needs solving within it—an objective point in which each individual must become involved, whether it be to reach a goal or to flip a chip into a glass. There must be group agreement on the rules of the game and group interaction moving towards the objective if the game is to be played.

Players grow agile and alert, ready and eager for any unusual play as they respond to the many random happenings simultaneously. The personal capacity to involve one's self in the problem of the game and the effort put forth to handle the multiple stimuli the game provokes determine the extent of this growth.

Growth will occur without difficulty in the student-actor because the very game he plays will aid him. The objective upon which the player must constantly focus and towards which every action must be directed provokes spontaneity. In this spontaneity,

---

[1]Neva L. Boyd, *Play, a Unique Discipline.*

personal freedom is released, and the total person, physically, intellectually, and intuitively, is awakened. This causes enough excitation for the student to transcend himself—he is freed to go out into the environment, to explore, adventure, and face all dangers he meets unafraid.

The energy released to solve the problem, being restricted by the rules of the game and bound by group decision, creates an explosion—or spontaneity—and as is the nature of explosions, everything is torn apart, rearranged, unblocked. The ear alerts the feet, and the eye throws the ball.

Every part of the person functions together as a working unit, one small organic whole within the larger organic whole of the agreed environment which is the game structure. Out of this integrated experience, then, a total self in a total environment, comes a support and thus trust which allows the individual to open up and develop any skills that may be needed for the communication within the game. Furthermore, the acceptance of all the imposed limitations creates the playing, out of which the game appears, or as in the theater, the scene.*

With no outside authority imposing itself upon the players, telling them what to do, when to do it, and how to do it, each player freely chooses self-discipline by accepting the *rules of the game* ("it's more fun that way") and enters into the group decisions with enthusiasm and trust. With no one to please or appease, the player can then focus full energy directly on the problem and learn what he has come to learn.

Approval/Disapproval

The first step towards playing is feeling personal freedom. Before we can play (experience), we must be free to do so. It is necessary to become part of the world around us and make it real by touching it, seeing it, feeling it, tasting it, and smelling it— direct contact with the environment is what we seek. It must be investigated, questioned, accepted or rejected. The personal freedom to do so leads us to experiencing and thus to self-awareness (self-identity) and self-expression. The hunger for self-identity and self-expression, while basic to all of us, is also necessary for the theater expression.

Very few of us are able to make this direct contact with our

*In education, the release of intelligence—learning!

6

selves. Our simplest move out into the environment is interrupted by our need for favorable comment or interpretation by established authority. We either fear that we will not get approval, or we accept outside comment and interpretation unquestionably. In a culture where approval/disapproval has become the predominant regulator of effort and position, and often the substitute for love, our personal freedoms are dissipated.

Abandoned to the whims of others, we must wander daily through the wish to be loved and the fear of rejection before we can be productive. Categorized "good" or "bad" from birth (a "good" baby does not cry too much) we become so enmeshed with the tenuous treads of approval/disapproval that we are creatively paralyzed. We see with others' eyes and smell with others' noses.

Having thus to look to others to tell us where we are, who we are, and what is happening results in a serious (almost total) loss of personal experiencing. We lose the ability to be organically involved in a problem, and in a disconnected way, we function with only parts of our total selves. We do not know our own substance, and in the attempt to live through (or avoid living through) the eyes of others, self-identity is obscured, our bodies become misshapened, natural grace is gone, and learning is affected. Both the individual and the art form are distorted and deprived, and insight is lost to us.

Trying to save ourselves from attack, we build a mighty fortress and are timid, or we fight each time we venture forth. Some in striving with approval/disapproval develop egocentricity and exhibitionism; some give up and simply go along. Others, like Elsa in the fairy tale, are forever knocking on windows, jingling their chain of bells, and wailing, "Who am I?" In all cases, contact with the environment is distorted. Self-discovery and other exploratory traits tend to become atrophied. Trying to be "good" and avoiding "bad" or being "bad" because one can't be "good" develops into a way of life for those needing approval/disapproval from authority—and the investigation and solving of problems becomes of secondary importance.

Approval/disapproval grows out of authoritarianism that has changed its face over the years from that of the parent to the

7

teacher and ultimately the whole social structure (mate, employer, family, neighbors, etc.).

The language and attitudes of authoritarianism must be constantly scourged if the total personality is to emerge as a working unit. All words which shut doors, have emotional content or implication, attack the student-actor's personality, or keep a student slavishly dependent on a teacher's judgment are to be avoided. Since most of us were brought up by the approval/disapproval method, constant self-surveillance is necessary on the part of the teacher-director to eradicate it in himself so that it will not enter the teacher-student relationship.

The expectancy of judgment prevents free relationships within the acting workshops. Moreover, the teacher cannot truly judge good or bad for another, for *there is no absolutely right or wrong way to solve a problem:* a teacher of wide past experience may know a hundred ways to solve a particular problem, and a student may turn up with the hundred and first![2] This is particularly true in the arts.

Judging on the part of the teacher-director limits his own experiencing as well as the students', for in judging, he keeps himself from a fresh moment of experience and rarely goes beyond what he already knows. This limits him to the use of rote-teaching, of formulas or other standard concepts which prescribe student behavior.

Authoritarianism is more difficult to recognize in approval than in disapproval—particularly when a student begs for approval. It gives him a sense of himself, for a teacher's approval usually indicates progress has been made, but it remains progress in the teacher's terms, not his own. In wishing to avoid approving therefore, we must be careful not to detach ourselves in such a way that the student feels lost, feels that he is learning nothing, etc.

True personal freedom and self-expression can flower only in an atmosphere where attitudes permit equality between student and teacher and the dependencies of teacher for student and student for teacher are done away with. The problems within the *subject matter* will teach both of them.

---

[2]See Evaluation, pp. 295–297.

Accepting simultaneously a student's right to equality in approaching a problem and his lack of experience puts a burden on the teacher. This way of teaching at first seems more difficult, for the teacher must often sit out the discoveries of the student without interpreting or forcing conclusions on him. Yet it can be more rewarding for the teacher, because when student-actors have truly learned through playing, the quality of performance will be high indeed!

The problem-solving games and exercises in this handbook will help clear the air of authoritarianism, and as the training continues, it should disappear. With an awakening sense of self, authoritarianism drops away. There is no need for the "status" given by approval/disapproval as all (teacher as well as student) struggle for personal insights—with intuitive awareness comes certainty.

The shift away from the teacher as absolute authority does not always take place immediately. Attitudes are years in building, and all of us are afraid to let go of them. Never losing sight of the fact that *the needs of the theater are the real master*, the teacher will find his cue, for the teacher too should accept the *rules of the game*. Then he will easily find his role as guide; for after all, the teacher-director knows the theater technically and artistically, and his experiences are needed in leading the group.

Group Expression

A healthy group relationship demands a number of individuals working interdependently to complete a given project with full individual participation and personal contribution. If one person dominates, the other members have little growth or pleasure in the activity; a true group relationship does not exist.

Theater is an artistic group relationship demanding the talents and energy of many people—from the first thought of a play or scene to the last echo of applause. Without this interaction there is no place for the single actor, for without group functioning, who would he play for, what materials would he use, and what effects could he produce? A student-actor must learn that "how to act," like the game, is inextricably bound up with every other person in the complexity of the art form. Improvisational theater requires very close group relationships because it is from group

9

agreement and group playing that material evolves for scenes and plays.

For the student first entering the theater experience, working closely with a group gives him a great security on one hand and becomes a threat on the other. Since participation in a theater activity is confused by many with exhibitionism (and therefore with the fear of exposure), the individual fancies himself one against many. He must single-handedly brave a large number of "malevolent-eyed" people sitting in judgment. The student, then, bent on proving himself, is constantly watching and judging himself and moves nowhere.

When working with a group, however, playing and experiencing things together, the student-actor integrates and finds himself within the whole activity. The differences as well as the similarities within the group are accepted. A group should never be used to induce conformity but, as in a game, should be a spur to action.

The cue for the teacher-director is basically simple: he must see that each student is participating freely at every moment. The challenge to the teacher or leader is to activize each student in the group while respecting each one's immediate capacity for participation. Though the gifted student will always seem to have more to give, yet if a student is participating to the limit of his powers and using his abilities to their fullest extent, he must be respected for so doing, no matter how minute his contribution. The student cannot always do what the teacher thinks he should do, but as he progresses, his capacities will enlarge. Work with the student where he is, not where you think he should be.

Group participation and agreement remove all the imposed tensions and exhaustions of the competitiveness and open the way for harmony. A highly competitive atmosphere creates artificial tensions, and when competition replaces participation, compulsive action is the result. Sharp competition connotes to even the youngest the idea that he has to be better than someone else. When a player feels this, his energy is spent on this alone; he becomes anxious and driven, and his fellow players become a threat to him. Should competition be mistaken for a teaching tool, the whole meaning of playing and games is distorted. Playing allows a person to respond with his "total organism within a total environment." Imposed competition makes this harmony impossible;

for it destroys the basic nature of playing by occluding self and by separating player from player.

When competition and comparisons run high within an activity, there is an immediate effect on the student which is patent in his behavior. He fights for status by tearing another person down, develops defensive attitudes (giving detailed "reasons" for the simplest action, bragging, or blaming others for what he does) by aggressively taking over, or by signs of restlessness. Those who find it impossible to cope with imposed tension turn to apathy and boredom for release. Almost all show signs of fatigue.

Contest and extension, on the other hand, is an organic part of every group activity and gives both tension and release in such a way as to keep the player intact while playing. It is the growing excitement as each problem is solved and more challenging ones appear. Fellow players are needed and welcomed. It can become a process for greater penetration into the environment.

With mastery of each and every problem we move out into larger vistas, for once a problem is solved, it dissolves like cotton candy. When we master crawling, we stand, and when we stand, we walk. This everlasting appearing and dissolving of phenomena develops a greater and greater sight (perceiving) in us with each new set of circumstances. (See all transformation exercises.)

If we are to keep playing, then, natural extension must exist wherein each individual strives to solve consecutively more complicated problems. These can be solved then, not at the expense of another person and not with the terrible personal emotional loss that comes with compulsive behavior, but by working harmoniously together with others to enhance the group effort or project. It is only when the scale of values has taken competition as the battle cry that danger ensues: the end-result—success—becomes more important than process.

The use of energy in excess of a problem is very evident today. While it is true that some people working on compulsive energies do make successes, they have for the most part lost sight of the pleasure in the activity and are dissatisfied with their achievement. It stands to reason that if we direct all our efforts towards reaching a goal, we stand in grave danger of losing everything on which we have based our daily activities. For when a goal is superimposed on an activity instead of evolving out of it, we often feel cheated when we reach it.

When the goal appears easily and naturally and comes from growth rather than forcing, the end-result, performance or whatever, will be no different from the process that achieved the result. If we are trained only for success, then to gain it we must necessarily use everyone and everything for this end; we may cheat, lie, crawl, betray, or give up all social life to achieve success. How much more certain would knowledge be if it came from and out of the excitement of learning itself. How many human values will be lost and how much will our art forms be deprived if we seek only success?

Therefore, in diverting competitiveness to group endeavor, remembering that process comes before end-result, we free the student-actor to trust the scheme and help him to solve the problems of the activity. Both the gifted student who would have success even under high tensions and the student who has little chance to succeed under pressure show a great creative release and the artistic standards within the workshop rise higher when free, healthy energy moves unfettered into the theater activity. Since the acting problems are organic, all are deepened and enriched by each successive experience.

Audience

The role of the audience must become a concrete part of theater training. For the most part, it is sadly ignored. Time and thought are given to the place of the actor, set designer, director, technician, house manager, etc., but the large group without whom their efforts would be for nothing is rarely given the least consideration. The audience is regarded either as a cluster of Peeping Toms to be tolerated by actors and directors or as a many-headed monster sitting in judgment.

The phrase "forget the audience" is a mechanism used by many directors as a means of helping the student-actor to relax on stage. But this attitude probably created the fourth wall. The actor must no more forget his audience than his lines, his props, or his fellow actors!

The audience is the most revered member of the theater. Without an audience there is no theater. Every technique learned by the actor, every curtain and flat on the stage, every careful analysis by the director, every coordinated scene, is for the enjoyment of the audience. They are our guests, fellow players, and the last spoke in the wheel which can then begin to roll. They make the performance meaningful.

When there is understanding of the role of the audience, complete release and freedom come to the player. Exhibitionism withers away when the student-actor begins to see members of the audience not as judges or censors or even as delighted friends but as a group with whom he is sharing an experience. When the audience is understood to be an organic part of the theater experience, the student-actor is immediately given a host's sense of responsibility toward them which has in it no nervous tension. The fourth wall disappears, and the lonely looker-in becomes part of the game, part of the experience, and is welcome! This relationship cannot be instilled at dress rehearsal or in a last minute lecture but must, like all other workshop problems, be handled from the very first acting workshop.

If there is agreement that all those involved in the theater should have personal freedom to experience, this must include the audience—each member of the audience must have a personal experience, not artificial stimulation, while viewing a play. If they are to be part of this group agreement, they cannot be thought of as a single mass to be pulled hither and yon by the nose, nor should they have to live someone else's life story (even for one hour) nor identify with the actors and play out tired, handed-down emotions through them. They are separate individuals watching the skills of players (and playwrights), and it is for each and every one of them that the players (and playwrights) must use these skills to create the magical world of a theater reality. This should be a world where every human predicament, riddle, or vision can be explored, a world of magic where rabbits can be pulled out of a hat when needed and the devil himself can be conjured up and talked to.

The problems of present-day theater are only now being formulated into questions. When our theater training can enable the future playwrights, directors, and actors to think through the role of the audience as individuals and as part of the process called theater, each one with a right to a thoughtful and personal experience, is it not possible that a whole new form of theater presentation will emerge? Already fine professional improvising theaters have evolved directly from this way of working, delighting audiences night after night with fresh theatrical experiences.

Theater Techniques

Theater techniques are far from sacred. Styles in theater change radically with the passing of years, for *the techniques of the theater are the techniques of communicating*. The actuality of the communication is far more important than the method used. Methods alter to meet the needs of time and place.

When a theater technique or stage convention is regarded as a ritual and the reason for its inclusion in the list of actors' skills is lost, it is useless. An artificial barrier is set up when techniques are separated from direct experiencing. No one separates batting a ball from the game itself.

Techniques are not mechanical devices—a neat little bag of tricks, each neatly labeled, to be pulled out by the actor when necessary. When the form of an art becomes static, these isolated "techniques" presumed to make the form are taught and adhered to strictly. Growth of both individual and form suffer thereby, for unless the student is unusually intuitive, such rigidity in teaching, because it neglects inner development, is invariably reflected in his performance.

When the actor knows "in his bones" there are many ways to do and say one thing, techniques will come (as they must) from his total self. For it is by direct, dynamic awareness of an acting experience that experiencing and techniques are spontaneously wedded, freeing the student for the flowing, endless pattern of stage behavior. Theater games do this.

Carrying The Learning Process Into Daily Life

The artist must always know where he is, perceive and open himself to receive the phenomonal world if he is to create reality on stage. Since theater training does not have its practice hours in the home (it is strongly recommended that no scripts be taken home to memorize, even when rehearsing a formal play), what we seek must be brought to the student-actor within the workshop.[3] This must be done in such a way that he absorbs it, and carries it out again (inside himself) to his daily living.

Because of the nature of the acting problems, it is imperative to sharpen one's whole sensory equipment, shake loose and free one's self of all preconceptions, interpretations, and assumptions (if one is to solve the problem) so as to be able to make direct and fresh contact with the created environment and the objects and the people within it. When this is learned inside the theater world, it simultaneously produces recognition, direct and fresh contact with the outside world as well. This, then, broadens the student-actor's ability to involve himself with his own phenomenal world and more personally to experience it. Thus *experiencing* is the only actual homework and, once begun, like ripples on water is endless and penetrating in its variations.

When the student sees people and the way they behave when together, sees the color of the sky, hears the sounds in the air, feels the ground beneath him and the wind on his face, he gets a wider view of his personal world and his development as an actor is quickened. The world provides the material for the theater, and artistic growth develops hand in hand with one's recognition of it and himself within it.

Physicalization

The term "physicalization" as used in this book describes the means by which material is presented to the student on a physical, non-verbal level as opposed to an intellectual or psychological approach. "Physicalization" provides the student with a personal concrete experience (which he can grasp) on which his further development depends; and it gives the teacher and student a working vocabulary necessary to an objective relationship.

Our first concern with students is to encourage freedom of physical expression, because the physical and sensory relationship with the art form opens the door for insight. Why this is so is hard to say, but be certain that it is so. It keeps the actor in an evolving world of direct perception—an open self in relation to the world around him.

---

[3] See pp. 339–340.

Reality as far as we know can only be physical, in that it is received and communicated through the sensory equipment. Through physical relationships all life springs, whether it be a spark of fire from a flint, the roar of the surf hitting the beach, or a child born of man and woman. The physical is the known, and through it we may find our way to the unknown, the intuitive, and perhaps beyond to man's spirit itself.

In any art form we seek the experience of going beyond what we already know. Many of us hear the stirring of the new, and it is the artist who must midwife the new reality that we (the audience) eagerly await. It is sight into this reality that inspires and regenerates us. This is the role of the artist, to give sight. What he believes cannot be our concern, for these matters are of intimate nature, private to the actor and not for public viewing. Nor need we be concerned with the feelings of the actor, for use in the theater. We should be interested only in his direct physical communication; his feelings are personal to him. When energy is absorbed in the physical object, there is no time for "feeling" any more than a quarterback running down the field can be concerned with his clothes or whether he is universally admired. If this seems harsh, be assured that insisting upon this objective (physical) relationship with the art form brings clearer sight and greater vitality to the student-actors. For the energy bound up in the fear of exposure is freed (and no more secretive) as the student intuitively comes to realize no one is peeping at his private life and no one cares where he buried the body.

A player can dissect, analyze, intellectualize, or develop a valuable case history for his part, but if he is unable to assimilate it and communicate it physically, it is useless within the theater form. It neither frees his feet nor brings the fire of inspiration to the eyes of those in the audience. The theater is not a clinic, nor should it be a place to gather statistics. The artist must draw upon and express a world that is physical but that transcends objects—more than accurate observation and information, more than the physical object itself, more than the eye can see. We must all find the tools for this expression. "Physicalization" is such a tool.

When a player learns he can communicate directly to the audience only through the physical language of the stage, it alerts his whole organism.[4] He lends himself to the scheme and lets this physical expression carry him wherever it will. For improvisational theater, for instance, where few or no props, costumes, or set pieces are used, the player learns that a stage reality must have space, texture, depth, and substance—in short, physical reality. It is his creating this reality out of nothing, so to speak, that makes it possible for him to take his first step into the beyond. For the formal theater where sets and props are used, dungeon walls are but painted canvas and treasure chests empty boxes. Here, too, the player can create the theater reality only by making it physical. Whether with prop, costume, or strong emotion the actor can only *show* us.

---

[4]"Direct communication" as used in this text refers to a moment of mutual perceiving.

II. Workshop Procedures

A system of work suggests that, by following a plan of procedure, we can gather enough data and experience to emerge with a new understanding of our medium. Those who work in the theater with any success have their ways for producing results; consciously or unconsciously they have a system. In many highly skilled teacher-directors, this is so intuitive that they have no formula to give another. While this may be exciting to observe, it narrows the field to the naturally "gifted" teacher-director only, and this need not be so. How often upon viewing demonstrations and lectures on the theater have we thought, "The words are right, the principle correct, the results wonderful, but how can we do it?"

All acting problems in this handbook are charted steps in a system of teaching/learning which is a procedure that begins as simply as the realization of the first step on a path or the knowledge that one and one make two. A "how to do it" procedure will become apparent with the use of the material. Yet, no system should be a system. We must tread carefully if we are not to defeat our aims. How can we have a "planned" way of action while trying to find a "free" way?

The answer is clear. It is the demands of the art form itself that must point the way for us, shaping and regulating our work and reshaping all of us as well to meet the impact of this great force. Our constant concern then is to keep a moving, living reality for ourselves, not to labor compulsively for an end-result. Whenever we meet, whether in workshops or in performance, in

18

that meeting must be the moment of process, the moment of living theater. If we let this happen, the techniques for teaching, direction, acting, developing material for scene improvisation, or the way to handle a formal play will come from our very core and appear as if by accident. It is out of willingness to understand organic process that our work becomes alive. The exercises used and developed in this handbook grew out of this focus. For those of us who serve the theater and not a system of work, what we seek will evolve as a result of what we do to find it.

Especially in the new and exciting development of scene improvisations is this true. Only from meeting and acting upon the changing, moving present can improvisation be born. The material and substance of scene improvisation are not the work of any one person or any one writer but come out of the cohesion of player acting upon player. The quality, range, vitality, and life of this material is in direct ratio to the process the individual student is going through and what he is actually experiencing in spontaneity, organic growth, and intuitive response.

This chapter attempts to clarify for the teacher-director how to organize material for training in the theater conventions and how we can all stay away from rote teaching and meet in the area of the yet unknown. Though many may pull away, fearful of leaving the familiar cage, some of us will find each other and together preserve the vital spirit of the theater.

To come to this understanding, the teacher-director must keep a dual point of view towards himself and the student: (1) observation of the handling of the material presented in its obvious or outward use as training for the stage; (2) constant close scrutiny of whether or not the material is penetrating and reaching a deeper level of response—the intuitive.

To keep the word "intuitive" from becoming a catch-all word which we throw around or use for old concepts, use it to denote that area of knowledge which is beyond the restrictions of culture, race, education, psychology, and age; deeper than the "survival dress" of mannerisms, prejudices, intellectualisms, and borrowings most of us wear to live out our daily lives.[1] Let us rather embrace one another in our basic humanness and strive in the workshops to release this humanness in ourselves and our stu-

---

[1]Today the area commonly referred to as "the right brain."

dents. Here, then, the walls of our cage, prejudices, frames of reference, and predetermined right and wrong dissolve. We look with an "inward eye." In this way there will be no fear that a system becomes a system.

Problem-Solving

The problem-solving technique used in workshop gives mutual objective focus to teacher and student. In its simplest terms it is *giving problems to solve problems*. It does away with the need for the teacher to analyze, intellectualize, dissect a student's work on a personal basis. This eliminates the necessity of the student having to go through the teacher or the teacher having to go through the student to learn. It gives both of them direct contact with the material, thereby developing relationship rather than dependencies between them. It makes experiencing possible and smoothes the way for people of unequal backgrounds to work together.

When one has to go through another to learn something, his learning is colored by both his and the teacher's subjective needs, often creating personality difficulties and the whole experience (view) is altered in such a way that direct experiencing is not possible. The approval/disapproval critique of authority becomes more important than the learning, and the student-actor is kept in old frames of reference (his own or the teacher's), behaviorisms and attitudes remain unchanged. Problem-solving prevents this.

Problem-solving performs the same function in creating organic unity and freedom of action as does the game and generates great excitement by constantly provoking the question of procedures at the moment of crisis, thus keeping all participating members open for experiencing.

Since there is no right or wrong way to solve a problem, and since the answer to every problem is prefigured in the problem itself (and must be to be a true problem), continuous work on and the solving of these problems opens everyone to their own source and power. How a student-actor solves a problem is personal to him, and, as in a game, he can run, shout, climb, or turn somersaults as long as he stays with the problem. All distortions of character and personality slowly fade away, for true self-identity is far more exciting than the falseness of withdrawal, egocentricity, exhibitionism, and need for social approval.

This includes the teacher-director and group leader as well. He must be constantly alerted to bring in fresh acting problems to solve any difficulties that may come up. He becomes the diagnostician, so to speak, developing his personal skills, first, in finding what the student needs or is lacking for his work and, second, finding the exact problem that will work for the student. For example: if your players cannot handle more than four on stage at one time, and all talk at once creating cluttered stage picture and general confusion, presenting the exercise named TWO SCENES will clear this up for everybody. Once the problem in TWO SCENES is solved, it can only result in the students' organically understanding some of the problems of blocking. From then on, all the teacher-director needs to do (should the difficulty arise again) is to side-coach "TWO SCENES!" for the players to understand and act accordingly.[2]

And so with all the other exercises. Problems to solve problems, voice projection, characterization, stage business, developing material for scene improvisation—all are manageable through this way of working. Dogmatism is avoided by not giving lectures on acting; language is used for the purpose of clarification of the problem. This can be considered a non-verbal system of teaching insofar as the student gathers his own data within a first-hand experience. This mutual involvement with the problem instead of each other frees the air of personalities, judgment values, recriminations, fawning, etc. and is replaced by trust and relationship making artistic detachment a strong probability.

This is the challenge for all members of the workshop. Each from his own point of view mutually focuses on the problems at hand. In time the last vestiges of authoritarianism leave as all work to solve the problems of the theater. When the youngest actors are told that they will never be asked a question that they cannot answer or given a problem they cannot solve, they can well believe it.

The Point of Concentration (Focus)

The Point of Concentration releases group power and indi-

---

[2]See TWO SCENES, p. 160.

vidual genius. Through Point of Concentration, theater, the most complicated of art forms can be taught to the young, the newcomers, the old, to plumbers, school-teachers, physicists, and housewives. It frees them all to enter into an exciting creative adventure, and thus it makes theater meaningful in the community, the neighborhood, the home.

The Point of Concentration is the focal point for the system covered in this handbook, and it does the work for the student. It is the "ball" with which all play the game. While its uses may be manifold, the four following points help clarify it for use in workshops. (1) It helps to isolate segments of complex and overlapping theater techniques (necessary to performance) so as to thoroughly explore them. (2) It gives the control, the artistic discipline in improvisation, where otherwise unchanneled creativity might become a destructive rather than a stabilizing force. (3) It provides the student with a focus on a changing, moving single point ("Keep your eye on the ball") within the acting problem, and this develops his capacity for involvement with the problem and relationship with his fellow players in solving it. Both are necessary to scene improvisation. It acts as a catalyst between player and player and between player and problem. (4) This singleness of focus on a moving point used in solving the problem—whether it be the very first session where he counts the boards or chairs (EXPOSURE) or later, more complicated ones—frees the student for spontaneous action and provides the vehicle for an organic rather than a cerebral experience. It makes perceiving rather than preconception possible and acts as a springboard into the intuitive.

(1) Presenting material in a segmented way frees a player for action at every stage of his development. It sorts theater experience into such minute (simple and familiar) bits of itself that each detail is easily recognizable and does not overwhelm or frighten anyone away. In the beginning the POC may be a simple handling of a cup, a rope, a door. It becomes more complex as the acting problems progress, and with it the student-actor will eventually be led to explore character, emotion, and complicated events. This focusing upon a detail in the over-all complexity of the art form, as in a game, gives everyone something to do on stage, creates playing by totally absorbing the players and

shutting off fear of approval/disapproval. Out of this something to do (playing), teaching, directing, acting, and scene improvisation techniques arrive. As each part (detail) unfolds, it becomes a step towards a new integrated whole for both the individual's total structure and the theater structure as well. By working intensely with parts, the group is also working on the whole.

With each acting problem intrinsically interrelated to another, the teacher keeps two, three, and sometimes more guide points in mind simultaneously. While it is most essential that the teacher be aware of the part of the theater experience explored in each acting problem and where it fits into the whole fabric, the student need not be so informed. Many stage techniques may never be brought up as separate exercises but will develop along with the others. Thus rendering of character, for instance, which is carefully and deliberately avoided in the early training, grows stronger with each exercise, even though the main focus is on something else.[3] This avoids cerebral activity around an acting problem and makes it organic (unified).

(2) The Point of Concentration acts as an additional boundary (rules of the game) within which the player must work and within which constant crises must be met. Just as the jazz musician creates a personal discipline by staying with the beat while playing with other musicians, so the control in the focus provides the theme and unblocks the student to act upon each crisis as it arrives. As the student need work only on his POC, it permits him to direct his full sensory equipment on a single problem so he is not befuddled with more than one thing at a time while actually he is doing many. Occupied with the POC, the student-actor moves unhesitatingly to anything that presents itself. He is caught unaware, so to speak, and functions without fear or resistance. Because each problem is solvable and is also a focus outside the student which he can see and grasp, each successive POC acts as a stabilizing force and soon frees everyone to "trust the scheme" and let go, giving themselves over to the art form.

(3) All players, while individually working on the POC, must at the same time, as in a game, gather around the object (ball)

---

[3]See Chapter XII.

and play together to solve the problem, acting upon the POC and interrelating. This makes a direct line from player to problem (similar to the line from teacher and student to problem). This total individual involvement with the object (event or project) makes relationship with others possible. Without this object involvement, it would be necessary to become involved with one's self or one another. In making ourselves or another player the object (the ball), there is grave danger of reflection and absorption. Thus we might push each other around the field (the stage) and exhibit ourselves instead of playing ball. Relations keep individuality intact, allowing breathing space (play) to exist between everyone, and prevent us from using ourselves or each other for our subjective needs. Involving ourselves in the POC absorbs our subjective needs and frees us for relation. This makes stage action possible and clears the stage of play-writing, emoting, and psycho-drama. In time, when artistic detachment is a fact, we can then make ourselves or others the object without misuse.

(4) The Point of Concentration is the magical focus that preoccupies and blanks the mind (the known), cleans the slate, and acts as a plumb-bob into our very own centers (the intuitive), breaking through the walls that keep us from the unknown, ourselves, and each other. With singleness of focus, everyone is intent on observing the solving of the problem, and there is no split of personality. For both players and audience the gap between watching and participating closes up as subjectivity gives way to communication and becomes objectivity. Spontaneity cannot come out of duality, out of being "watched" whether it be the player watching himself or fearful of outside watchers.

This combination of individuals mutually focussing and mutually involved creates a true relation, a sharing of a fresh experience. Here old frames of reference topple over as the new structure (growth) pushes its way upwards, allowing freedom of individual response and contribution. Individual energy is released, trust is generated, inspiration and creativity appear as all the players play the game and solve the problem together. "Sparks" fly between people when this happens.

Unfortunately, understanding the Point of Concentration as

an idea is not the same as letting it work for us (accepting it wholeheartedly). Time is needed if the principle of POC is to become a part of the total integration of ourselves and our work. While many people concede the value of using POC, it is not easy to restructure one's self and give up the familiar, and so some resist in it every way they can. Whatever the psychological reasons for this, it will show itself in refusal to accept group responsibilities, clowning, playwriting, jokes, immature evaluation, lack of spontaneity, interpretation of everyone else's work to meet a personal frame of reference, etc. A person with high resistance will try to manipulate those around him to work for him and his ideas alone rather than entering into the group agreement. It oftens shows itself in resentment of what is considered a limitation imposed by the teacher or sometimes in referring to the game exercises as "kid stuff." Exhibitionism and egocentricity continue as the student-actor ad-libs, "acts," plays "characters," and "emotes" rather than involving himself in the problem at hand.

It is axiomatic that the student who resists working on the Point of Concentration will never be able to improvise and will be a continuous discipline problem. This is so because improvising is openness to contact with the environment and each other and willingness to play. It is acting upon environment and allowing others to act upon present reality, as in playing a game.

Sometimes resistance is hidden to the student himself and shows itself in a great deal of verbalization, erudition, argument, and questioning as to "how to do it" within the workshops. With skilled and clever players this is often difficult to pinpoint and uncover. Lack of discipline and resistance to the Point of Concentration go hand in hand, for discipline can only grow out of total involvement with the event, object, or project.[4]

However, at no time is the student-actor to misuse the stage, no matter what his subjective resistance may be. A firm hand must be used, not to attack or impose one's will, but to maintain the integrity of the art form. If students train long enough, they will realize this way is not a threat to them, will not destroy their "individuality"; for as the transcending power in keeping

---

[4]See Discipline Is Involvement, pp. 286–288.

the Point of Concentration is felt by everyone and results in greater theatrical skills and deeper self-knowledge, their resistance will in time be overcome.

Evaluation

Evaluation takes place after each individual team has finished working on an acting problem. It is the time to establish objective vocabulary, and direct communication made possible through non-judgmental attitudes, group assistance in solving a problem, and clarification of the Point of Concentration. All the members of the workshop as well as the teacher-director enter into it. This group help in solving problems removes the burden of anxiety and guilt from the player. Fear of judgments (one's own as well as those from others) slowly leave the players as good/bad, right/wrong reveal themselves to be the very chains that bind us, and they soon disappear from everyone's vocabulary and thinking. In this loss of fear rests release; in this release rests the abandonment of restrictive self-controls (self-protection) by the student. As he abandons these and lends himself willingly to a new experience, he trusts the scheme and takes a further step into the environment.

The teacher-director must also evaluate objectively. Was concentration complete or incomplete? Did they solve the problem? Did they communicate or interpret? Did they show or tell? Did they act or react? Did they let something happen?

Evaluation that limits itself to a personal prejudice is going nowhere. "Policemen don't eat celery," or "People don't stand on their heads in a situation like that," or "He was good/bad, right/wrong"—these are the walls around our garden. It would be better to ask: "Did he show us who he was? Why not? Did he stay with the problem? Whose good/bad, right/wrong—mine, Jonathan's, or yours? Did he keep his Point of Concentration?"[5]

In time mutual trust makes it possible for the student to give himself over to the evaluation. He is able to keep a *single* purpose in mind, for he no longer needs to watch himself, and he becomes eager to know exactly where the problem might have

---

[5]See p. 297.

gotten away from him. When he is the audience, he evaluates for his fellow actors; when he is the actor, he listens to and allows the student audience to evaluate for him, for he stands with his peers.

The kind of evaluation made by the student audience is dependent upon their understanding of the Point of Concentration and the problem to be solved. If the student is to have a greater understanding of his stage work, it is most essential that the teacher-director does not make the evaluation himself but, rather, asks the questions which all answer—including the teacher. Did they playwrite? Did he pretend or make it real? Did he move the object or let the object move him? Did he cry with his feet? Did he make contact or make assumptions? Did they solve the problem?

The student audience is not to sit by and be entertained, nor are they to protect or attack the players. If they are to help one another, Evaluation must be on what was actually communicated, not what was "filled in" (by either the actor or the audience) and not any personal interpretation of how something should be done. This furthers the whole point of process as well, for it keeps the audience busy watching not a play or story but the solving of a problem. As the student audience come to understand their role, the communication lines from audience to actor as well as from actor to audience are strengthened. Those in the audience change from passive observers to active participants in the problem.

"Assume nothing. Evaluate only what you have actually seen!" This keeps throwing the ball back to the players and sharpens their eye and their hand in finer selectivity in clarifying the stage reality. The student audience does not compare, compete, or clown; they are there to evaluate the acting problem presented and not a performance of a scene. Thus audience responsibility for the actors becomes part of the organic growth of the student. When a scene does evolve, it is added pleasure for all.[6]

The point of accepting a direct communication without interpretation and assumption is difficult for students to understand in the beginning work. It may be necessary to work hard to get this point across. Asking each member of the audience, "What did

---

[6]See Points of Observation, No. 4, in the BEGIN AND END exercise, p. 80.

the player communicate to you?" may clarify this point. It is at this time that what the student-audience "thought" the player did or "assumed" he did out of his (the student's) frame of reference can be identified as interpretation rather than the receiving of a direct communication. A player on stage either communicates or does not. The audience sees the book in his hand or does not see it. This is all we ask. The very simplicity of this is what confounds most students. If the player did not make a direct communication to the audience, the next time on stage he will make every effort to do so. If the student-audience did not receive a communication, they didn't—that is all.

Sometimes members of the student audience hold back on Evaluation, for the following reasons: first, they do not understand the Point of Concentration and so do not know what to look for; second, many students confuse Evaluation with "criticism" and are reluctant to "attack" their fellow students. Once it is understood, however, that Evaluation is an important part of the process and is vital to the understanding of the problem for both the actor and his audience, the reticence which some students might feel about expressing themselves will disappear. Third, the teacher-director may not truly "trust the scheme" himself and is unknowingly squelching the students' Evaluation by taking it over himself. The teacher-director must become the audience together with the student-actors in the deepest sense of the word for Evaluation to be meaningful.

Side Coaching

Side Coaching alters the traditional relationship of teacher-student, creating a moving relation. Side Coaching allows the teacher-director an opportunity to step into the excitement of playing (learning) in the same space, with the same focus, as the players.

It is a method used in holding the student-actor to the Point of Concentration whenever he may have wandered away. *(Keep your eye on the ball!)* This gives the student-actor self-identity within the activity and keeps him functioning at a fresh moment of experience, and, further, it gives the teacher-director his place and makes him a fellow player.

Side Coaching keeps the stage space alive for the student-actor. It is the voice of the director seeing the needs of the over-all presentation; at the same time it is the voice of the teacher seeing the individual actor and his needs within the group and on the stage. It is the teacher-director working on a problem together with the student as part of the group effort.

Side Coaching reaches the total organism, for it arises spontaneously out of what is emerging on stage and is given at the time players are in action. Because it is a further method of keeping the student and teacher relating and must therefore be objective, great care must be taken to see that it does not disintegrate into an approval/disapproval involvement instead—a command to be obeyed!

A simple, direct calling out is best. *Share the stage picture! See the buttons on John's coat! Share your voice with the audience! Write with a pen, not your fingers!* (When writing is done early in training, most players pretend by using fingers.) *You walked through a table! Contact! See it with your feet! No playwriting!* Such comments are worth a dozen lectures on blocking, projection, giving reality to space objects, etc. For they are given as part of the process, and the student-actor effortlessly moves out of a huddled position, gives the table space, and sees his fellow player. Our voice reaches his total self, and he moves accordingly.

The player who looks out inquiringly when first hearing our Side Coaching need only be coached *Listen to my voice but don't pay any attention to it,* or *Listen to my voice but keep right on going. Just stay with the problem!*

Side Coaching gives the student-actor his self-identity within the activity because it keeps him from wandering off into isolation within his subjective world: It keeps him in present time, in the time of process. It keeps him aware of the group and himself within the group.[7]

Do not confuse players with a barrage of Side Coaching. Wait for the emerging play. Remember you are a fellow player.

Side Coaching is also used to end an exercise when necessary. When "One minute!" is called out, the players must solve the problem they are working on within an approximation of that time.

---

[7]See "Detachment," p. 380.

Teams And Presentation Of Problem

All the exercises are done with teams chosen at random. Students must learn to relate with everyone and anyone. Dependencies in the smallest areas must be constantly observed and broken. This is related to the acting itself, for many actors become dependent upon mannerisms as well as on people and things. Removing crutches whenever they appear helps students to avoid developing these problems. This is why changing rooms, using circle staging as well as proscenium, and improvising in front of "cameras" and "microphones" are highly recommended.

"Counting off" is a simple device accepted by all age groups in dividing up for teams. If the teams fall into the same groupings too often, then alter the method of selection (vary numbers in counting), so that students are never quite certain just where to sit in order to fall in with their friends. This counting method eliminates the negative exposure which the slower members of a group may experience if the teams are chosen by the students themselves (captain system or whatever). It is very painful for a student to sit and wait to be asked to join a team, and such procedures should be avoided in the beginning workshops. This is as true of the student-actor of fifty as it is for one eight years old.

However, if there is a good deal of uneven development within the group in the beginning of workshops, it may be necessary to match players so as to keep everyone with as challenging partners as possible. Ways must be found to do this without pointing it up at all.

Presenting the Problem

The teacher-director is advised to present the acting problem quickly and simply. Sometimes merely writing the daily problem on the blackboard is enough. If explanations are necessary, do not try to give a long and detailed description. Simply clarify the Point of Concentration and cover the necessary material quickly as you would explain the playing of a game. Whenever feasible, give a demonstration with a few actors guided by you. Do not do this too often, however, for it may become a way of *showing* how and preventing self-discovery in the students. Do not be too concerned if all do not seem to "get it" immediately. Working on the problem itself and the group preparation (with teacher-director guiding when necessary) before doing the exercise will bring clarification to many students. If there is still confusion, Evaluation will make it quite clear for those who are slower to understand.

Along the same line, do not tell students why they are given a problem. This is particularly important with young actors and lay actors. Such verbalized predeterminations place the student in a defensive position, or his Point of Concentration will be on giving the teacher what the teacher wants instead of working at the problem. Indeed, there should be no verbalization of "what we are trying to do" for the student personally. All language is to be directed to clarify the structure of the problem alone. Let the student-actor stay with what seem to be the simple externals of the problem. He will know himself in time what Neva L. Boyd termed "the stimulation and release that is happening to his full nature."

Physical Set-Up Of The Workshops
Environment in Workshop Training

"Environment" in workshop training refers to both the physical set-up and the atmosphere existing within that set-up. Physically, whenever possible workshop sessions should be held in a well-equipped theater. While "well-equipped" does not mean an elaborate stage, the workshop area should have at least one lighting dimmer and a simple sound system (amplifier, speaker, phonograph, perhaps a microphone). If such a physical set-up is provided, then student-actors are given full opportunity to develop skills which add up to the total theater experience: acting, developing scene material, and creating technical effects.

The exercises in this handbook allow for set pieces, costumes, sound effects, and lighting to be used spontaneously during the solving of the problems. The elements needed to achieve these effects should be readily available to your student-actors as they prepare their situations. Large wooden set blocks are extremely useful, since they can be quickly transformed into counters, thrones, altars, sofas, or whatever called for. A costume rack with specially selected costume parts should be close at hand, loaded with hats of all types (chef, police, medieval, clown, etc.),

31

cloaks, robes, scarves, and a beard or two. The sound corner should be equipped with some gadgets for creating manual sound effects (cowbells, wooden sticks or blocks, tin cans, chains, buckets, etc.) as well as a few sound-effects recordings such as autos starting, trains, sirens, wind and storms, etc. Each team should choose one member to act as technician and provide whatever sound or lighting effects may be needed while improvising (see Chapter VIII).

While it is true that improvisational theaters, for the most part, use few or no real props or set pieces, the actor who is training specifically for this form should handle real props as suggested by some of the exercises in the text. Learning to use sets, costumes, lights, etc. with no more time for planning than the actors have for structuring their scenes is simply a way of stirring up action in another area of the theater—another road to the intuitive.

The atmosphere during the workshop session should always be one of pleasure and relaxation. Student-actors are supposed to absorb not only the techniques they gain from the workshop experience but also the accompanying moods.

Preparation For the Acting Problem

The student-actors should make their own decisions and set up their own physical world around the problems given them. This is one of the keys to this work. The players create their own theater reality and become masters of their "fate," so to speak (at least for fifteen minutes).

Once the teacher-director or group leader has introduced the acting problem, he retires to and becomes part of the group. As such, he should move around from group to group during the early workshop sessions, clarifying the problem and procedure wherever necessary, helping individual members to group agreement.

In Orientation, for example, even the simplest group decision on such things as group listening (p. 55) will be hard to come by. Individuals on the team will toss ideas back and forth. Some will try to tell everyone "how to do it." Moving from team to team, the teacher-director will be able to help them to come to group agreement.

This time may also be used to clarify any misunderstandings about the problem. In the first workshop, for instance, many will ask, "How do I show listening?" The teacher should not allow anyone to show them, and he remains noncommittal himself; for everyone physicalizes "listening" through his own individual structure, and there should be no chance for imitation. Encourage them to "just listen." They will soon discover that they already know how to "listen" (or "see" or "taste").

The simple group agreement of the first exercise will open the way to far more complicated situations in later exercises. If the groundwork is carefully laid, agreement on later problems—such as place (Where), character (Who), and problem (What)—will come more easily with each successive exercise.

Again, for those interested in the development of scene improvisation, this is the only way of working. Because of the nature of this art form, the finding of and use of material for scenes must evolve out of the group itself, during the process of solving a problem along with every other technique the student-actors are developing.

Timing

An acting problem must be ended when the action has stopped and the players are simply ad-libbing, making jokes, etc. This is the result of not working on the problem or not playing with one another. Side-coaching "One minute!" will let students know they must finish their scene or end their problem. This sometimes accelerates action, and the scene may continue for a while. When this does not happen, it is sometimes necessary to then call, "Half-minute!" and sometimes it may be necessary to stop the improvisation immediately.

In the early work inform students that when "One minute!" is called, they must try to solve the problem they are working on within that time. This, then, revives the POC for them and usually accelerates the scene simultaneously, which becomes an excellent point to bring up in Evaluation. When players are working on the POC, "One minute!" rarely has to be called. Interest as to what is happening on the stage remains high, as in playing a game.

Calling "One minute!" develops an intuitive sense of pace

and timing in players. For this reason it is sometimes useful to allow the student audience or chosen members of it to call time. When this is done, group evaluation on this point should be made. As a group develops this time sense, "One minute!" need rarely be called, for the players bring their scenes to their natural endings.

Timing is perceiving (sensing); it is an organic response which cannot be taught by lecture. It is the ability to handle the multiple stimuli occurring within a setting. It is the host attuned to the individual needs of his many guests. It is the cook putting a dash of this and a flick of that into a stew. It is children playing a game, alerted to each other and to the environment around them. It is to know objective reality and to be free to respond to it.

Labels and/or Concepts

The acting workshop is concerned with process, not information. And so, the teacherdirector must avoid using labels in early sessions. Keep away from technical terms such as "blocking," "projection," etc. Instead, substitute phrases such as "share the stage picture," "share your voice," etc. Far from eliminating analytical thought, the avoiding of labels will free it, for it allows the player to "share" in his own unique way; for imposing a label before its organic meaning is fully understood prevents direct experiencing, and there are no data to analyze. For instance, only when "share your voice" is understood by the actor organically and dynamically after months of use as his responsibility to his audience (making them part of the game) should the term "projection" be introduced to him. A label is static and prevents process.

In some cases, the workshop will contain student-actors with previous theater experience who will initially use the conventional stage technology. However, these terms will gradually disappear as the teacher-director establishes the general vocabulary to be used throughout training. Because the whole workshop system is based on self discovery, the undesirability of labels should be very clear in the teacher-director's mind at the outset.

Avoiding The How

It must be clear in everybody's mind from the very first

workshop session that How a problem is solved must grow out of the stage relationships, as in a game. It must happen at the actual moment of stage life (Right now!) and not through any pre-planning. Pre-planning how to do something throws the players into "performance" and/or playwriting, making the development of improvisers impossible and preventing the player in the formal theater from spontaneous stage behavior.

In almost every case a student new in the theater workshops thinks he is expected to perform. Sometimes the group leader himself is confused on this point and mistakes "performance" for growth (although in some cases this can be true). With new students pre-planning results in awkwardness and fear; with the skilled, it continues their old patterns of work. In either case very little is learned, for at best whatever comes to the student must be but a trickle struggling its way through old frames of reference and set attitudes.

Performance is confused with learning, end result with process. No matter to what extent the need for spontaneity and the taboo of the planned How are stressed, it is a very difficult point to grasp and will require constant clarification for everyone. However, when everyone understands that How kills spontaneity and prevents new and untried experiences, they will avoid conscious repetition of old actions and dialogue and trite ideas, either "borrowed" from the current TV show or from old plays they themselves have been in.

Direct communication prevents How. This is why in Evaluation each individual audience member is asked to open himself for this communication. The player makes the communication or does not, the audience sees it or does not. This, then, continues to clear up the whole problem of How; for a member of the audience cannot then decide How in his terms (interpretation) the player should have made the communication.

Pre-planning How constitutes the use of old material even if that material is but five minutes old. Pre-planned work on stage is the result of a rehearsal even if that rehearsal was but a few seconds of mental visualization. Any group of student-actors laughingly give up their hold on How when they realize that if they want to rehearse and perform they should be with a group doing a show instead of a workshop. For the unskilled, whose rehearsal can at best bring only anxious performance, a great sense of relief is evident when they realize all they have to do is play the game.

Real performance, however, opens players up for deeper experiences. When this moment arrives, it is apparent to everyone. It is the moment of the total organism working at its fullest capacity—right now! Like a flash fire, real performance is all-consuming, burning away all the subjective needs of the player and creating a moment of great excitement throughout the theater. When this occurs, spontaneous applause will come from the workshop members. (See Performance, p. 387).

Pre-planning is necessary only to the extent that the problems should have a structure. The structure is the Where, Who, and What plus the POC. It is the field upon which the game is played that is pre-planned. How the game will go can be known only when the players are out on the field.

Reminders And Pointers

The following list of reminders and pointers for both teacher (or group leader) and student rightfully should be weighed after the exercises have been used. However, a quick glance at them now will alert everyone, and the list should be reviewed while a group is working through the exercises.

1. Do not rush student-actors. Some students particularly need to feel unhurried. When necessary, quietly coach. "Take your time." "We all have lots of time." "We are with you."

2. Interpretation and assumption keep the player from direct communication. This is why we say *show*, don't *tell*. Telling is verbally or in some other indirect way indicating what one is doing. This then puts the work upon the audience or the fellow actor, and the student learns nothing. Showing means direct contact and direct communication. It does not mean passively pointing to something.

3. Note that many exercises have subtle variations. This is important, and they should be understood, for each variation is solving a very different problem for the student. Each teacher-director will find that he will make many of his own additions as he goes through the work.

4. Repeat problems at different points in the work, to see

how student-actors handle early work differently. Also, this is important when relationships with the environment become fuzzy and detail is lost.

5. How we do something is the *process of doing* (right now!). Pre-planning How makes process impossible and so becomes resistance to the Point of Concentration, and no "explosion" or spontaneity can take place, making any change or alterations in the student-actor impossible. True improvisation re-shapes and alters the student-actor through the act of improvising itself. Penetration into the POC, connection, and a live relation with fellow players result in a change, alteration, or new understanding for one or the other or both. In time, during the solving of the acting problem the student becomes aware that he is acted upon and is acting, thereby creating process and change within his stage life. The intuition gained remains with him in his everyday life, for whenever a circuit is opened for anyone, so to speak, it is usable everywhere.

6. Without exception, all exercises are over the moment the problem is solved. This may happen in one minute or in twenty, depending on the growing skills of students in playing. The solving of the problem is the scene's life force. Continuing a scene after problem is solved is *cerebration* instead of *process*.

7. Try always to keep an environment in the workshop where each can find his own nature (including the teacher or group leader) without imposition. Growth is natural to everyone. Be certain that no one is blocked off in the workshops by an inflexible method of treatment.

8. A group of individuals who act, agree, and share together create strength and release knowledge surpassing the contribution of any single member. This includes the teacher and group leader.

9. The energy released in solving the problem, flowing through the Where, Who, and What, forms the scene.

10. If during workshop sessions students become restless and static in their work, it is a danger sign. Refreshment and a new focus is needed. End the problem immediately and use some simple warm-up (object) exercise or game. Skip around the handbook and use anything that will keep up the vitality level of the group. Just be careful not to use any advanced exercises

until the group is ready for them. Be certain that Orientation and Where exercises are given students in the beginning work, however. This is as true for the professional company as it is for the lay actor and newcomer to the theater.

11. Become familiar with the many game books useful in this work.

12. Remember that a lecture will never accomplish what an experience will for student-actors.

13. Be flexible. Alter your plans on a moment's notice if it is advisable to do so, for when the foundation upon which this work is based is understood and the teacher knows his role, he can find an appropriate theater game and/or games to meet an immediate problem.

14. Just as the teacher-director watches his students for restlessness and fatigue, so he must watch himself. If following workshop he finds himself drained and exhausted, he must go carefully over his work and see what he is doing to create this problem. A fresh experience can only create refreshment.

15. While a team is working on stage, the teacher-director must observe audience reaction as well as the players' work. The audience (including himself) should be checked for interest levels and restlessness; the actors must interrelate, communicate physically, and be seen and heard as they solve the acting problem. When an audience is restless, uninterested, the actors are responsible for this.

16. The heart of improvisation is transformation.

17. Avoid giving examples. While they are sometimes helpful, the reverse is more often true, for the student is bound to give back what has already been experienced.

18. If the environment in the workshop is joyous and free of authoritarianism, everyone will play and become as open as young children.

19. The teacher-director must be careful to always stay with the POC. The tendency to discuss character, scene, etc. critically and psychologically is often difficult to stop. The POC keeps both the teacher and the student from wandering too far afield.

"Did he solve the problem?"

"He was good."

"But did he solve the problem?"

20. No outside device is to be used during playing. All stage action must come out of what is actually happening on stage. If actors invent an outside device to create change this is avoidance of relation and the problem itself.

21. Actors in improvisational theater, like the dancer, musician, or athlete, require constant workshops to keep alert and agile and to find new material.

22. Act, don't react. This includes the teacher and group leader as well. To react is protective and constitutes withdrawal from the environment. Since we are seeking to reach out, a player must act upon the environment, which in turn acts upon him, catalytic action thus creating interaction that makes process and change (building of a scene) possible. This is a most important point of view for members of the workshop to have.

23. If the student-actors are to develop their own material for scene improvisations, group selection and agreement on the simplest objects in the beginning work are essential to developing this group skill.

24. The response of an audience is spontaneous (even when the response is boredom), and with rare exception (as when large numbers of friends and relatives are present), can be considered just. If the actors realize that they do not face a "put-on" response, they can then play with the audience as they would with another team. An actor can be reassured, "If they were a bad audience, then, of course, they deserve to be punished."

25. Watch for excessive activity in early sessions of workshop; discourage all performing, all cleverness. Students with previous training, natural leadership, or special talent will often ignore the POC just as the fearful one will resist it. Keep everyone's attention focused on the problem at all times. This discipline will bring the timid ones to fuller awareness and channel the freer ones towards greater personal development.

26. Let all scenes develop out of the agreed stage environment. The players must help each other "make do" with what is at hand if they are to truly improvise. As in games, the student-actors can play only by giving complete attention to the environment.

27. Discipline imposed from the outside (emotional tug-of-war for position) and not growing out of involvement with the

problem produces inhibited or rebellious action. On the other hand discipline freely chosen for the sake of the activity becomes responsible action, creative action; it takes imagination and dedication to be self-disciplined. When the dynamics are understood and not superimposed, rules are abided by, and it is more fun that way.

28. Keep the fine line between emoting and perceiving always clear within the workshop by insisting upon concise physical expression (physicalizing) and not vague or stale feeling.

29. The sensory equipment of students is developed with every tool at our command, not to train for mechanical accuracy in observation, but for strengthening perception towards their expanding world.

30. Unless needed to solve a specific problem in a play, re-membered experiences (recalls) are avoided as the group works for immediate (right now) spontaneous ones. Every individual has enough muscular memory and stored-away experience that can be used in a present-time situation without deliberately abstracting it from the total organism.

31. If student and teacher are freed from ritual and authoritarianism and allowed to share this freeing of their creativity, no one needs to dissect and examine his emotions. They will know that there are many ways of expressing something—that cups, for instance, are held differently by different people and different groups.

32. By helping to free the student-actor for the learning process and by inspiring him to communicate in the theater with dedication and passion, it will be found that the average person will not fail to respond to the art form.

33. Warm-ups should be used before, during, and after work-shop sessions when necessary. They are brief acting exercises that refresh the student as well as catering to particular needs as seen by the teacher-director during each session.

34. Stage life comes to the player by his giving life to the object. Giving life to the object prevents him from mirroring himself.

35. Invention is not the same as spontaneity. A person may be most inventive without being spontaneous. The explosion does

not take place when invention is merely cerebral and therefore only a part or abstraction of our total selves.

36. The teacher-director must learn to know when the student-actor is actually experiencing, or little will be gained by the acting problems. Ask him!

37. Never use the advanced acting exercises as a bribe. Wait until students are ready to receive them.

38. Allow students to find their own material.

39. Self-discovery is the foundation of this way of working.

40. Do not be impatient. Don't take over. Never force a nascent quality into false maturity through imitation or intellectualization. Every step is essential for growth. A teacher can only estimate growth, for each individual is his own "center of development."

41. The more blocked, the more opinionated the student, the longer the process. The more blocked and opinionated the teacher or group leader, the longer the process.

42. Tread gently. Keep all doors open for future growth. This includes the teacher and leader of the group as well.

43. Do not be concerned if a student seems to be straying far from the teacher's idea of what should be happening to him. When he trusts the scheme and has pleasure in what he is doing, he will give up the bonds that keep him from release and full response.

44. Every individual who involves himself and responds with his total organism to an art form usually gives back what is commonly called talented and creative behavior. When the student-actor responds joyfully, effortlessly, the teacher-director will know that the theater is, then, in his very bones.

45. Always work to achieve the universal selection, the essence understood by all who see it.

46. Ad-libbing and wordiness during the solving of problems constitutes withdrawal from the problem, the environment, and each other. Verbalizing becomes an abstraction from total organic response and is used in place of contact to obscure the self, and when cleverly done, this is difficult to catch. Dialogue, on the other hand, is simply a further expression of a total human communication (connection) onstage

47. Train actors to handle theatrical reality, not illusion.

48. Do not teach. *Expose* students to the theatrical environment through playing, and they will find their own way.

49. Nothing is separate. In the unity of things rests growth and knowledge. Technical facts about the theater are available to everyone through many books. We seek far more than information about the theater.

50. In the seed rests the flowering tree. So must the acting problems hold within them the prefiguring of their results from which "the individual in the art and the art in the individual" can flourish.

51. To evolve problems to solve problems requires a person with rich knowledge of his field.

52. Creativity is not rearranging; it is transformation.

53. Sentiment, tear-jerking, etc. are cultural weapons. On our stages, let us cry and laugh not from old frames of reference but from the sheer joy of watching human beings explore a greater beyond.

54. Imagination belongs to the intellect. When we ask someone to imagine something, we are asking them to go into their own frame of reference, which might be limited. When we ask them to *see*, we are placing them in an objective situation where reaching out into the environment can take place, in which further awareness is possible.

55. Tension should be a natural part of the activity between players without every scene ending in a conflict to make something happen (release can come out of agreement). This is not easily understood. A rope between players might set up opposite goals (conflict) in a tug-of-war, yet a rope between players pulling them all up a mountain could have similar tension with all pulling together towards the same goal. Tension and release are implicit in problem-solving.

56. For improvisational theater, a player must always see and direct all action to his fellow players and not to the character he is playing. In this way each player will always know to whom to throw the ball, and players can help each other out. During performance and workshop, knowing this, when one has gone astray, the other can pull him back into the scene (game).

57. Some students find it very difficult to keep from "writing a play." They remain separate from the group and never inter-

relate. Their withdrawal blocks progress during the group-planning sessions and while working onstage. They do not enter into relationships but manipulate their fellow students and the stage environment for their own purposes. This "playwriting" within the group violates the group agreement, prevents process with the other players, and keeps the user from achieving an expanding creative experience of his own. Playwriting is not scene improvisation. Scene improvisation can only evolve out of group agreement and playing. If playwriting continues as the session progresses, the players do not understand the POC. Sometimes a whole group, not understanding this point, will all be playwriting.

58. The player must be aware of himself in the environment equally with other players. This gives him self-identity without the need for exhibitionism. This is equally true of the teacher or group leader.

59. Work for equality in the workshops and retreat from imposing the teacher's authority. Allow the acting exercises to do the work. When students feel they "did it themselves," the teacher has succeeded in his role.

60. Caution: if students consistently fail to solve the problem and fall back on ad-libbing, playwriting, joke-making, and working separately, with body and body movement misshapened and distorted, their whole foundation is shaky. They have been rushed, or the function of group agreement and the POC has never been understood. They must go back to the earlier exercises and work on the simplest object involvements until they are sure enough of the beginning material to advance successfully.

61. No one can play a game unless he is intent on both the object and his fellow player.

62. Improvising in itself is not a system of training. It is one of the results of the training. Natural unrehearsed speech and response to a dramatic situation are only part of the total training. When "improvising" becomes an end in itself, it can kill spontaneity while fostering cleverness. Growth ceases as the performers take over. The more gifted and clever the players, the more difficult it is to discover this. Everyone ad-libs every waking hour of the day and responds to the world through his senses. It is the enriching, restructuring, and integration of all of these daily life responses for use in the art form that makes up the

training of the actor for scene improvisation and formal theater.

63. A moment of grandeur comes to everyone when they act out of their humanness without need for acceptance, exhibitionism, or applause. An audience know this and responds accordingly.

64. It takes a penetrating eye to see the environment, one's self within it, and make contact with it.

65. All of us must constantly dig around, above, and below, cutting away the jungle to find the path.

66. In playing, for better or for worse we all throw ourselves into the same pool.

67. An audience is neither refreshed nor entertained when not included as part of the playing.

68. A fixed attitude is a closed door.

69. When urgency (anxiety) appears, find the POC and hang on. It is the tail of the comet.

70. Individual freedom (expressing self) while respecting community responsibility (group agreement) is our goal.

71. The game exercises train for formal theater as well. Keep students working with both formal and improvisational theater for a rounded experience.

72. Rote response to what is going on is a treadmill.

73. Student-actors hang on to themselves out of sheer desperation, fearful they might "fall off the cliff."

74. Acting is doing.

75. Right of individual choice is part of group agreement.

76. No one player can decide by himself that a scene (game) is ended even if his theater sense is correct. If for any reason a player wishes to leave the scene, he may do so by inciting action within the group to end the scene by solving the problem, or, failing that, he may find a reason to exit within the structure of the scene.

77. Group agreement is not permissiveness; it simply keeps everyone playing the same game.

78. Let the object put us in motion.

79. It is difficult to understand the need for a "blank" mind free of preconceptions when working on an acting problem. Yet everyone knows that you cannot fill a basket unless it is empty.

80. Contact comes out of our sensory equipment. Self-protection (assumption, prejudices, etc.) keeps us from contact.

81. It takes courage to move out into the new, the unknown.

82. The theater games are interactive. If students do not show some integration of earlier exercises when working on new ones, the workshops may be pushing ahead too quickly.

83. When players are always alerted and willing to come to each other's aid as needed, each member of the cast is given a sense of security. This mutual support brings a feeling of well-being to the audience.

84. Any player who "steals" a scene is a thief.

85. A close-working group in improvisational theater often communicates on a non-verbal level with uncanny skill and swiftness.

86. Improvisation is not exchange of information between players; it is communion.

87. Any player who feels urgent about the game and plays it alone does not trust his fellow players.

88. Many want only to reaffirm their own frame of reference and will resist a new experience.

89. Players must learn to use any and every break made during the solving of problems for the onstage event. Breaks, for the most part, are momentarily pulling away from the stage environment and relationships. If this happens through laughter, for instance, the teacher-director simply side-coaches, "Use your laughter." This is easily picked up by the player, and he utilizes the energy and "legalizes" it within the scene. A student-actor soon learns that there is no such thing as a break on stage, for anything that happens is energy that can be channeled into the mainstream of the playing.

90. On stage, one's *taking* is the other's *giving*.

91. Everyone, including the teacher-director, is strengthened and moves towards action and leadership when reasons for not doing something (or doing something) are not acceptable. The simple statement, "There is always a reason," keeps the student from verbalizing reasons further. It is important to know that each and every reason is valid, whether it be socially acceptable or not, whether it be in truth "a sick grandmother" or just dilly-dallying, for in every case the reason created the present problem, whether

it be lateness to rehearsal or a quarrel between players. When the youngest actor knows that the only thing that matters is to keep the game going and that a reason is but a past step that holds up the playing, he is freed from the need to be servile. Reasons have value to us only when they are an integral part of and help us to understand the present situation. Any other reason is imposed. It is a private matter and therefore useless except for possible subjective reasons.

92. An object can be put in motion only through it's own nature and will not respond to manipulation. To transform or alter an object requires total absorption without meddling. Let it happen! Stay out of it!

93. The question often arises, "Is the child more fanciful, freer than the adult?" Actually, when the adult is freed for the experiencing, his contribution to scene improvisation is far greater.

94. No one knows the outcome of a game until he plays it.

95. Without the other player, there is no game. We cannot play tag if there is no one to tag us.

96. Scene improvisation will never grow out of the artificial separation of players by the "star" system. Players with unusual skills will be recognized and applauded without being separated from their fellow players. Group harmony pleases an audience and brings a new dimension to the theater.

Exercises

*The workshop sessions in this section
can be used in progressive sequence.*

III. Orientation

Orientation must be given to each new student, particularly in the case of lay actors. The first exercise in Exposure and the subsequent exercises of Involvement provide the foundations upon which all following problems are laid.

This chapter contains an outline for five Orientation sessions. It should be noted that the material set up within each session may be covered completely at two or three meetings or may require additional sessions, depending upon the size of the group and their response. The teacher-director would do well to take her time in covering this material, no matter how many sessions this entails.

Orientation Purposes

Orientation is not to be looked upon as a mere introductory or "getting acquainted" process. It is, instead, the important first step set before the student-actor; and, as such, it has significant value for the beginner. Indeed, student-actors who do not receive a proper Orientation are generally much slower to grasp the subsequent acting problems. This is particularly true when they have missed Exposure. Even highly trained actors benefit from the clarified communication and the definition of terms which the Orientation experience brings them.

1. It establishes the non-acting, problem-solving approach by bringing the first organic awareness of self, space, and environment to the student. It is the first step in removal of the subjective pretend/illusion response.

49

2. It helps the student begin to relate to Space Objects.

3. It takes the students over the first step in Involvement with Space Objects. It sets the reality of the Invisible among them.

4. It sets up the technique of theater games and brings fun and spontaneity into the acting exercises.

5. It encourages group agreement and individual participation in making decisions.

6. It establishes group agreement and the necessity of interdependent action to solve the problem.

7. It is the first step in breaking the student's dependency upon the teacher by establishing the teacher as part of the group.

8. It introduces the actors' responsibilities to the audience and shows them how to include the audience as part of the game.

9. It introduces the audience's responsibility towards the actors and presents the audience (students and teacher-director alike) as an evaluator, not as a judge, for it removes judgmental words from the evaluation. It eliminates personal interpretations and assumptions which spring from limited frames of reference and shows how to turn evaluation away from the personalities of both the actors and the audience. It creates mutual focus on the problem at hand.

10. It introduces the student-actor to the Point of Concentration and to the need for directed (focused) energy while on stage. "Keep your eye on the ball!"

11. It establishes a working vocabulary between the teacher-director and the student.

12. It induces the student to meet himself and make his first personal physical analysis of his "feelings" (in determining tensions) and reduces his fears of the audience, the activity, and the teacher director.

13. It gives each student the right to his own observations and allows him to select his own material.

14. It sets the tone for the work to follow—adventuring and non-forcing, the awakening of the intuitive.

First Orientation Session

If the following outline is thoroughly understood and absorbed into our reading attitude when going through this handbook, we will have no trouble in making the exercises our own. Simply stated, here are the components which we bear in mind as we go through each exercise:

1. Introduction to the exercise
2. Point of Concentration
3. Side Coaching
4. Example
5. Evaluation
6. Points of Observation

Exposure

Divide the total group into halves. Send one half to stand in a single line across the stage, while the other remains in the audience. Each group—audience and on stage—is to observe the other. Coach: "You look at us. We'll look at you." Those on stage will soon become uncomfortable. Some will giggle and shift from foot to foot; others will freeze in position or try to appear nonchalant. If the audience starts to laugh, stop them. Just keep coaching: "You look at us. We'll look at you."

When each person on stage has shown some degree of discomfort, give the group that is standing a task to accomplish. Counting is a useful activity, since it requires focus: tell them to count the floorboards or the seats in the auditorium. They are to keep counting until you tell them to stop, even if they have to count the same things over. Keep them counting until their discomfort is gone and they show bodily relaxation. Then their bodies have a natural look, although at first they continue to show signs of years of held muscles.

When the initial discomfort has disappeared and they have become absorbed in what they are doing, reverse the groups: the audience is now on stage, and the actors have become the audience. Handle the second group just as you did the first. Do not tell them that you will give them anything to do. The direction to count (or whatever is useful) should be given only after they too have become uncomfortable.

Exposure Group Evaluation

When both groups have been on stage, instruct all the students to return to the audience. Now question the whole group about the experience they have just had. *Be careful not to put words into their mouths.* Let players discover for themselves how they felt. Discuss each part of the exercise separately.

How did you feel when you were first standing on stage?

There will be few answers at first. Some might say, "I felt self-conscious" or "I wondered why you had us standing there." Such answers are generalities which indicate the student's resistance to the exposure he has just experienced. Try to break down the resistance. For instance, ask the audience:

How did the actors look when they first stood on stage?

The members of the audience will be quick to respond, since they will readily forget that they also were "the actors" themselves. Although they may also use generalities, they will speak up more freely when talking about the others.

Encourage the actors to describe their physical responses to their first experience on stage. It is far easier for them to say "The calves of my legs were tight" or "My hands felt bloated" or "I felt out of breath" or "I felt tired" than it is to admit "I was afraid." But you may not get even this physical description until you ask directly:

How did your stomach feel?

When these physical descriptions are flowing freely, then allow all the students to speak up in as much detail as they wish. You will find that the student who previously covered up and insisted he was comfortable when first standing on stage will suddenly remember that his lips were dry or the palms of his hands were moist. Indeed, as their concern about self-exposure subsides, they will speak about their muscular tensions almost with relief. There will always be a few who will remain resistant; but they will be influenced by the group's freedom in time and should not be singled out at the beginning.

Keep the discussion brief and on a group level. Steer them away from emotional responses and generalities. If a student says, "I felt self-conscious," just reply: "I don't know what you mean—how did your shoulders feel?"

When the first part of the exercise has been fully discussed, then move on to the second part.

How did you feel when you were counting the boards?

Be careful not to refer to it as "when you had something to do." Let this realization come to each student in his own way, particularly when working with lay actors and children. (Presumably, all professional actors already know that "something to do" on stage is what we seek. This "something to do" allows the player to receive the environment.)

What about the fluttering in your stomach? What happened to your watery eyes? Did the stiffness leave your neck?

The answer will be, "It went away"; and why it went away will soon become evident: "Because I had something to do."

And it is this "something to do" (focused energy) that we call the actor's Point of Concentration. Quickly explain to your students that counting the boards (their "something to do") will be replaced by a different acting problem each time they do an exercise; and that this acting problem, this something-to-do, will be called their Point of Concentration.

Sensory Awareness[1]

At this point, the group should be greatly released and receptive—ready for a short discussion of the senses and their value as tools. When it is pointed out that, in stage life, mashed potatoes are often served as ice cream and stone walls are actually made of wood and canvas (indeed, in improvisational theater, props and scenery are rarely used at all), students will begin to understand how an actor through his sensory (physical) equipment must make visible for an audience what is not visible.

This physical or sensory involvement with objects should be firmly established in the student-actor in the beginning sessions. It is a first step on the path to building other and more complex stage relationships. The object agreed upon is the *one* reality between the players around which they gather. This is the first step in group agreement. The following exercises provide the basis for developing this sensory awareness.

---

[1] RANDOM WALK used with sensory-awareness exercises is especially valuable for children (Chapter IX).

SEEING A SPORT

Two teams. Players divide by counting off in twos. This is the first random team grouping and is most important.

By *group agreement*, the team decides what sport they are going to watch. When group agreement has been reached, the team goes on stage. Players themselves are to call "Curtain!" when they are ready.

POINT OF CONCENTRATION: on seeing

SIDE COACHING: *See with your feet! See with your neck! See with your whole body! See it 100 times larger! Show us, don't tell us! See with your ears!*

POINTS OF OBSERVATION

1. Tell the students beforehand that the event they are going to watch is taking place some distance away from them (so they must concentrate on watching closely). This is the first step in getting them out into the environment. If distance is not stressed, they will sit with their eyes cast downward, never venturing away from their immediate surroundings.
2. While the group is watching, side-coach frequently. If a student looks at you wonderingly when you first call out, tell him to hear your voice but to keep his concentration on watching. If the POC (seeing) is sustained (as in the counting of the boards during EXPOSURE), tension will be released, fear will be well on the way out.
3. The individuals on a team are not to have any interplay during the "seeing" but are to individually watch the event. This is a simple way of getting single or individual work while all are still within the security of a group.

SEEING A SPORT, RECALL

Full group.

All sit quietly and think of a time when they were seeing a sport, whether ten years ago or last week.

POINT OF CONCENTRATION: on the whole scene—seeing the colors, hearing the sounds, watching the people, following the movement, etc.

SIDE COACHING: *Focus on colors! Listen for sounds! Concentrate on smells! Now put them all together! See movement! Focus on what's above, below, around you.*

POINTS OF OBSERVATION

1. Recalls for the most part should be avoided, since they are more useful clinically than for the art form. Sensory exercises are given to provide the student-actors with a quick example of the vastness and availability of past experience. Present experience is the aim of the workshops, but recalls will arise and be spontaneously selected when needed. (See Reminders and Pointers, No. 30, p. 40, and Definition of Terms.)
2. "Seeing" homework: Tell the students to take a few moments out of each day to concentrate on seeing the things around them, noticing colors, listening to sounds, observing the environment.

LISTENING TO THE ENVIRONMENT

All are to sit quietly for one minute and listen to the sounds of the immediate environment. They then compare the sounds they heard: birds, traffic, creaking chairs, etc.

POINT OF CONCENTRATION: on hearing the sounds around them.

POINT OF OBSERVATION

Assign this exercise as homework, to be done a few minutes each day.

WHAT AM I LISTENING TO?

Two teams

Each team decides (by group agreement) what they will listen to. They are to choose either a lecture or a musical program and should decide specifically what type of lecture or concert it is to be (e.g., classical music, psychology, jazz).

POINT OF CONCENTRATION: on listening.

See SEEING A SPORT, p. 54, for side coaching and points of observation.

Listening homework: Tell the students to take a moment or two out of every day to concentrate on the sounds around them.

FEELING SELF WITH SELF

Group remains seated in audience.

Beginning with the bottoms of the feet, players are to feel what is against their bodies at each point. The feet feel the stockings, the shoes, and the floor beneath them; the legs feel the slacks or the stockings; the waist feels the belt; the finger feels the ring; the teeth feel the lips; etc.).

POINT OF CONCENTRATION: on feeling self with self.

SIDE COACHING: *Feel self with self! Feel your feet with your feet, your legs with your legs! Feel the space! Let the space feel you!*

When they have felt all the parts of their body, then coach players to stand up and walk through the space. (See SPACE SUB-STANCE, p. 81.)

POINTS OF OBSERVATION
1. Warn the students not to touch the parts with their hands but to feel with the various parts of their bodies.
2. Coach continuously throughout the exercise.
3. "Feeling" homework: Tell the students to take a moment each day to feel themselves pushing through the atmosphere while walking. Tell them to reach out into the atmosphere with the surface of their body.

IDENTIFYING OBJECTS GAME

Players stand in circle. One player is called to center, where he stands with his hands behind his back. Teacher-director slips some object into his hands. Using his sense of feel, he is to discover what the object is.

Ask the player: *What color is it? How is it shaped? How big is it? What is it for?*

POINT OF OBSERVATION

It is best to choose objects that are fairly recognizable, although not well known or used every day (e.g., poker chip, playing card, paper of pins, pencil sharpener, comb case, rubber stamp, apple).

GROUP TOUCH EXERCISE #1

Have the group feel a single object that they all have used hundreds of times, such as soap.

Ask the players: *Do you think your hand remembers the feel of soap?* The answer will be a unanimous "yes!"

Change objects after a time, keeping them familiar.

POINT OF CONCENTRATION: on feeling the object.

SIDE COACHING: *Let your hand remember!*

POINT OF OBSERVATION

Go directly into the next exercise after the players have solved this problem.

GROUP TOUCH EXERCISE #2

Two teams.

Each group is to select some familiar object or substance (sand, clay, etc.) through group agreement. When group agreement has been reached, team goes on stage. All members use the same objects or substances simultaneously.

POINT OF CONCENTRATION: to focus all energy on the object—its size, shape, texture, temperature, etc.

SIDE COACHING: *Feel the texture! Feel its temperature! Feel its weight! Feel its shape!*

POINT OF OBSERVATION

"Touch" homework: Tell the students to take a few minutes out of every day to pick up and handle an object, then put the object down and try to recall how it felt.

TASTE AND SMELL

Two teams.

Each group is to select something very simple to eat. When group agreement has been reached, first team goes on stage and proceeds to eat, smelling and tasting the food as they go along.

POINT OF CONCENTRATION: to taste and smell the food.

SIDE COACHING: *Chew the food! Feel its texture in your mouth! Taste the food! Let it go down your throat!*

POINT OF OBSERVATION

"Taste" and "Smell" homework: While eating at home, the students are to take a few minutes to concentrate on the taste and smell of their food.

EVALUATION OF SENSORY EXERCISES

Was concentration complete or incomplete? It probably varied, since it takes time to learn concentration on stage. Stress that when concentration on the problem was complete, we, the audience, could *see*.

What were they handling, seeing, listening to, etc.? Keep this discussion centered on the whole group effort, not on individuals.

Did they *show* us or *tell* us? Even if they did not speak but used very obvious physical actions rather than focusing energy on the problem, they were telling rather than showing. For instance, if a player "pantomimed" what he saw while watching a baseball game, then he was telling. If, on the other hand, he held on tightly to the problem of seeing, he made good use of the Point of Concentration.

Showing becomes a physicalization of seeing and is not a pantomime. It grows out of the problem and is not imposed upon it. Telling is calculated and comes from the head; showing is spontaneous and comes from the intuitive.

POINTS OF OBSERVATION FOR SENSORY EXERCISES

1. These exercises use the first random team-groupings which will be part of all subsequent workshop sessions. In this case, with only two large teams, the students can simply count off in twos.
2. Each team must come to group agreement before going on

stage. There should be no interplay or dialogue on stage between players during these exercises. In this way, premature situations are avoided and thus "acting." They are working alone together, you might say.

3. Each student is to work individually on the sensory problems while remaining a part of the group. Do not ask separate individuals to perform during this first session. The group security is essential if the individual is to release his muscle hold (fears).

4. When "Curtain!" must be called by a team ready to start an exercise, do not appoint anyone to do this, but let them—as individuals or a group—step spontaneously into the theater experience by calling for their curtain. As simple as this may seem, it is most important. The call for "Curtain!" is, in effect, the magical rising of the actual theater curtain, even though the "theater" may be nothing more than a row of chairs and an open space at the end of a large room.

5. If some students look to see what their neighbors are doing after "Curtain!" has been called, side-coach: *Everyone listens in his own way! Keep your point of concentration on the problem, not on your neighbor!* While a percentage of every age group of students will "peek" in this way, it is more prevalent among children (see The Uncertain Child, p. 289). Stopping the exercise momentarily to explain that it is not a MIRROR (imitation) EXERCISE should clear it up for students. Do not point out the player who is doing the peeking. He does it out of a need to "do right" and will soon learn that there is no right or wrong way to solve a problem.

6. Do not begin Evaluation until all the students have had their chance on stage.

7. It is during the Evaluation that the students' value judgments of good/bad–right/wrong are replaced with the impersonal terms of complete/incomplete.

8. Do not dwell on the problem too long. These exercises are the first step in helping the student to recognize that physical memory exists within him and can be called up intuitively whenever he needs it. They show him that he need not withdraw into a subjective world—that he need not move into a cloud of past memories—when working in the theater or the classroom.

9. Side coaching during these exercises should help to free bodily response in the student-actors. If an individual resists this side coaching, call out: *Don't think about what I'm saying! Let your body listen!*
10. It is advisable for the teacher-director to end the exercises at this early stage, rather than waiting for the student-actors to end them.
11. Discourage all jokes, premature situations, etc. by keeping the students' concentration on the reality.
12. Avoid the parlor-game attitude which these exercises might provoke. The audience is not to guess—the audience must know through what the actors show (communicate).
13. Although sensory awareness will be a part of every Evaluation from now on, it will rarely be the main Point of Concentration. Instead, it will be considered a secondary part of every problem, to be developed along with other skills.

MIRROR EXERCISE #1

Two players.

A faces B. A is the mirror (the follower), and B initiates. A reflects all B's movements and facial expressions. While looking into the mirror, B takes a simple activity such as washing or dressing. After a time, reverse the roles with B playing the mirror and A initiating the movement.

POINT OF CONCENTRATION: mirror reflections of the initiator's movements, from head to foot. Direct seeing.

SIDE COACHING: *Reflect only what you see—not what you think you see! Change! Change!*

POINTS OF OBSERVATION

This exercise can give you a quick index into each student's natural sense of play, clowning, inventiveness, ability to create tension, and timing. Look for:

In A	1.	body alertness
(follower)	2.	direct seeing (no imitation)
	3.	ability to stay with B and not make assumptions; e.g., if B takes a familiar activity like putting on

makeup, does A anticipate and therefore assume the next action, or does A stay with B?

4. ability to provide true reflection; e.g., if B uses right hand, does A use right hand or opposite hand?

In B
(initiator
of activity)

1. inventiveness (are his actions more than pedestrian?)
2. exhibitionism (does he joke to get audience laughing?)
3. humor (does he "fool" the mirror and alter actions?)
4. variation (does he, without coaching, change movement rhythms?)

WHO IS THE MIRROR?

Have student-actors use this exercise without telling their audience which one of the two is the mirror. This effort to confound the audience demands a heightened concentration and produces a penetrating involvement with each other. The flowing movement dissolves the walls between players, reflecting themselves being reflected. They look and *see* their fellow player.

FOLLOW THE FOLLOWER

Two players.

Players begin by playing the "Mirror" game. When players are initiating and reflecting with large movements, side-coach *"On your own."* Players then reflect each other without initiating. This is tricky—players are not to initiate but are to follow the initiator. Both are at once the Initiator and the Mirror (or follower). Players reflect themselves being reflected.

POINT OF CONCENTRATION: on following the follower.

SIDE COACHING: *You are on your own! Follow the follower! Reflect only what you see! Not what you think you see! Reflect! Keep the mirror between you! Don't initiate! Follow the initiator! Follow the follower!*

POINTS OF OBSERVATION

1. Start players on their own only when players are in full-body motion.

2. This exercise may seem confusing at first, but keep with it. As each player reflects the other, there will naturally be body variation due to different body structure, so each player is reflecting himself being reflected.

TUG-OF-WAR

Two players.

The players must play tug-of-war with a space rope. The "rope" is the connection between them.

POINT OF CONCENTRATION: to give the space rope connection.

SIDE COACHING: *Pull! Pull! Stay in the same space!*

POINTS OF OBSERVATION

1. Body action should come out of the rope's connection. If full concentration is put on the object between the players, they will use as much energy as they would pulling an *actual* rope.
2. Watch for the performer who "fits in" by guiding himself more by the action of his partner than by the POC. No matter how clever he may be, he is avoiding the problem.
3. This is a very important exercise, since it shows both actors and audience that—as in a game—almost all the problems they will work on can be solved only through interaction with another player. No player can do the exercise alone. It also points up the need to give the object space for the interaction to take place.
4. Your players should leave this exercise with all the physical effects of having actually played tug-of-war (i.e., warm, out of breath, pink cheeks, etc.). If this has not occurred even partially, then you may be sure that your players were pretending.
5. Players should choose partners of equal strength!

ORIENTATION GAME #1

One person goes on stage, picks a simple activity, and begins doing it. Other players come on stage one at a time and join him in this activity.

POINT OF CONCENTRATION: on showing the activity.

POINTS OF OBSERVATION

1. The simple activity might consist of painting a fence, beating a rug, scrubbing a floor, raking leaves.
2. Players are not to know ahead of time what the first player is doing.
3. This group interaction should create flow and energy. Repeat the game until this takes place.

Second Orientation Session
OBSERVATION GAME[2]

A dozen or more real objects are placed on a tray, which is set in the center of the circle of players. After ten or fifteen seconds, the tray is covered and/or removed. The players then write individual lists of the names of as many of the objects as they can remember. The lists are then compared with the tray of objects.

PLAY BALL

The group first decides on the size of the ball; and then the members toss the ball among themselves on stage. Once the game is in motion, the teacher-director calls out that the ball is becoming various weights.

POINT OF CONCENTRATION: on the weight and size of the ball.

SIDE COACHING: *The ball is one hundred times lighter! The ball is one hundred times heavier! The ball is normal again!*

EVALUATION

Did all players concentrate on the weight of the ball? Did they show us or tell us?

POINTS OF OBSERVATION

1. Watch for students who use body to show relationship to the ball. Did the body become light and float with the lighter ball? Did the body become heavy with the heavier ball? Do not bring this to the students' attention, however, until all have worked the problem. If Evaluation is given before all the students have been on stage with the problem, many will try

---

[2]Neva L. Boyd, *Handbook of Games* (Chicago: H.T. Fitzsimons Co., 1945), p. 84.

to perform to please the teacher and will act out lightness or heaviness rather than keeping with the Point of Concentration (which spontaneously produces the result we are after).
2. In conjunction with this exercise, have the group play a game together (e.g., jumping rope, baseball, ping pong).

INVOLVEMENT IN TWOS

Two players.

Players agree on an object between them and begin an activity with it (as in TUG-OF-WAR). In this case, the object they choose determines the activity (e.g., spreading a sheet, pulling a blanket between them in bed, taffy pulling).

POINT OF CONCENTRATION: on the object (space) between them.

POINTS OF OBSERVATION
1. One way to prevent student-actors from planning How (see p. 35) is to have each team write the name of an object on a slip of paper. The slips of paper are then collected and placed in a hat; and each team picks from the hat just prior to going on stage. This is enjoyable for everyone.
2. For this first involvement, suggest that the object be one which ordinarily brings forth a tactile response.

INVOLVEMENT IN THREES OR MORE

Three or more players.

Group agrees on an object which cannot be used without involving all of them. They are to participate in a joint action in which all move the same thing.

POINT OF CONCENTRATION: to make the object visible in space.

EXAMPLES: pulling a fishnet, tugging a boat, portaging a canoe, pushing a stalled car, taffy pulling.

EVALUATION

Did they work together? If three people pushed a car and the fourth sat behind the wheel, the problem was not solved, for all did not physically move the car.

Did they need each other to solve the problem, or could one of them have managed the problem alone? If one of the players could have managed the problem alone, then the group's choice of an object was incorrect for the problem presented.

Did they work together or separately? If three people were using the activity of painting an object, then they were working separately even though they were working on the same project. However, if the people needed each other to move the object, then they would be working on the problem.

POINTS OF OBSERVATION

1. INVOLVEMENT WITH TWOS will almost automatically keep players involved together. INVOLVEMENT IN THREES OR MORE may tend to confuse them. Do not give any examples, however; allow them to discover the solution to the problem themselves.
2. Watch to see that the students do not work separately while in the group.

INVOLVEMENT WITHOUT HANDS

Two or more players.

Players agree on an animate or inanimate object between them. Players are to set object between them in motion without using their hands.

POINT OF CONCENTRATION: to show and manipulate the object between them without using their hands.

EXAMPLE: pushing a rock, pushing a car, getting a toboggan to move, mountain climbing (rope tied to waist), raising a board to shoulder.

EVALUATION

Did they show us the object or tell us?

POINTS OF OBSERVATION

1. Do not let the students take a built-in no-hands object such as mashing grapes with the feet, for this is resistance to the POC.
2. Watch for spontaneity and unusual ways of putting the objects in motion.

3. Remember, giving examples is telling How to your students!
4. As a first step to the above exercise it might be advisable to have something that ties all the players together such as a chain gang. The third step is WHERE WITHOUT HANDS, p. 145, to be used sometime after the introduction of Where.

MIRROR EXERCISE #2

Four players on a team.

Team divides into sub-teams. Sub-teams reflect each other. Sub-team A is mirror; sub-team B initiates all movement. Sub-team that initiates movement must agree on an activity involving both players. Play as in MIRROR EXERCISE #1, p. 60. After a time, reverse the teams. SIDE COACH: *Change!*

POINT OF CONCENTRATION: mirror sub-team is to reflect all movements *exactly*.

EXAMPLE: Barber shaving customer. Sub-team A then becomes the reflection of the barber and customer and must follow the shaving activity exactly.

POINT OF OBSERVATION

This exercise should be given again when the student-actors come to the problems on seeing.

ORIENTATION GAME #2 (WHO)

One player goes on stage and starts an activity. Other players join him one at a time, as definite characters (Who), and begin an action related to his activity.

EXAMPLE: First player is a surgeon. Other players are nurse, scrub nurse, anesthetist, intern, etc.

POINTS OF OBSERVATION

1. Players are not to know ahead of time what the first player is doing or who he is.
2. At each session, play the ORIENTATION GAME until your student-actors are entering into the problem with excitement and fun, just as they would in any game. This releases a flow of energy that results in group interaction and brings a natural

quality in speech and movement. If this does not happen, you are not communicating the Point of Concentration. If the scene becomes too verbal or if the players move around aimlessly, then they are not focused on group activity but are singly ad-libbing or playwriting. Should this occur, have your first player start a game (ping pong, baseball, etc.) and encourage the others to join in.

3. While Who is added here, take care that the activity is kept in the foreground, or students will begin to "act."

Third Orientation Session
WHO STARTED THE MOTION?[3]

Players are seated in a circle. One player is sent from the room while the others select a leader to start the motion. The player is then called back. He stands in the center of the circle and tries to discover the leader, whose function it is to make a motion—tapping foot, nodding head, moving hands, etc.—and to change motions whenever he wishes. The other players reflect these motions and try to keep the center player from guessing the leader's identity.

When the center player discovers the leader, two other players are chosen to take their place.

DIFFICULTY WITH SMALL OBJECTS
(Use at intervals throughout training.)

A. Single player
   Player becomes involved with small object.

POINT OF CONCENTRATION: having difficulty with object.

EXAMPLES: Opening a bottle, opening a stuck purse, forcing a drawer open, tearing open a cigarette pack.

B. Single player
   Player becomes involved with a piece of clothing

EXAMPLES: stuck zipper on back of dress, tight boots, a ripped lining in coat sleeve.

---

[3]*Ibid*, p. 84.

C. Two or more players

This is the same as A and B except that it involves more players.

POINTS OF OBSERVATION

Resistance to the POC will show itself in a player who intellectualizes the problem. Instead of having a physical difficulty with the object, he may, for instance, have a hole in his shoe and take a dollar bill out of his wallet to place in the shoe to cover up the hole. This is a "joke" and total avoidance of the exercise presented.

HOW OLD AM I?

Single player

Teacher-director sets up a simple Where, preferably a corner bus stop. Set includes bench downstage and a storefront background. Player writes down age on slip of paper and hands it to teacher-director before going on stage. Player comes on stage and waits for bus. Each player is given one or two minutes for exercise.

POINT OF CONCENTRATION: on the age chosen.

SIDE COACHING: *The bus is half a block down! It's coming closer; It's here!* Sometimes adding, *It's held up in traffic!* gives added insight to the character.

EXAMPLE I (done by an adult): A character skips on stage, chewing gum. He glances down the street, sees nothing, sits on bench, and begins blowing bubbles with gum. He gets it stuck on his nose, cleans up the sticky mess with tongue and finger, glances down street again but sees nothing. He twirls around, notices shop windows, goes to them and peers in, pressing his hands against the glass. He moves downstage, blowing more bubbles, fumbles in his pocket searching for something, but cannot find it. Disturbed, he goes quickly through all his pockets, pulls out a yo-yo, and starts playing with it. The bus arrives. He quickly puts yo-yo back into his pocket and anxiously fumbles around for bus fare.

EXAMPLE II (done by an 11-year-old boy): A character comes on stage with a firm, aggressive step. He is carrying something in his hand. He glances down the street, sees nothing coming, and sits down on the bench. He puts what he is carrying on his lap and opens what seems to be a briefcase. He thumbs through a few of the sections, pulls out a paper, glances at it, takes a pen out of his inside coat pocket, makes a note on the paper, puts it back into the briefcase, zips it closed, looks down the street, and, seeing no bus, places briefcase on the ground. He looks down the street restlessly—still no bus. He rises, walks up and down, notices the show windows, glances in them, and smoothes his hair. He comes back as the bus is arriving and grabs up his briefcase.

EVALUATION

How old was he? Did he show us or tell us? Are age qualities always physical? Are age differences part of an attitude toward life? Did he see the bus or was he just listening to coaching?

POINTS OF OBSERVATION

1. At this early stage a student-actor will usually give some bodily rhythms and a good deal of activity (business) to help clarify age.
2. Discourage "acting" and/or "performing" during this exercise by stopping the action whenever necessary.
3. When doing HOW OLD AM I? REPEAT during the tenth or twelfth session of Where, recall this first solving of the problem to your student-actors.
4. Coach "Held up in traffic" only when you want to explore student-actor's work further.

HOW OLD AM I? REPEAT

Single player.

Player sits quietly on bench waiting for bus and concentrating on age only. When age emerges in the body, what is needed for the problem will come up for use.

POINT OF CONCENTRATION: focusing on age only, repeating it over and over again to himself.

SIDE COACHING: *Concentrate on the problem! Put the age in your feet! Your upper lip! Your spine!*

When age appears: *Bus is a block away! Held up in traffic!*

POINTS OF OBSERVATION

It is difficult for the student-actor to believe that:

1. The blank mind (free of preconception) is what we are after. Adventuring!
2. If concentration is truly on age only, student-actors and audience alike will have a most inspirational experience as the bodies of players become older or younger spontaneously with little or no overt action or need for stage business.
3. This exercise will work only if the student-actor truly blanks his mind of any imagery relating to this age (repeating this age over and over with the assist of the Side Coaching will help in this).
4. Concentrating on the age alone serves to release body memory to such an extraordinary degree that the player shows us age with the minutest of body movements and gesture, subtleties that one would expect to see in only the most accomplished and experienced of actors. Again we see that to experience new adventures, we must trust the scheme and let the Point of Concentration do the work.
5. If the problem was solved, the student-actor should come from this exercise with more body grace evident because of some loss of rigidity, with muscular release and shiny eyes. New sources of energy and knowledge were truly released. "They showed age without doing anything!" is an excited comment often heard by student-actors.
6. To prepare himself for action, the player should concentrate on exhalation as in EXCURSION INTO THE INTUITIVE, pp. 191–192.

OBJECT MOVING PLAYERS[4]

Any number of players.

Players agree on object which is to move them. They are to be an interrelated group.

---

[4]See also USING OBJECTS TO EVOLVE SCENE, p. 212.

POINT OF CONCENTRATION: on the object that is moving them.

SIDE COACHING: *Feel the object! Let the object move you! You're all in it together!*

EXAMPLES: sailboat, car, merry-go-round, ferris wheel.

EVALUATION

To audience: Did they allow the object to move them, or did they initiate movement independent of the object? Did they move by watching the other players?

To actors: Did you make this a mirror game (reflection of others), or did you work on the point of concentration?

POINTS OF OBSERVATION

1. See whether the players *feel* the object (space) between them. This sometimes occurs to an extraordinary degree when the students have played together many months or when they are concentrating deeply on the problem.
2. Many students will ask: "Should we watch the other players to know when to move?" This is the student asking the teacher "How do I do it?" which indicates a dependency. A simple "Let the object move you" repeated over and over again aids in breaking this dependency.
3. If the Point of Concentration is kept on the object (space), a group connection appears that is felt by the actors and evident to the audience.
4. It may be that the players will finally "let go" and let the object move them only after constant coaching. Most of them will "let go" if the Point of Concentration is understood and if the side coaching reaches them; moreover, each team should be kept on stage until this does happen for most of them.
5. Repeat this exercise throughout the training.

IT'S HEAVIER WHEN IT'S FULL[5]

EXERCISE

Three or more players.

Players agree on an activity in which receptacles must be filled, emptied, and filled again.

---

[5]See also GIVING REALITY WITH OBJECTS, pp. 291-92.

POINT OF CONCENTRATION: on showing the variations in weight when things are full or empty.

EXAMPLES: picking apples, filling a treasure box, carrying water.

VARIATION A

Handling things of different weights.

EXAMPLES: shoveling sand, pitching hay, lifting weights.

VARIATION B

This variation is to be used after the beginning exercises in Where. Where, Who, and What are agreed upon, and the problem of varying weights is placed within the agreed context.

ORIENTATION GAME #3

One player goes on stage and starts an activity. Other players come on, one at a time. This time they know who they are as they enter the scene; and the first player (who does not know who they are) must accept them and relate to them.

POINT OF CONCENTRATION: on the activity, with Who as an addition but not as the main focus.

EXAMPLE: Man hanging drapes. Woman enters. Woman: "Now, dear, you know that's not the way I want them hung!" Man accepts that woman is playing his wife; and he plays accordingly. Actors continue to enter, playing the couple's children, the next-door neighbor, the family minister, etc.

EVALUATION

Did she show or tell us that she was the wife, neighbor, etc.? Did they all stay with the activity?

POINTS OF OBSERVATION

1. By this time, ORIENTATION GAME should show the primitive beginnings of a scene growing out of the Point of Concentration as well as the first sign of relationship rather than mere simultaneous activity.

2. Let the players enjoy ORIENTATION GAME even if the stage is somewhat chaotic because of the large group of "characters" in the scene, with everyone moving and talking at once as all

very earnestly play the game. This childlike stage behavior releases pleasure and excitement and is essential to the social growth of the group (necessary to improvisational theater). Refrain (no matter how tempted) from trying to get an orderly scene. Subsequent exercises will slowly do this for the student. TWO SCENES in particular (p. 160) will help.

PART OF A WHOLE[6]

(Can be used for an orientation game.)

One player goes on stage and becomes part of a large animate or inanimate moving object. As soon as the nature of the object becomes clear to another player, he joins the player on stage and becomes another part of the whole. This continues until all the audience have participated and are working together to form the complete object.

POINT OF CONCENTRATION: on being a part of a larger object.

EXAMPLE: One person goes on stage and curls up with arm moving from the shoulder like a piston. Another player lines up with first player, about two feet from him, and assumes similar position. Two other players join, and four wheels are now moving. Other players quickly become whistles, engines, and finally a semaphore which stops the train.

POINTS OF OBSERVATION

1. This exercise generates a great deal of spontaneity and fun. Every age group responds to it with equal energy. You will notice that sound effects arise spontaneously when needed.
2. Other examples: a statue grouping, a flower, an animal, body cells, inside of a clock. Give no examples, however. If the game is presented clearly, players will come up with most delightful objects.

Fourth Orientation Session
THREE CHANGES

Two rows of players facing each other

Each player is to observe the person opposite him and note

---

[6]Many users call this "The Machine."

his dress, hair, etc. Players then turn backs on each other. Each player changes three things on his person (e.g., unties his tie, parts his hair, unties shoelaces, switches watch from right to left arm).

Players then face each other again. Each player must now identify what changes his opposite has made. Change partners and ask that players make four changes. Continue to change partners after each change until you reach seven, eight or more.

POINT OF OBSERVATION

Do not let players know that you plan to increase the changes until after the first playing. Many are worried how to find three changes. Four or more will create a good deal of excitement. This is an excellent exercise for players, taxing their powers of making do (improvising) on a simple physical level. Players are forced to look at a "barren" land as it were and find things to use for the game their eye did not see at first glance. This has been called the Survival Game.

WHAT DO I DO FOR A LIVING?

Same setting and procedure as in HOW OLD AM I? (see p. 68).

POINT OF CONCENTRATION: on showing what he does for a living.

EVALUATION

Is it only through activity that we can show age? Is it only through activity that we can show what we do for a living? Does the body structure alter in some professions? Is there a difference between a salesman and a teacher? Would 20 years as a laborer make a man look and act differently than 20 years as a doctor? Is it an attitude that creates change? Is it the work environment?

POINTS OF OBSERVATION

1. This questioning in Evaluation should provoke the first insight into physicalizing character aspects. It should be most casual. Because these exercises are done early in the work, do not belabor the whole point of character—in fact, *avoid* it until it grows naturally out of the acting problems.
2. If the group is large, two or three players may work simulta-

neously on stage. However, they are to work separately and are not to have any interplay of any kind.

3. Jokes, "acting," clowning, etc. are evidence of a resistance to the problem.
4. To prevent How, have student-actors sit quietly concentrating on the profession each has chosen—nothing more. If concentration is complete, what he needs for the problem will arrive for his use.

MIRROR EXERCISE #3 (PENETRATION)

(This exercise should be given throughout the training, especially before giving CONTRAPUNTAL ARGUMENT, p. 180, those which follow it, and CHARACTER AGILITY, p. 269. It is the first two-part exercise given, the first step toward PREOCCUPATION.)

Two players.

Players are seated facing each other. They agree on a simple relationship (employer-employee, husband-wife, teacher-student) and choose a topic for discussion or argument.

After they have begun the discussion, the director calls one of them by name. The player called then assumes the facial structure of the player opposite him while, at the same time, continuing the conversation. He is not to reflect movement and expression, as in the earlier MIRROR exercises, but is to try to make his face *look* like the opposite player's.

POINT OF CONCENTRATION: player called is to concentrate on re-molding his own face inside out to look like the other player's.

EXAMPLE: A's mouth is thin, his chin recedes, his eyes are small. B's lips are full, his jaw juts out, he has large eye sockets. When A's name is called, he is to concentrate on restructuring his own face to look like B's. While continuing the discussion, he must work to get his jaw out, his lips full, etc., much like a sculptor.

SIDE COACHING: *Rebuild your nose like his. Jawbone! Forehead! Change your chin line! Eyeballs! Concentrate on him! On upper lip! On jaw line! As you are!* (Bring players back and forth and to their own faces throughout the exercise.)

POINTS OF OBSERVATION

1. Keep changing the "mirror." Do not let the students know when their names will be called. Coach to see that the discussion or argument never stops while players rebuild their faces. Remind them to keep away from superficial expressions. They must *penetrate* each others faces.
2. In selecting teams, ask players to pair off with faces of dissimilar structure. Short noses with long noses, heavy faces with thin ones. Ask students to exaggerate the opposite face.
3. Some players may be apprehensive about seeing how they look to another person. Handle this by stressing the solving of the problem and pointing out that exaggeration was asked for.
4. When this exercise is given this early in the training, resistances will appear. For the most part, the players will show very little physical change and will play the exercise similar to MIRROR EXERCISE #1 (reflecting instead of penetrating). However, the exercise does have value when given here, for it forces the players to look at each other and see their fellow player.
5. Resistance to such close eye contact with another player this early will show itself in irritation with the exercise, almost no attempt to change facial structure, and verbalization as to, "How is it possible to keep talking?"
6. When repeated at a later time in the training, the early resistance to this exercise should be brought to the attention of the student-actors.
7. Here for the first time students are thrown into an explicit talking relationship—a Who and a What. They should be so occupied with penetration, however, that they take the problem in stride.

CONVERSATION WITH INVOLVEMENT

Two or more players.

Players agree on simple discussion topic. They then proceed to eat and drink a large meal while keeping up a continuous discussion.

POINT OF CONCENTRATION: giving life to the object through the smelling, seeing, tasting, etc.

SIDE COACHING: *Taste the food! Feel the texture of the napkin! What is the temperature of the drinking water? Chew your food! Smell the food!*

EVALUATION

Did the players give sensory reality to the objects? Did they show us or tell us? What kind of soup were they drinking? Was the meat hot?

POINTS OF OBSERVATION

1. See that the players show relationships (Who).
2. If resistance to the Point of Concentration is high (with many jokes, gags, etc.), then the group is not yet ready. Leave this problem and come back to it at another time.
3. Do not allow players to make a situation out of this exercise. If this occurs, they "perform" the situation and resist working on the problem (objects).
4. Make a plan of the immediate environment.
5. The scene can be broken down into three or more parts (e.g., first taste and smell, then feeling objects, then seeing, etc.).
6. This is the second two-way problem. (See p. 394)
7. Use all senses together.

Fifth Orientation Session

INVOLVEMENT WITH LARGE OBJECTS

Single player.

Player becomes involved with a large entangling object.

POINT OF CONCENTRATION: on the selected object.

EXAMPLES: spider web, boa constrictor, tree branches in forest or jungle, octopus, parachute, man-eating plant.

POINT OF OBSERVATION

Watch the wording when stating the POC to be certain that the player's concentration is on the object and not on disentangling himself from the object. This is an important difference and one that comes up continuously throughout the work.

DRAWING OBJECTS GAME

Two teams. (To first be used sometimes in Orientation.)

Players divide into two teams. Each team sets up a table with plenty of paper and pencils (in the event one of the pencil points breaks during the excitement of playing the game) at an equal distance from the group leader. The group leader has a prepared list of objects such as Christmas tree, window, cow, train, airplane, cat, mouse, apple, house—any object that has an outstanding characteristic. One player from each team comes to the center. The group leader exposes only one of the objects to the team members, who then quickly run back to their team and draw the object for their teams, who are all gathered around trying to identify it. As soon as any member of a team recognizes the object drawn, it is called out by name. The team naming the most objects first wins the game. The game continues until each member of each team has had a chance of drawing the object.

The ability to draw has nothing to do with this game, for it is a game of selectivity that shows which students can quickly pick from their "file" to make a communication. In fact, artists within a group are often less facile. This game can be repeated at intervals making the objects more and more difficult. A variation of this game, using abstractions, can be found in Neva L. Boyd's *Handbook of Games* (p. 101).

TRAPPED

Single player.

Player chooses a Where from which he is trying to escape.

EXAMPLES: caught in bear trap, tree trunk, elevator, etc.

PHYSICALIZING AN OBJECT

Single player.

Player selects an object, animate, or inanimate, which he handles and uses. He is to communicate to the audience the life or movement of this object.

POINT OF CONCENTRATION: giving life or movement to the object.
EXAMPLE: If the object is a bowling ball, the student actor

throws the ball down the alley, and the audience must know what happens to the bowling ball once it has left his hands. Other objects which can be used are: trying to hold a fish, playing a pinball machine, playing billiards, flying a kite, playing with a yo-yo.

SIDE COACHING: *What is the ball doing? Give life to the fish!*

EVALUATION

Did they physicalize the object? Did they show or tell?

POINT OF OBSERVATION

Be careful that this exercise does not become watching a sport. The distinction between giving life to the object and manipulating the object is subtle. Be careful in presentation and side coaching not to tell student-actors How.

MAINTAINING SURFACE HEIGHTS

Single player.

Player establishes a surface (table, counter top, etc.) on which he puts many small objects, setting them down with strong impact. The objects may be books, pencils, glasses, etc.

POINT OF CONCENTRATION: on keeping the height of the surface stable and constant while setting various objects on it.

POINT OF OBSERVATION

Resistance to the POC will show itself by players piling objects one upon the other instead of placing them singly on the surface.

BEGIN-AND-END WITH OBJECTS

Single player.

Player selects a small object such as a pack of cigarettes.

PART A

Teacher-director instructs player to perform a simple action with the object (e.g., taking a cigarette from the pack).

PART B

Teacher-director instructs player to repeat the action, this time calling out "Begin!" each time he makes fresh contact with the object and "End!" when each detail is completed.

PART C

Teacher-director instructs player to repeat the action as before, this time doing it as fast as he can and without being told to begin and end.

POINT OF CONCENTRATION: on the object.

EXAMPLE OF PART B: He touches the pack: "Begin!" He grasps the pack: "End!" He touches a cigarette: "Begin!" He grasps the cigarette: "End!" He begins to remove the cigarette from the pack: "Begin!" He removes the cigarette from the pack: "End!" He moves the cigarette toward his mouth: "Begin!" He grasps the cigarette with his mouth: "End!"

EVALUATION

To actor: Was the first or third action visible in the space for you? To audience: do you agree?

POINTS OF OBSERVATION

1. If Part B is done correctly, each detail will be like an individual no-motion frame within a strip of movie film. You should coach the student to do his beginning and ending with great bursts of energy.
2. The third action (Part C) should be out of the head, into the space; thus visible. It will be much clearer and sharper than the first (Part A).
3. This exercise is especially helpful in developing sharp detail in handling objects and should be repeated frequently throughout training. A larger variation of the exercise, where the same technique is used to bring out detail and the intent of a scene appears on p. 135.
4. The reality the audience sees is what must be accepted in the Evaluation. When an actor is used to "acting," that often becomes *his* reality; and the audience is his checkpoint against this.

5. This exercise is related to SPACE SUBSTANCE and should be done prior to it.

SPACE SUBSTANCE

After the preliminary exercises in object involvement have been used, SPACE SUBSTANCE should be introduced and repeated for at least eight more sessions as a warm-up. It is valuable for freshening up groups at all times. Since there are many possible variations of this exercise, what to use in subsequent sessions should be determined by the teacher-director. The oftener it is used, the more perfect student-actors will become in creating, finding, and building "objects out of thin air" and "letting things happen."

A. EXPLORATION

Large group (no audience necessary).

Ask student-actors to move around the stage, giving substance to space as they go. They are not to feel or present space as though it were a known material (water, mud, molasses, etc.) but are to explore it as a totally new and unknown substance.

SIDE COACHING: *Move through the substance and make contact with it. Don't give it a name—it is what it is! Use your whole body to make contact! Feel it against your cheeks! Your nose! Your knees! Your hips! Let it (space) feel you!*
If players tend to use hands only, have them keep their arms close to their bodies so as to move as a single mass.
Keep side-coaching: *Push the substance around. Explore it! You never felt it before. Make a tunnel! Move back into the space your body has shaped. Shake it up! Make the substance fly. Stir it up! Make it ripple.*

B. SUPPORT AND EFFORT

Large group with audience.

Start players walking around stage, pushing through the space substance.

SIDE COACHING: *Let the space substance support you. Lean on it. Rest on it. Let it hold your head. Your chin. Your arms. Your eyeballs. Your upperlip, etc.*

After the players are in motion and responding to the problem, give a new understanding to the space substance they are contacting.

SIDE COACHING: *You are holding yourself up. You would fly into a thousand pieces if you quit holding yourself up. You are hanging on to your arms. Your mouth. Your forehead.* (Call out the various parts of the body that the students hold rigid.) Now have the students go back to letting the space substance "support" them. Change back and forth until the student-actors obviously feel the difference. While calling out parts of the body, help the students to release muscle holds. (One student who customarily had a tight expression on his face that gave him what might be called a "mean" look first became aware of his rigidity through this exercise.)

EVALUATION

To players: how did you feel when space was supporting you? When you were your own support?

To audience: did you notice a difference between support and no support in the way players walked and looked?

POINTS OF OBSERVATION

1. When players hold themselves together, are their own gravity line, so to speak, some shrink up, some seem to be afraid of falling, while others appear anxious, lonely, and still others look aggressive. In fact, many "character qualities" appear. When, on the other hand, the players lean on space, an expansion and fullness can be noted as they move through the environment. Smiling faces, peacefulness, and an air of gentleness appear. It is as if they know the environment will support them if they allow it to.
2. "Put your signature in space" is a good side-coaching remark to place the player in the environment. The object is for the player to leave a mark in space—a footprint, the outline of his head, etc.—and then see that mark.

C. SHAPING SPACE
Single players.

Ask players one by one to find any object they wish out of

the space substance.

POINT OF CONCENTRATION: to find an object from space substance.
POINT OF OBSERVATION

Most players gather the space substance and handle it as they would any other pliable mass. With confidence and certainty the student finds his object with incredible exactness and reality. Where in the earlier creating of objects only a few students achieved this, this exercise is successful with almost all. Perhaps this is so because the player intuits; he does not construct (invent) the object from the imagination but discovers it as it comes up out of space.

Next ask each player to pull the space substance around as though it could not be separated from itself. This sometimes results in the presentation of elastic or ribbony material. Side-coach the players to experiment with it.

D. ENSEMBLE SPACE-SHAPING

Two or more players.

Ask players to find one object animate or inanimate, together out of space substance and then use it. Then have the players pull the space substance about, keeping it attached in space, swing on it, let it pull them up, wind it around each other, etc.

POINTS OF OBSERVATION

1. Players move out of the immediate environment with ease after this exercise. (In manipulating space substance, a group of players once ended up doing a maypole dance, and the reality was so sharp for the players that when the ribbons became tangled, the student audience "saw it."
2. Be certain the players are making contact with the space substance and not imposing upon it.

E. TRANSFORMATION OF OBJECTS

Large group of players.

First person creates an object and passes it on to the next player. This next player is to handle the object until it changes shape and then pass it on. The exercise differs from TRANSFORM-

ING THE OBJECT (p. 214) in that here the player is *not* to make a story or situation around the object but is simply to handle it until something happens. If nothing happens, he is to pass it to the next player and so on down the line. For instance, if a player is handed a yo-yo and uses it, it might transform itself into a bird or an accordion. Following this: two players create together (as in ENSEMBLE SPACE-SHAPING) a continuous flow of changing objects.

This is a tricky exercise and must be clearly understood by the players. They are not to change the object—it either transforms itself, or they do nothing about it. No associations should be used to lead to a story. If a player is handed a comb, for instance, he is not to make a mirror and use the comb.

POINT OF OBSERVATION

A great deal of excitement is felt if an object seems to transform itself. When a student has this experience, it should be pointed out to him that this is exactly what POC must do for players.

F. TOUCH AND BE TOUCHED/SEE AND BE SEEN

SIDE COACHING: *Allow the space to flow through you and you flow through the space. Allow your mind to flow through your brain. Allow your sight to flow through your eye. Allow the space to flow through you and your fellow player. Take a ride on your own body and view the scenery around you. Touch an object in the space—a tree, a cup, a piece of clothing, a chair. When you touch the object, feel it, allow it to touch (feel) you!* (vary objects). *Touch a fellow player and allow your fellow player to touch you. Touched and be touched!* (vary players). *Flow through the space and allow the space to flow through you and your fellow players. See an object. The moment you really see it, allow the object to see you!* (vary objects). *See a fellow player. Allow the fellow player to see you. Look full face at your fellow player and occlude: do not see him or let yourself be seen. Change! See and be seen.* Repeat several times. Vary players.

POINTS OF OBSERVATION: Remember to keep players moving and to allow time between each side coaching. Was it difficult to allow yourself to be touched. . . to be seen? Avoid analysis.

NO-MOTION WARM-UP

Any number of players.

The following exercise should be given just prior to NO MOTION (p. 189). It should also be given in conjunction with SPACE SUBSTANCE, however, and so is presented at this point in the text.

Ask players to raise their arms up and down. Now ask them to concentrate on No Motion while continuing to raise their arms up and down in the normal way. Use the image of a flip-book—a series of stills which when riffled create a moving picture. Now ask them to see the series of "stills" the raising of their arms has left behind in space. When they grasp this, go on to the same approach to walking, climbing stairs, ladders, etc. Properly executed this exercise gives the players a physical feeling and understanding of keeping out of their own way. By concentrating on No Motion hands, legs, etc. move effortlessly without conscious volition. This can be used as a physicalization to show how, with lack of interference, the POC can work for us. As one player remarked, "It is as if someone else is moving us about!" Another player said, "It's like being on a vacation."

POINT OF CONCENTRATION: on the still moments between the movement.

POINT OF OBSERVATION

Homework for this exercise will be useful and help accelerate workshop training. (1) Ask students to take a few minutes out of each day to catch a moving scene and see it as a momentary still picture: a street view; an office; an ambulance racing past; a moment of themselves and another person in some emotional situation. (2) Ask students to keep a "log" of their daily experience—just a simple word or two set down in a notebook at the moment of something happening. For instance, if a person is irritated because he can't find his shoes, at that moment he writes down "irritated—shoes, 9:30." If an hour later he runs for the bus and misses it, he may write "out of breath—missed bus, 10:30." Each individual, if he does the exercise, will intuitively know what moments to log.

This homework does not bring up introspection or subjectivity in the student's work. On the contrary, it gives him an extraordinary sense of his environment and himself within it. Like the POC in NO MOTION, it gives him a sharp perception of the moving world about him. Immediacy and brevity are necessary, however. If the student makes an elaborate record as in a diary, he will change the exercise into something else. Wordiness will carry everyone into emotionalism, judgments, sentiments, withdrawal. Wordiness will take the person beyond the moment of the event and expose him to subjectivity and stale experience.

PENETRATION

Any number of players.

While the following exercise could be integrated as part of the side coaching during certain of the sense exercises, it might be useful as a special warm-up during Orientation sessions. Note that this is not a complete exercise, it is simply a suggestion for emphasizing an important part of playing.

Give the POC to teams and tell them they may do what they wish with it before the audience.

POINT OF CONCENTRATION: to penetrate the environment. Ask students to think of their sensory equipment as an extended tool —something that can move out, cut through, *penetrate*.

SIDE COACHING: *Penetrate that color! Penetrate that taste! Let your ear penetrate the sound.*

ADD A PART

(Can be used as an orientation game)

Whole group.

A player goes on stage and places an object which is a part of a larger object. Each successive player adds a part until everyone has had a turn.

EXAMPLES: The first player places a steering wheel on stage. The second player adds a windshield, the third player adds a back seat. And so on.

The first player places a window frame, the second player adds a curtain, etc.

ADD AN OBJECT WHERE #1
Whole group.

First player goes on stage and places an object in the general environment around which a Where can be built. Each successive player uses all the objects already placed and then adds one himself.

EXAMPLE: First player places a wash basin on stage, second player adds a bath tub. And so on.

POINT OF OBSERVATION

This exercise is a preliminary step to Where.

Summary

Continue to urge student-actors to make a conscious integration of the physical world around them. Encourage them to receive how things taste, feel, smell, sound and look. Open consciousness of the world around is a necessary tool in the improvisational theater, the classroom, the home and the arts.

Should students lose detail and generalize objects and relationships at any time during the workshops, it would be well to stop the class for a moment and interject one of the exercises previously covered in Orientation. Almost every one of them is useful for warm-ups at all times.

The teacher-director may also suggest that students take the exercises home. While the exercises are best not done outside the workshops, here they can provide much fun for friends and family.

Pleasure and enthusiasm must set the tone throughout these exercises. If students are apprehensive, anxious, and constantly looking to see if they are doing "right," then there has been some error in presentation. In his urgency, the teacher may be a pedant rather than the leader or guide of the group. He may be imposing his own frame of reference on "results." He may be giving too many problems in one session and not allowing students to have the experience of flow as they would from a game.

Try to always begin sessions with a game and to end them, if possible, with an exercise which will give the players a non-verbal summation of the earlier problems. ORIENTATION GAME, ADD A PART, PART OF THE WHOLE are just such exercises. They quickly show the teacher to what extent the earlier exercises have been organically integrated by the students. If clowning, "acting," and exhibitionism persist, then it is obvious that involvement with or understanding of the Point of Concentration has not yet taken place.

Do not use exercises involving single players until after the student-audience is "part of the game." This should take place by the end of the second orientation session. If not, delay singles.

IV. Where

Introduction

The Three Environments

Many actors find it difficult to "reach beyond their noses" and must be freed for a wider physical relationship with the environment. For purposes of clarification, three environments should always be kept in mind: immediate, general, larger.[1]

The *immediate* environment is that area close upon us—the table where we are eating, with its food, utensils, ashtrays, etc. The *general* environment is the area in which the table is placed —the room, restaurant, etc., with its doors, windows, and other features. The *larger* environment is the area beyond—the space outside the window, the trees in the distance, the birds in the sky, etc.

All the exercises in environment (Where) are designed to awaken the players to all three areas and to help them move out, penetrate, and work comfortably.

Involvement With Where

The first Where exercise will provide the student-actor with the basic structure he will use for all subsequent game exercises. It is the "field" upon which he plays. It brings him the full stage environment and shows him how he must play within it and let

---

[1]See SPACE SUBSTANCE, p. 81.

:ople, the objects, and the events he meets within this en-
nent work for him.

‿‿cause of the importance of thoroughly familiarizing the student-actor especially interested in scene improvisation with this
basic form, it is wise to spend a good deal of time on this problem and the variations and additions suggested in the text. (Do
not use every exercise in Where before going to other parts of the
book. Many of the exercises in the latter part of this chapter are
for very advanced students only.)

For the player in formal theater, Where exercises serve to
place him inside the stage set where he will understand that stage
movement is organic rather than remembered.

First Where Session

Establishing Focus on Where, Who and What

Prior to presenting the WHERE EXERCISE, hold a discussion
with the group to establish focus on the primary (Where) and
secondary (Who and What) Points of Concentration.

Begin by discussing Where (relationships with physical objects).

How do you know where you are? If you get no response, try
a different approach.

Is it true that you always know where you are? "Sometimes
you don't know where you are."

*True, you may be in an unfamiliar place. How do you know
it's unfamiliar? How do you know when you are in a familiar
place? How do you know where you are at any moment of the
day?* "You just know." "You can always tell." "There are signs."

How do you know when you are in the kitchen? "You can
smell the cooking."

If there were nothing cooking, how would you know? "By
where it is."

What do you mean? "By where it is in the house."

*If every room in your house were moved around, would you
still know which room was the kitchen?* "Of course!"

How? "By the things in the room."

What things? "The stove. The refrigerator."

Would you know a kitchen if it had no stove or refrigerator in it? If it were in the jungle, for instance? "Yes."

How? "It would be a place where food is prepared."

And so, through discussion and the presentation of exacting questions, the student-actors conclude that "we know where we are by the physical objects around us." When this basic premise has been agreed upon, become more specific.

What is the difference between an office and a den? "An office has a desk and a telephone."

Isn't this also true of most dens? "Yes."

What might a den have that an office would not have? "Photographs, rugs, lamps."

Couldn't those be in an office?

On a large blackboard, set up two columns under the headings of den and office. Now ask the group to call out items which might be found in each place, listing them under the proper heading as they are mentioned. Eventually, it will become apparent that differences do exist; for, while both locations might have a desk, a water cooler and intercom system are more likely to be found in an office than in a den.

Continue along this same line. *How do you know the difference between a park and a garden?* The more detailed these discussions become, the more your students will realize that refined selection (capturing the essence) adds brilliance to the theater communication.

When the Where discussion has been completed, the Who and What points should be covered rather quickly.

In Who, we are interested in establishing human relationships —in encouraging the player to realize whom he is working with and to get some understanding of their mutual roles.

Do you usually know the person in the same room with you? Would you know a stranger from your brother? Your uncle from the corner grocer? "Of course!"

When riding on a bus, can you tell the difference between two school friends and a mother and child? Between two strangers and a husband and wife? "Yes."

How can you tell? "You can tell by the way they act together."

What do you mean, "by the way they act together"? The

youngest actor replies, "Mothers are bossy . . . sweethearts look silly . . . husbands and wives argue." Sad commentary, indeed.

In discussing this further, the students will agree that people show us who they are through their behavior (as opposed to telling us). When they have arrived at this point, bring in the fact that actors, to communicate to the audience, must show Who through relationships with their fellow players.

When Who has been covered, move on to the last of the three Points of Concentration. What is the play of the players on stage.

Why do you usually go into a kitchen? "To make a meal." "To get a glass of water." "To wash the dishes."

Why do you go into a bedroom? "To sleep." To change clothes."

The living room? "To read." "To watch TV."

As the questioning progresses, the students will agree that we usually have a need for being where we are and for doing what we do—for handling certain physical objects, for going into certain places or rooms. And so must the actor have his needs for handling certain props on stage, for being in a certain place, for acting in a certain way. When Where, Who, and What have been thoroughly covered, move into the WHERE EXERCISE.

WHERE EXERCISE[2]

Special Materials

1. Number of small blackboards (may be painted plywood) and chalk. Paper can be substituted, but blackboards are desirable for younger actors.
2. An easel or stand for placement of an onstage blackboard.
3. A few chairs.

Two players (number to be increased after second or third session)

Each team of two is supplied with a blackboard and chalk. They then agree on a place (Where) and plot out a floorplan of it on the blackboard (i.e., if the team chose a living room, they would plot out the sofa, chairs, coffee table, ashtrays, fireplace,

---

[2]See ONCE UPON A TIME, p. 307, for the children's version of introduction to Where.

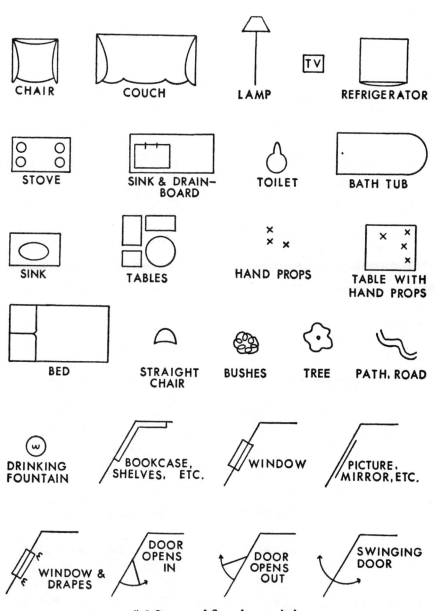

1 Suggested floorplan symbols

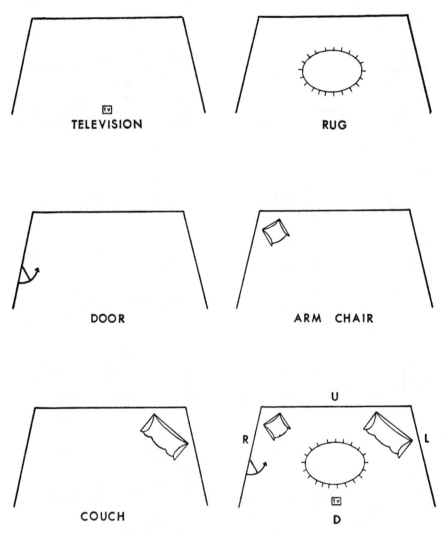

2 Building the floorplan through suggestions

etc.). Each player should be encouraged to contribute a share of the items, using the standard floorplan symbols (see illus. #1.

When the first team has completed their floorplan, their blackboard should be propped on an easel facing the stage, where the onstage players can see it easily. The teacher-director should tell them that they need not remember any of the items but are to refer to the floorplan as often as they wish during the exercise.

This is a deliberate step to ease players from remembering (blanking the mind) and will give a great sense of relief if stressed. "Don't keep it in your heads, refer to the blackboard!" It is also another step in helping the student relax his cerebral hold on himself.

They are now to play within their Where, establishing a simple Who relationship between them—such as two friends, a husband and wife, a brother and sister, etc.—and deciding upon a simple What (reason for being there). This Who, Where, and What should also be written on the bottom of the floorplan, along with the Point of Concentration.

POINT OF CONCENTRATION: (1) The players must show where they are by making physical contact with all the objects drawn on the floorplan. (The only physical objects actually needed for on the stage will be chairs. The other objects are simply represented by chalk marks on the blackboard and must be created on stage by the students as they go along.) In other words, each player must in some way handle or touch on stage everything drawn on the blackboard, sharing with the audience its visibility while using. (2) To show Where (as above) through Who and What (relationship and activity).

EXAMPLE: It is probably wise to demonstrate the exercise to the class prior to their involvement with the problem. The teacher-director should spend whatever time is necessary on this introduction. Remember, drawing the floorplan is the beginning of the student-actor's disciplined focus on or awareness of detail. Through it, he learns to avoid generalities. Don't rush the learning process!

Set up a large blackboard. Have the class agree on a Where. Now have each member of the group call out an item to be placed on the floorplan. Draw them in as they are called out (compare illus. #2). When the floorplan is completed to everyone's satisfaction, ask the question: Who shall we have in the Where? When they have decided, select two players to go on stage and play the Who. Now ask the final question: What are they doing there? When this has been agreed upon, show the class how the floorplan works. With the help of the two players, walking through the scene and using the props, the exercise should become clear to them. Encourage the rest of the class to watch carefully.

Are they sharing what they are doing with the audience? Are they showing and not telling us where they are? Do they both handle the objects the same way? Did they walk through tables?[3] When the total class is involved to the teacher's satisfaction, then it is time to pass out the individual blackboards or paper and get to work on the problem.

EVALUATION

Was concentration complete or incomplete? Did the team solve the acting problem? Did we know Where they were? Did they handle all the objects? Did they refer to the floorplan when necessary? Did they talk about using the objects ("I think I'll close the window" etc.), or did they use them?

Check the actors' floorplan against what the audience observed (compare illus. #3). In the early stages of the exercise, the players will often be confused and will not use all the objects. As the exercise is repeated, this confusion will be overcome. Just coach to use *everything* on stage and continue side-coaching to refer to their blackboards as often as they wish.

Did they handle (contact) their objects so that we could un-

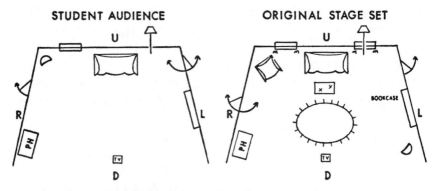

3 Players' original floorplan compared to
audience's floorplan drawn from players'
use of WHERE

---

[3]For the first session, put all the players in the same Where and have the group as a whole choose Who.

derstand What they were doing? Try to determine what actions were missed. Encourage volunteers to demonstrate how various objects might have been handled. Try to show them the differences in object handling (e.g., the difference in weight and construction between a book and a magazine). If SPACE SUBSTANCE EXERCISE has been done frequently up to this point, creating space objects will be very sharply detailed.

Could they have used their objects in a more interesting manner? Are hands the only way of touching objects? Is it necessary to handle (contact) objects in a pedestrian manner? Objects can be fallen against, leaned on, etc. Noses can be pressed against windows as easily as hands can open them. Could the bottles behind the bar be contacted? "A drunk could fall on them." "He could have a fight with the bartender." As much as possible, the teacher should let the students discover principles for themselves. As a warm-up exercise select a specific object and have single players use it. Evaluation would then be on the variations possible with the simplest of objects. (see USING OBJECTS TO EVOLVE SCENES, p. 212.)

Did they show us Where they were by the use of the physical objects, or did they tell us? Did they show first and then tell? An action usually precedes dialogue.

Did they share what they were doing with us? This exploration into "sharing with the audience" will lead to a discussion of stage arrangements and self-blocking. Ask individual students to go on stage and demonstrate other ways of clarifying action.

Was the stage setting interesting? Would the fireplace have given more room if it had been stage right? Encourage them to think in terms of rooms they are familiar with. This will simplify working on floorplans and will enable them to spread the props and furniture over the entire stage area.

When a satisfactory evaluation has been made of the first team's work, have another team go through their where. Since the evaluation helps both the team on stage and the members of the audience, each team will be helped by the past evaluations of the other teams.

After the second team has worked, begin their evaluation by asking: did they benefit from our discussion with the first team?

1. In developing floorplans, it is important that *each* team member have a piece of chalk and be encouraged to make use of it, for this allows even the most timid person to contribute at least one object to the floorplan. This is the organic beginning of group involvement.

2. Introduced here for the first time, the floorplan immediately becomes an integral part of all future exercises. It is a visualization of the actor's Where. It is important that the student-actor's initial floorplan be compiled correctly and purposefully. For this reason, the teacher-director would do well to wander from group to group during the first planning session, offering suggestions and encouragement wherever needed. At first, the student-actors will place their items haphazardly, some putting too many on the board and some too few. As time goes on, they will become more selective and will choose and place items with an eye toward the total stage picture.

3. Before beginning a problem, be sure that the completed blackboard floorplan is in full view of the players on stage. Encourage them to refer to it freely and often. This gradual release from remembering will allow them to concentrate on the handling of the objects themselves, eliminating the need for remembering their location on stage. Always check the audience's perceptions against the actual floorplan after each exercise.

4. Constantly remind the actors to show where they are by using all the physical objects on the stage. Through this coaching, the actor's Point of Concentration will become clear to him.

5. When talking is mumbled or the actors hide in bunches outside the line of vision, side-coach: *Share the stage picture! Share your voice with your audience!* In almost every instance, students will respond.

6. These early scenes will almost certainly contain too much talking in the place of action—telling instead of showing. Relationships will be sketchy, object contact will be pedestrian, "sharing" will be negligible, concentration will be

sporadic. This will all be remedied with time, discovery, and coaching.

7. To avoid early playwriting, do not allow the players to plan a situation. Observe the teams closely during preparation of the exercise. If How they will manipulate the set is discussed, if scene is planned rather than What, if Point of Concentration (Where) is not observed, then the exercise becomes an unspontaneous, rehearsed activity.[4] Keep What (play) a simple physical activity between players.

8. Have the student-actors add more and more detail to their floorplans each time the exercise is given. Pictures, candy dishes, ashtrays, radios—all should be included. As they move around the room, channeling their energies to solve the problem, self-blocking will appear, awareness of fellow players will emerge, and they will gain entrance into their full stage environment.

9. Be sure that contact is made by each player with all the objects during this early period. Later, they no longer need to touch every object on stage—indeed, it will interfere with their work. But the discovery of this freedom and subsequent leveling off rests entirely with the teacher's judgment.

10. The Where, Who, and What, Point of Concentration, and additional information as the scenes become more complex should be written at the bottom of each floorplan. A file of completed floorplans is useful for reference when planning a performance.

11 . In the first few sessions of Where, have students use familiar interiors such as rooms in a house, offices, etc.

12. Players, being more on their own in these exercises than heretofore, may pull away from each other and work the POC separately although in the same situation. To avoid this, have the group show us Where through Who (relationship) and What (activity). If, for example, Where is a living-room and Who girl and boy friend, objects in the general environment might be used in many ways. The books in the bookcase might be taken to read poetry to the girl friend. The girl friend might use the chair by coming over and putting

---

[4]See discussion of How, p. 34.

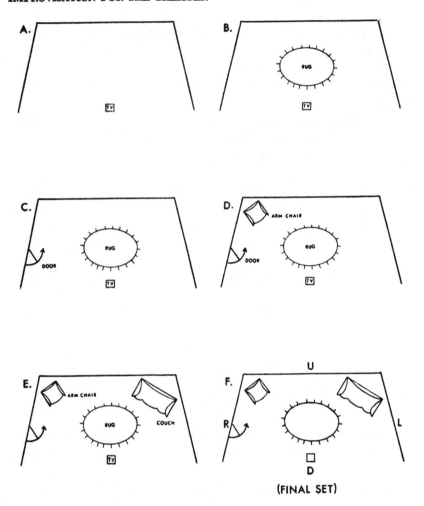

4 Additional information on floorplans

her arms around her boy friend who is sitting in the chair. It is the same problem of letting the POC move the players rather than imposing anything upon it. This is the only road to true scene improvisation, for it is only through relationship that stage action appears.

13. If players persist in using a built-in activity when doing Where, they are resisting the POC and relationship. For instance, if a bedroom is chosen as the Where and the players are housecleaning, this then becomes a built-in or non-chal-

lenging use of Where. To avoid this, suggest a problem where the players use a What more or less unrelated to the objects within the Where. The bedroom could be a place where two students are studying. A machine shop, for instance, could have two players playing checkers on their lunch hour. These unrelated activities (What) then keep total absorption with the game, and the preoccupation (POC) getting to the objects becomes the energy source.

THE WHERE GAME

(This is similar to the ORIENTATION GAME, but now the players concentrate on Where rather than on activity.)

Player goes on stage and shows Where through the physical use of the objects. When another player thinks he knows Where the first player is, he assumes a Who, enters the Where, and develops a relationship with the Where and the other player. Other players join them, one at a time, in a similar fashion.

POINT OF CONCENTRATION: on Where.

EXAMPLE: Player goes on stage and shows the audience rows and rows of bookshelves. Second player enters and stands behind counter. He begins stamping cards which he removes from inside cover of books. Third player enters, pushes cart to shelves, and begins stacking books. Other players enter the library Where. Other settings for WHERE GAME: train station, supermarket, airport, hospital waiting room, street scene, beach, schoolroom, art gallery, restaurant.

Second Where Session

The following WHAT'S BEYOND? A, B, and C exercises should be given in one session if possible. While the first handling of the exercise by new students will be primitive for the most part, repetition at intervals throughout the training period (e.g., after WORD GAME, during problems of Emotion) will bring added richness to the student-actor's work. When two more WHAT'S BEYOND exercises, D and E, are given later, repeat A, B, and C. These exercises heighten exits and entrances.

WHAT'S BEYOND? A

Single player.

Player is either to leave or enter a room (or both). Stage is used only to walk through; no action is to take place other than what is necessary to communicate to the audience what room he has come from and what room he is going to. (Suggest that stage is simply an empty hallway leading to and from doors.)

POINT OF CONCENTRATION: to show what room he has come from, what room he is going to.

EXAMPLE I (done by an adult): The character walks briskly on stage, wiping her hands on what seems to be a towel that she is holding. She unties something around her waist and hangs it on the doorknob. She moves across stage, stopping momentarily to take what appears to be a hat, puts it on her head, glances into a mirror, and briskly exits out another door.

EXAMPLE II (done by a 12-year-old): A character comes walking on stage, yawning and stretching. As he walks across the stage, he is slowly unbuttoning and easing out of what seems to be a loose-fitting garment. He rubs his tongue over his teeth as he exits out another door.

EVALUATION

What room did he come from? What room did he go to? Did he show us or tell us? Is it possible to show What's Beyond without some onstage activity? Keep the evaluation on the Point of Concentration only! We are not interested in anything but what was in the area the actor came from and what is in the area he is going to.

POINTS OF OBSERVATION

1. After the players have worked within this "room" situation, the exercise may be given again—this time with the player entering or leaving a specific location (such as a forest clearing, a department store, etc.).
2. WHAT'S BEYOND should be added to the floorplan.
3. As in HOW OLD AM I? REPEAT and WHAT DO I DO FOR A LIVING? REPEAT, try this exercise and the subsequent WHAT'S BEYOND? at a later date using the same suggested technique to see how

much of WHAT's BEYOND can be shown with the greatest of subtlety by "letting it happen."

WHAT'S BEYOND? B

Single player.

Played same as WHAT's BEYOND? A.

POINT OF CONCENTRATION: suggest what went on in the place (off stage) the player has just left.

EVALUATION

What happened off stage?

POINT OF OBSERVATION

If this exercise is given early in the Where session, the actors should keep it simple (e.g., a simple activity such as shoveling snow off the driveway). When repeated later on in the training, the offstage scene should then be based on a relationship with other people (e.g., a quarrel with a sweetheart, a theft of a purse, a death scene, etc.).

WHAT'S BEYOND? C

Single player.

Exact reversal of WHAT's BEYOND? B.

POINT OF CONCENTRATION: on what the player is going to do in the other room (off stage).

EVALUATION

What will happen off stage?

WHERE WITH HELP

Two players.

Where, Who, and What agreed upon. Players do scene with Contact, helping each other solve the problem.

POINT OF CONCENTRATION: to help each other make contact with everything in the Where while playing out Who and What.

Did they make contact with the objects through who they were and what they were doing, or did they make contact at random just for the sake of "touching" the objects?

POINTS OF OBSERVATION

1. Tell players to use a great deal of detail in drawing their floorplans (e.g., doors, windows, rugs). Keep What very simple with no particular tension between players (e.g., in a beauty shop getting hair done, in a living room just watching TV, etc.).
2. Players are to keep their own floorplan on stage for reference. Another floorplan is put on blackboard for audience. If no blackboard is available, an extra floorplan—without statement of relationships or What—should be passed around to audience.
3. Exercise is over the minute both players have made contact with everything in the Where. It may be necessary to call "One minute!" to end the exercise, although in some instances the exercise will end naturally by itself.

WHERE WITH OBSTACLES

Same team as in WHERE WITH HELP

Where, Who, and What agreed upon. This time each player is to try to keep the other from contacting all the objects.

SIDE COACHING: *Work on the problem!*

EVALUATION

Which exercise gave Where more reality—helping the other actor or putting obstacles in his way? Which gave Who more reality?

POINTS OF OBSERVATION

1. Stress to players that they are to make contact with objects through the What and Who of the scene. They are not just to dash around touching objects. Their actions must come out of a relationship.

2. Watch to see how relationships are strengthened. This exercise is similar to GIVE AND TAKE (p. 230). If heightened reality and relationships are not evident, continue the simple Where for a few more sessions.
3. Note that players must watch each other most intently so as to solve the problem.

Third Where Session

FINDING OBJECTS IN THE IMMEDIATE ENVIRONMENT

Three or more players.

A simple stage relationship and a likely discussion which keeps everyone involved are agreed upon. This could be a committee meeting, office workers, family council, etc. During the course of this meeting, each player is to handle dozens of objects in the immediate environment. They do not plan ahead what these objects will be.

POINTS OF CONCENTRATION: on receiving the objects the agreed environment has to offer (letting the environment work for the players).

SIDE COACHING: *Take your time! Don't meddle, let the objects appear! Keep the discussion going! Work on the problem! Keep in contact with each other!*

EVALUATION

Did the actors invent objects or did they wait for them to appear? Did players see each other's objects and use them? Is it possible to do this exercise without being intent upon each other? Did they talk their objects or contact them? To actors: did objects come through association, or did they appear?

POINTS OF OBSERVATION

1. Suggest players select a gathering seated around a table.
2. This exercise is related to SPACE SUBSTANCE and belongs in the transformation group.
3. Resistance to working this problem will show itself in players using only the most obvious things and continuously pulling

away from the environment and the other players. Inventing, they soon run out of things to handle. When the problem is solved, however, much to everyone's excitement, endless objects are the result: bread becomes crumbs, paper scraps, lint appears on a neighbor's coat, dust floats through the air, and pencils come from behind ears. Let your players discover this for themselves.

4. This is another of the two-way problems. The on-stage occupation, the meeting, must be continuous, while the preoccupation, the POC, must be worked on at all times. Some players will keep the meeting going and neglect the POC, others will work only on the POC and neglect the meeting. Side-coach accordingly.

WHERE WITH UNRELATED ACTIVITY

Two players.

Where and Who agreed upon. What is to be a mutual activity not dependent upon Where they are (e.g., a dancing lesson in the bedroom, building a boat in the living room).

POINTS OF CONCENTRACTION: players must make physical contact with all the objects in the general environment as drawn on the floorplan while pursuing their mutual activity.

POINT OF OBSERVATION

This exercise was developed to help players understand that it is only through relationship (Who) and activity (What) that the stage environment (Where) comes to total life for audience and actor alike. This two-way problem gives the players both occupation (activity) and preoccupation (POC). It would seem that a two-way problem consistently stirs up stage action because it temporarily removes the censoring mechanism that holds players to old frames of reference and pedestrian or stereotyped behavior.

WHERE GAME

See First Where Session, p. 101.

WHAT TIME IS IT? A

Single player.

Bare stage. No detailed Where. Player writes a time on a slip of paper and hands it to teacher before going on stage.

POINT OF CONCENTRATION: on the time of day.

EXAMPLE I: Man enters and closes door with exaggerated quiet, He leans down and removes his shoes. Putting them under his arm, he stealthily and unsteadily crosses the stage. Accidentally bumping into a chair, he stands frozen and listens intently. Nothing happens. Silently hiccoughing, he moves with high steps toward an inside door, puts his head in very carefully, listens, and hears—with great satisfaction—a snore. He exits, still hiccoughing.

EXAMPLE II (done by a ten-year-old): Girl comes sleepily on stage, crosses, opens the refrigerator, and takes out what appears to be a bottle. Yawning, she takes a pan from a cupboard shelf and partially fills it with water from the sink faucet. She then places the bottle in the pan and lights the stove. As she stands watching it, her head nods sleepily in a doze. She picks up the bottle and shakes it on her forearm, yawningly puts it back in the pan, and again nods her head, heavy with sleep. Once more she picks up the bottle, shakes it on her forearm, seems satisfied, turns off the stove, and sleepily exits.

EXAMPLE III: A man enters and sets himself to work building something. After a time, he puts his tools aside, opens his lunch-pail, and proceeds to eat its contents. When he has finished eating, he returns to work.

EVALUATION

What time was it? Did he show us or tell us? If audience says he was a drunken husband afraid of his wife, repeat: What time was it?

Is it possible to show time without an accompanying activity? Is lunchtime always noon? What about the night worker? Is it possible to show time without using our cultural frames of reference (i.e., in our 9-to-5 culture, we have set ways of showing 6 A.M., noon, 5 P.M., *etc.*)?

WHAT TIME IS IT? B

(To be given immediately after WHAT TIME IS IT? A.)
Large group of players.

Players sit or stand on stage. Teacher-director gives same time to all of them. They are to sit quietly on stage, working separately. They may move only if they are pushed to do so by the Point of Concentration; but they are not to bring in activity just to show time.

POINT OF CONCENTRATION: to feel time through their bodies, muscularly and kinesthetically.

SIDE COACHING: *Feel the time in your feet. In your spine.*

EVALUATION

Is there bodily reaction to time? Is the drowsiness of late afternoon different from midnight drowsiness? Is there only sleep-time, work-time, hungry-time? Is clock-time a cultural pattern? Is it possible to communicate time without handling props, setting up Where, etc.?

POINTS OF OBSERVATION

1. Actors will vary considerably in feeling time. For instance, 2:00 A.M. will put some actors to sleep; but the night-owl in the group will become wide awake.
2. Time should now be added to the Where floorplan.
3. This exercise should be handled the same as HOW OLD AM I? REPEAT and WHAT DO I DO FOR A LIVING? REPEAT.

WHAT TIME IS IT? C

Three or more players

Players agree upon Where, Who, What, and Time.

POINT OF CONCENTRATION: on time, allowing it to determine the way the scene will develop. Evaluation and Side Coaching follow the usual line.

WHO GAME[5]

Two players.

A seated on stage. B enters. B has pre-planned definite character relationship with A but has not told him what it is. By the way B relates to A, A must discover Who he is. When players have finished, reverse the scene, with B on stage and A choosing relationship.

POINT OF CONCENTRATION: to communicate relationship (Who) without telling a story; to find out Who you are (A); to show Who, the relationship (B).

EXAMPLE: A (girl) is seated on bench. B (girl) enters. B: "Hello, darling. How are you?" B starts fussing over A's hair. She then walks around A, looking her over most critically. B asks A to stand up. A does so. B turns her around, making clicking sounds. B "You look beautiful, darling; just beautiful!" B then puts her arms around A with great tenderness and rocks her back and forth. She stops, wipes a tear away, then hurriedly gets busy fussing with A again. She handles what looks like yards and yards of a bouffant skirt, then picks up a long, trailing piece of cloth which she places on A's hair. When A knows she is the daughter and this is in preparation for her wedding, she enters into the relationship.

EVALUATION

Did B show the relationship or tell?

POINTS OF OBSERVATION

1. This is one of the early steps in the direct handling of character relationship and should be repeated throughout the training period.
2. Use a bench, rather than a single seat, on stage.
3. The exercise can end the moment the problem is solved—when the relationship is known—or can continue. Sometimes an interesting involvement takes place and much can be gained by continuing.

See also SHOWING WHO THROUGH USE OF OBJECT, p. 139, and ART GALLERY, p. 139.

4. Suggest that the students play this as a parlor game with their friends.
5. If this game is given too early in the training, the student-actors may verbalize and make an intellectual game out of it. Should this occur, playing should be stopped and evaluated (show and not tell). Using gibberish here stops telling.
6. Repeating this game every few months provides an excellent picture of student-actors' development and in their growing selectivity and improvisational skills.
7. This game can be used for audience participation, where everyone but player knows Who he is.

Fourth Where Session

It is a good idea to begin each session with a warm-up exercise. Selections for warm-up are determined by the needs of the group—whether it is an object-involvement exercise repeated, a Who exercise, or whatever.

WHO'S KNOCKING? A

Single player.

Player is out of audience's view. They can only hear his knock.

Player is to know Who he is, Where he is, time, weather, etc. He is then to knock in a way that will communicate as much of this information to the audience as possible.

POINT OF CONCENTRATION: on knocking; to show Who, Where, and What, through knocking.

EXAMPLE: Different kinds of knocks might be: policeman at night, telegram, rejected sweetheart, messenger from the king, gangster entering a hideaway, spy, frightened neighbor, very young child, old man.

WHO'S KNOCKING? B

Single player

A variation especially valuable for young actors. After asking student audience the Where, Who and What of a knock, the teacher will find that many of them did not know the exact circumstances. After Evaluation, when the action has been clarified, have the player repeat WHO'S KNOCKING, and the audience will listen more intently and find communication clearer. Now ask the student-actor who was the person he was trying to get to and have him go off stage and knock again, also calling out to whomever he was trying to reach. Send another student-actor on stage (quickly set up a Where) and have him be the person being called.

EXAMPLE: A young boy coming home from school is knocking on a front door.

Teacher: *Whom are you trying to reach?*

Student: "My mother, but she is in the shower." ("In the shower" is "story-telling" or "playwriting".)

Teacher: *How do you know she is in the shower if you have just come home from school?* Now, the teacher asks again: *Where are you?*

Student: "Knocking on the front door of my house trying to get in."

Have student return to stage and knock and call again, (an extension of the outside Where is quickly designated to the one knocking : a kitchen window, back door, etc.). Have the young actor try to get in the house, calling to his mother as well as knocking. After he knocks and calls from the door with no answer he runs (continuing to call) to the window and then to the back door. Someone, then, can be sent on stage to be his mother and let him in.

EXAMPLE II: Player tells audience after initial knock that she is in a locked clothes closet trying to get out. Send someone on stage to be her mother; add obstacles to her getting out (she cannot open door, etc).

This is simply an example of how with the simple warm-up exercise WHO'S KNOCKING a player can move into Where, Who, and What and build a more complicated stage situation.

EVALUATION

Who knocked? Where was he? What was the reason for the knock? What age? What weight? Was it possible to tell the time? What color hair did he have?

1. Many questions in the Evaluation may be unanswerable; but it is interesting to ask, for many new insights often occur this way.
2. This exercise is designed to show the student-actor how a sense of character and where he is and what he is doing can be determined by something as simple as the quality of a knock.
3. Repeating the knock after Evaluation, as in the example shown, is especially valuable in keeping young student audiences "part of the game." Helping the very young student audience become more involved with what the other students are doing and really listen is often a serious problem for teachers and group leaders in the early work.

ADD AN OBJECT WHERE #2

Whole group.

Agree on Where. Each player is to go on stage and place something in the Where. However, player is not to add his object until he has used the other objects already placed in the Where. This process of addition continues until the players have all added an object. Now they continue just as in the WHERE GAME (p. 101).

POINT OF CONCENTRATION: To build a Where.

EXAMPLE: A pet shop. First player goes on stage and places a counter. Second player uses counter and places birdcage. Third player uses counter and birdcage and places aquarium. Fourth player uses counter, birdcage, and aquarium and places broom closet. And so on.

EVALUATION

How many just plunked objects on stage and neglected to build the Where? How many developed definite characters when they came in to add an object?

POINTS OF OBSERVATION

1. This exercise can be given when drawing floorplans is not

practical, as with very young students or very large groups of older children. If the workshop plan given in this handbook is followed, the exercise should be given after the WHERE GAME.

2. This exercise is much like ONCE UPON A TIME (see p. 307) except that real props are not used.

4. Following is a variation of the ADD AN OBJECT WHERE. One player goes on stage, puts an object in the Where, and uses it. Second player enters, relates to first player, and uses object first player has placed on stage. First player exits. Second player adds another object. Third player enters, relates in some way to second player, uses objects one and two. Second player exits. Third player adds an object. Fourth player enters, relates to player, uses objects one, two, and three. Third player exits. Fourth player adds an object. And so on.

Fifth Where Session

MIRROR EXERCISE #3
See Fourth Orientation Session, p. 75.

WEATHER EXERCISE #1
One player.

POINT OF CONCENTRATION: kind of weather or climate player is experiencing.

EVALUATION

Did the weather envelop him? Did he use his whole body to show us (e.g., was heat shown by his trousers sticking to his legs or did he just mop off his face)? Did he concentrate on the weather or a character? Did he concentrate on the weather or a situation?

Repeat this exercise at this time or at a later date, following the procedure of HOW OLD AM I? REPEAT and WHAT DO I DO FOR A LIVING? REPEAT.

WEATHER EXERCISE #2

Large group.

Group sits or stands on stage. Players agree upon, or are given by other students or teacher-director, a type of weather or climate. They are to show the audience the kind of weather they are experiencing, and they are to do it without using their hands.

POINT OF CONCENTRATION: on weather.

SIDE COACHING: *Feel the rain between your toes. Down your spine. At the end of your nose!*

EVALUATION To actors: Did you feel the rain differently without the use of your hands? To audience: was this a more interesting showing of weather?

POINT OF OBSERVATION

This exercise should be given immediately after all the players have completed WEATHER EXERCISE #1 and the Evaluation has been given.

WEATHER EXERCISE #3

(Should be given at same session with previous WEATHER EXERCISES.)
Two or more players. Where, Who, and What agreed upon.

POINT OF CONCENTRATION: around weather or climate

EVALUATION

Did concentration on weather create tension on stage? Did weather work for the actors, or was weather just thrown in? Did weather help develop the content of the scene?

POINT OF OBSERVATION

Weather should be added to all floorplans from now on. Include some mention of it in all evaluations, since it can add interesting nuances to any scene.

114

WHO GAME, ADDING WHERE AND WHAT

Same as who game, p. 109, with addition of Where and What.
EXAMPLE: A (girl) seated on stage. B (man) enters, looks
anxiously about stage. Sees girl and comes downstage right. Girl
is seated SL. Man stands a moment on SR, looks at girl, and then
moves toward her, moving in front of seats (as in a theater) to
get to her. He is now face to face with her. He gives her a quick
nod of recognition and a quick tender smile. He stops the smile
abruptly and with serious face sits down alongside her. Certain
no one is looking, he sidles close to her and surreptitiously takes
her hand, squeezes it, and then quickly drops it. He then sits
looking straight ahead with his head slightly bowed, taking sur-
reptitious glances at A from time to time.

EVALUATION

Where are they? Who is she? Who is he?

POINTS OF OBSERVATION

1. Watch for an increasingly interesting selection of detail from
   the actors.
2. A variation of the game would give the student-audience another aspect of the same problem. In the game just covered,
   they are involved with the unknown (A's point of view). As
   added fun, allow them in on the pre-planning, from the
   known (B's point of view). Simply have B write down Where
   and Who and pass it around the audience for them to read.
3. Another variation is to have many Where's and Who's on
   slips of paper. B selects one of each just prior to going on
   stage.
4. If student-actors have become skilled in playing, this exercise can go on for a very long time and stay in process. If,
   however, players tell a story instead of playing, stop them
   immediately. The moment we know Who and Where and
   What, the scene is over. This supplies an added challenge to
   the players.

Sixth Where Session

Choice of warm-up exercises will be determined by the needs
of students. Is their handling of objects sloppy? Do they need

work on Who? Do they need work on Seeing? Plan warm-ups accordingly.

EXPLORATION OF LARGER ENVIRONMENT

Two or more players.

Teacher-director begins session by suggesting environment around which Where is to be used. He may suggest a general environment (e.g., "Today we will work with the outdoors" or "with enclosed areas") Or he may designate a more specific environment (e.g., "Today we will work around water"). Students now agree on Who and What and play scene.

POINT OF CONCENTRATION: on relating to the larger over-all environment.

EXAMPLES: Outdoors—water, woods, forest, jungle, mountains. Enclosed—cave, tomb, boxcar, tower, prison cell.

EVALUATION

What was above them? Beneath them? What was beyond?

POINTS OF OBSERVATION

1. Many students will have difficulty relating to environments other than the immediate environments of home, office, school, bar, etc. In this exercise, they are forced out into the larger, more distant environments.
2. Some students, to avoid the exercise, will get side-tracked by a little detail at hand (no matter how large or what the environment, they will always end up building a fire). They must be made to see and communicate with the larger environment beyond them (e.g., space, water, an enclosure, lack of space, etc.).
3. This exercise helps the student, in exploring the larger environment, to make use of the space where the audience sits.

Seventh Where Session

QUICK SELECTION EXERCISE FOR WHERE

Paper and pencils.

Each student is to write down the names of three objects

which most readily indicate each of the following places. The object is not to be part of the decor (such as sawdust on the floor) but should be one physical inanimate object (i.e., an altar would suggest a church, a movable bed would suggest a hospital, etc.). When individual lists have been completed, they are to be compared and discussed.

POINT OF CONCENTRATION: to indicate Where through one related object

LIST OF PLACES

a jail	a church steeple
a dungeon	a tree house
a cellar	a cocktail lounge
a cave	a saloon
a boxcar	a greasy-spoon restaurant
a hospital room	a coffee shop
a child's bedroom	a dining room
a dormitory	a dentist's office
a mine	a library
an attic	a church
a tower	a drug store

EVALUATION

Did the object readily indicate the Where, or could the example have been more explicit? Can objects alone show Where? Is it attitude toward and use of objects that clarify Where?

POINTS OF OBSERVATION

1. This exercise should give the student some understanding of how a selected detail will help make an interesting communication with an audience.
2. This is *not* a game of association. It is an exercise in selectivity.

EXCHANGING WHERE

Two or more players per team. Try to keep equal distribution of sexes.

Each team agrees on Where, Who, What, time, weather, what's beyond, etc. and does a floorplan.

When all groups have finished, collect the floorplans and redistribute them so that each team has another's floorplan. Redistribution should occur at the moment the team is on stage—*not before*. Team may not go off stage for a discussion but must go right into the scene as structured by floorplan.

POINT OF CONCENTRATION: players must enter into scene without any forethought; they must remain with planned structure presented on floor plan.

EVALUATION

Did they follow the floorplan?

POINTS OF OBSERVATION

1. In spite of warnings, student-actors tend to plan How in advance. EXCHANGING WHERE will alleviate this tendency. It is also one of the steps toward developing skills in SUGGESTIONS BY THE AUDIENCE.
2. Do not tell students in advance that the floorplans will be collected and redistributed. Have them work on them as if they were going to carry them through.
3. Try to keep the same number and distribution of sexes on each team, so that the floorplans will have meaning for different teams.
4. Do not give the floorplan to the team until they are already on stage.

Eighth Where Session

INVOLVEMENT WITH THE IMMEDIATE ENVIRONMENT

Two players. Preferably seated. Relationships agreed upon.

POINT OF CONCENTRATION: to show Where through continuous picking at small objects (contact) in the immediate environment.

EXAMPLES: In the course of conversation at a restaurant, players might pick at napkins, swizzle sticks, crumbs, cigarette butts, flies, etc.

SIDE COACHING: *Keep focus on objects around you! Show us Who you are through the immediate environment!*

EVALUATION

Did the handling of small physical objects in the environment become part of the total scene, or did dialogue stop when objects were being handled? Did Where they were come to life through the objects? Did they show us or tell us? Who were they? What was the shape of the salt shaker? Was there a cloth on the table?

POINTS OF OBSERVATION

1. The purpose of the exercise is to make the players aware of, and coach them to integrate, their action with the small details in their immediate environment.
2. Caution the students that they are not to perform a full activity, such as eating a meal. If a restaurant is chosen for Where, suggest that the dialogue between them take place after the meal has been completed but before the dishes have been cleared away.
3. This exercise should be repeated after some work on ARGUMENT, p. 180.
4. If NO MOTION (p. 189) has been given early in workshop training (recommended if the group is naturally skilled), the present exercise need not be used; for NO MOTION A brings extraordinary life and detail to the minutest object in the immediate environment. With some groups, however, the present exercise is more desirable. As in all such matters, the judgment of the teacher-director is what counts.

WHERE THROUGH THREE OBJECTS

Single player. Goes on stage and shows audience Where through the use of three objects.

POINT OF CONCENTRATION: to build a Where through three objects.

EXAMPLE: Where—greasy-spoon restaurant. Objects—juke box, dining counter, phone booth.

EVALUATION

Did the three objects handled build the Where, or were they isolated objects? Did you see a greasy-spoon restaurant?

POINTS OF OBSERVATION

1. Repeat at regular intervals throughout training.
2. Watch to see that this exercise does not become an activity exercise, and side-coach accordingly. If the problem is solved the Where becomes a reality and an extraordinary sense of a total environment comes from the three objects alone, and is communicated to the audience.
3. This is a valuable exercise as a step towards developing on-the-spot scenes from suggestions by the audience.
4. This exercise should be used after QUICK SELECTION.

Ninth Where Session

Developing Organic Response Through Gibberish

Gibberish is an extremely valuable exercise and should be used throughout the workshops. For the director of the formal play, gibberish is a great aid in releasing the actor from the multitude of technical details surrounding the initial plunge into rehearsal and freeing him to move spontaneously and naturally within his role.

Gibberish is, simply enough, the substitution of shaped sounds for recognizable words. It should not be confused with "double talk," where actual words are inverted or mispronounced in order to scramble the meaning. Gibberish is a vocal utterance *accompanying an action*, not the translation of an English phrase. The meaning of a sound in gibberish should not be understood unless the actor conveys it by his action, expressions, or tone of voice; however, it is important that this should be left for the student-actor to discover.

A scene that cannot be understood in gibberish is usually nothing but gags, story, plot, or ad-libbing. Gibberish develops the expressive physical language vital to stage life, by removing the dependency on words alone to express meaning. Because gibberish uses sounds of language minus the symbols (words), this puts the problem of communication on a direct-experiential level.

The actor showing the most resistance to gibberish is usually the person who relies almost completely on words in place of experiencing and shows great anxiety when these words are taken away from him. Since he almost invariably fights contact in any form, his everyday body movement is stiff; and his isolation from his fellow actors is quite pronounced.

There will also be the student who will keep insisting that the teacher spell it out: "Should it be through action or gibberish that the communication is made?" The older and more anxious the student, the more he will prod the teacher to answer this question. One anxiety-ridden student who finally received great insight remarked: "You are on your own when you speak gibberish!" When asked if that wasn't also true when she used words, she thought a moment and replied: "No, when you use words, people know the words you are saying. So you don't have to do anything yourself."

Let students find this out for themselves. Gibberish, if communicated properly, can only bring about total physical response. But if the teacher *tells* the student he is to do it through action, he will then concentrate on action and will not get the experience he should have. We want integration of sound with physical or organic response; and it must come spontaneously from the student.

Because sound without symbols—except in the case of pain, joy, fear, or astonishment—cannot be recognized without body functioning, gibberish forces the student-actor to show and not tell. Because the sounds are meaningless, the player has no way of escaping. Then physicalizing mood, problem, relation, and character becomes organic. Body holds are released, for players must listen and watch each other closely if they are to understand one another.

Scenes without sound, loosely called "pantomime" (see Chapter V), will not achieve the same results as gibberish; for we must not abstract sound (dialogue) from action. Dialogue and action are interdependent: dialogue creates action, and action creates dialogue. The student-actor must be freed physically as he speaks. The insecurity which can keep the flow and intonation

121

of the dialogue static will disappear as the student-actors lessen their dependency on words.

Insight into useless dialogue (ad-lib) often appears at this time. Dialogue that is not part of the expressive physical language of the stage life, is, after all, only gibberish!

Introducing Gibberish

Developing fluency in "no-symbol" speech brings with it a release from word patterns that may not come easily to some student-actors. The teacher should illustrate what gibberish is before using it as a stage exercise. (He may have to practice his own fluency before presenting gibberish to the group.) Such an illustration might consist of simple communications initiated by the teacher. Using gibberish, ask a student to stand up. Go to him and, with a gesture, indicate the command. Use a sound to accompany the gesture—*Gallorusheo!* If he is slow to respond, repeat the sound or invent a new phrase and strengthen the gesture. Ask other students to sit down (*moolasay!*), move about (*rallavo!*), sing (*plagee?*). Make a student sing the scale by pointing to him and singing from "do" to "fa" using only the sound "o" and pointing again.

Have students turn to their neighbors and carry on conversations as if speaking an unknown language. They should converse as though making perfect sense. Keep the conversations going until everyone participates. Stress the use of as many different sounds as possible, exaggeration of mouth movements, and tonal variation. Have those who stick with a monotonous *dadeeda* sound with little lip movement converse with those who speak more easily.

Have the students who seem to speak gibberish with confidence ask others in the group to hold hands, open a window, pick up a book—simple actions which can be easily communicated. While most of the group should be over their initial fear of joining in the activity, there will be one or two student-actors who are so tied to speech for communication that they will be almost paralyzed, physically as well as vocally. Their gibberish will come out as defective speech, or they will retain exactly the word and sentence pattern of what they are saying and simply garble the individual word sound. Their actions will be jerky.

Do not belabor the point with them. Treat it most casually, and before the third session of gibberish is completed, flow of sound and body expression will be one.

GIBBERISH #1—DEMONSTRATION

One player.

Stands on stage. He is to sell or demonstrate something to the audience in gibberish. When he has finished, have him repeat but ask him to pitch what he is selling or demonstrating.

POINT OF CONCENTRATION: to communicate (show) to audience.

SIDE COACHING: *Sell directly to us! See us!*

EVALUATION

Was there variety in the gibberish? Did he maintain direct communication with the audience? Did he see the audience or stare at them? Was there a difference between the first selling and the second? Why did pitching bring greater intensity to the player's work?

POINTS OF OBSERVATION:

1. Demonstrating or selling *directly* to the audience must be insisted upon. At first, the player will stare out or look over the heads of the audience. If pitching does not alleviate this, it may be necessary to have the player repeat a few times until he really *sees* the audience.
2. It will become evident in the student-actor's work when his stares become seeing. (cf. Seeing and Not Staring, Chapter VII.) Both the audience and the player will experience the difference. An added depth, a certain quiet, will come into the work when this happens.
3. Pitching requires direct contact with others. Students will discover this for themselves. If the point is understood, even momentarily, it will be an important breakthrough for many of the students.

GIBBERISH #2—PAST INCIDENT

Two players.

Players on stage. Using gibberish, A tells B of a past incident (such as a fight he was in or a trip to the dentist). B then tells A of something that happened to him, also using gibberish.

POINT OF CONCENTRATION: on communication to each other.

EVALUATION

Ask A what B told him. Then ask B what A told him. (Neither player must *assume* what the other has related, since B's assumptions will not help A to make the clear communication necessary for solving the problem.) Ask the audience what was communicated to them.

POINTS OF OBSERVATION

1. To avoid preliminary discussion, the two players should be picked at random just prior to going on stage.
2. This exercise should be repeated at intervals throughout training.
3. When this exercise is first played, students will act out (tell) their incident in great detail. If relating a visit to the dentist's office, for instance, they will hold their jaw, open their mouth wide, poke at their teeth, groan, etc. When the exercise is re-done after months of workshop, however, the integration of sound and physical expression will be most subtly communicated. The players will be able to communicate the same events with a shrug of the shoulders or a slight dilation of the nostrils or a wiggle of the foot. They will be able to show, not tell.

GIBBERISH #3—TEACHING

TEACHING A

Two players.

Players each decide on a Where and Who. They both have the same What: to teach, using gibberish. Subject could be how to take pictures, play a guitar, etc.

POINT OF CONCENTRATION: to instruct another.

TEACHING B

Two or three large teams.

Teams are to be in schoolroom situations. Each team agrees

upon Where, Who, and What. Floorplans should be used to insure detailed environment. Students play scene in gibberish.

POINT OF CONCENTRATION: to instruct a group and experience their response.

EXAMPLES: children's first-grade class, medical students in dissection class.

GIBBERISH #4—THE GIBBERISH GAME

Played same as the WHERE GAME (p. 101).

One player goes on stage and sets up a Where, into which other players enter, after deciding upon specific characters for themselves. They speak in gibberish.

POINT OF CONCENTRATION: on the gibberish.

Exercises For Three More Where Sessions

TWO SCENES EXERCISE A, B, and C
See p. 160.

GIBBERISH #5—WHERE WITH GIBBERISH

Any size team

Floorplans prepared by each team as usual. Scenes are done in gibberish. After each team's performance, the players repeat the same scene in English.

POINT OF CONCENTRATION: on making everything that happens on stage understandable to the other actors.

SIDE COACHING: During gibberish, *Communicate to the other player! Don't expect him to interpret! What are you telling him?*

EVALUATION

Was the meaning of the English dialogue close to or the same as the gibberish communication?

POINT OF OBSERVATION

1. This exercise will very clearly show the student-audience where communications were clear and where the players as-

sumed or filled in for each other. Make it clear that we can only help each other by evaluating the reality that was exactly communicated, not a generality which the audience or the other players filled in for us.

2. Unnecessary verbalizing comes sharply to the students' attention when there are no understandable words between players.

3. Repeating in English is done simply to determine how exact the communication had been made in gibberish. During the English version of the exercise, stop the action continuously to ask the opposite player and the audience, "Did he communicate that in gibberish?" Once the point of unnecessary dialogue becomes clear through this means, the scene does not have to be completed.

WHAT DO I DO FOR A LIVING? REPEAT

Same as HOW OLD AM I? REPEAT.

GIBBERISH #6—FOREIGN LANGUAGE

FOREIGN LANGUAGE A

Team of four players.

Team sub-divides. Together, the sub-teams agree on Where, Who, and What. The two players within each sub-team speak the same language; however, each sub-team speaks a language not understood by the other.

EXAMPLE #1: Where—deck of ocean liner. Who—Sub-team A: young girl and companion; Sub-team B: husband and wife. What —relaxing in deck chairs.

EXAMPLE #2: Where—border customs office. Who—Sub-team A: mother and daughter. Sub-team B: official and countryman. What—mother, daughter, countryman seeking visas.

EVALUATION

Did the sub-teams understand each other? Did players speaking same language communicate freely to each other?

126

POINTS OF OBSERVATION:

1. It is interesting to note that if the student-actors are working on the POC (on the gibberish), when the sub-teams are speaking to each other the gibberish is very labored and accompanied by many large gestures. But when they are speaking within their own sub-teams (speaking the "same language"), they communicate fluently and with minimal gesturing. The fact that they are using gibberish in both instances does not seem to occur to them.
2. Tell the players not to give any particular language rhythms to their gibberish (such as French, Swedish, etc.).
3. This exercise should produce a complete breakthrough into gibberish by the most resistant student-actor. Sound should now flow and be completely integrated with bodily expression. Gibberish should not interfere with the total communication. If this does not happen in this exercise, gibberish has not been presented correctly to the students.

FOREIGN LANGUAGE B

Two players.

Exercise played same as FOREIGN LANGUAGE A, with each player speaking a different language.

POINT OF CONCENTRATION: on the gibberish.

GIBBERISH #7—TWO SCENES WITH GIBBERISH

Incorporate gibberish into the exercise called TWO SCENES (see Non-directional Blocking, p. 160). This exercise is particularly interesting. The teams must be alerted to give the Frame (close-up) to each other; and since they are speaking in gibberish, they must be greatly involved in the full stage action.

Additional Exercises For Heightening The Reality Of Where

Stop!

Before moving ahead into the following exercises, it is most important to go into WORD GAME (Chapter IX). We may find students at a loss for fresh material. They become tired of the familiar living room or schoolroom; development slows down if they constantly assume characters of schoolteachers and an occasional storekeeper. This is particularly true of the young actor.

WORD GAME releases more "playing" and generates a good deal of excitement and fun. Because it allows each team to play two or three scenes, it brings a flow to their work; it further shows the teacher-director (similar to the run-through in directing a play) how far students have come and what their needs are.

It would also be advisable to do a few exercises from Chapters V and VII before coming back to the additional Where exercises.

VERBALIZING THE WHERE

Two or more players.

Where, Who, and What agreed upon.

PART A

Players sit quietly on stage. Without leaving their chairs, they go through the scene verbally, describing their action and relation to the Where and to the other players. In short, they narrate for themselves. When dialogue is necessary, it is given directly to the other player, interrupting the narration. The entire scene, narration and dialogue, is done in present tense.

POINT OF CONCENTRATION: to state every involvement, relationship, observation, etc. while verbally playing the scene.

SIDE COACHING: *Keep it in the present! Give us a detailed description of that object! Describe the other players for us! See yourself in action! What color is the sky!*

EXAMPLE

Player #1: I tie my apron around my waist and reach for the red-and-white, cloth-covered cookbook on the table. I sit down at the table and open the book. I turn to the section on cookies and thumb through the smooth, shiny, white pages, looking for a recipe. *Hmmm, sugar cookies—that sounds pretty good.* I ponder over it a minute and then decide to look farther. I turn some more pages. I find two pages stuck together, the edges brown and stiff.

I wonder what's on this page—must be something good. I insert my finger between the two pages and unstick the corner. I find a recipe for chocolate-drop cookies. *Chocolate drop cookies . . . now let's see, do I have chocolate?* I put the book down on the table, get up, and walk to the yellow cabinets over the sink. I reach for the handle of the cabinet to the right of the window. One of the decals is loose. I fasten it and open the cabinet. I hear the screen door open and slam behind me.

Player #2: I open the screen door and run into the kitchen. Darn it, I let the door slam again! *Hey, mom, I'm hungry. What's for dinner?* (And so on.)

PART B

When the players have finished talking through the scene, they get up and actually play the scene through. This exercise provokes scene material.

POINT OF CONCENTRATION: to retain as much physical reality from the verbalization as possible.

EVALUATION

To actors: Did the verbalization of the scene help you in on-stage reality? Was the playing of the scene easier because of the verbalization?

To audience: was greater depth brought to the playing of the scene because of the verbalization? Was there more life in the playing of the scene than usual? Was involvement and relationship greater than usual?

POINTS OF OBSERVATION

1. This exercise serves a similar function to the Relaxed Rehearsal (see Directing for the Formal Theater, p. 336) in that it gives perspective to the actor and brings "self" back into the picture. It also brings the physical stage to life.
2. Except for the practice of side-coaching some of the mirror and space exercises, the exercises up to this point have attempted to objectify the student-actor, to make him a part of the group, the environment, and the exercise—to create a *loss of self.* In this exercise, we bring self back to the actor. He is made conscious of himself as a part of the environment. This is most important; for the actor, much like the player in a

game, must always know where he is in relation to what is happening on stage.

3. Note the complete absence of playwriting in these scenes as true improvisation appears.
4. It is not necessary that every detail covered in the narration be a part of the playing of the scene. This exercise gives an enrichment in detail and underlining which will be accomplished even if the narration is not followed to the letter.
5. Take care that this exercise is given only to those students who have become truly objective in their work. If it is given too early—before students have mastered "loss of self"—it will defeat its own purpose, in that it will bring subjectivity before objectivity has been grasped.[6]
6. This exercise has been played successfully with as many as ten players in a scene.
7. The problem must be handled carefully to avoid playwriting. If narration deals with what the players are thinking rather than on the detail of *physical* realities around them, this exercise can become a series of "soap operas."
8. VERBALIZING THE WHERE is valuable to use during rehearsals of improvisational theater and during a run when details and reality are lost or become sloppy. It is also valuable for the formal theater rehearsal.

WHAT'S BEYOND? D

Two players.

Simple Where agreed upon. A is on stage. B enters. A must find out where B has been and what he has done without B telling him. A must then start scene on stage related to what B was doing off stage.

POINT OF CONCENTRATION: what's beyond.

EXAMPLE: Where—dining room. Who—husband and wife. What —wife selecting food from a party buffet table.

Scene opens with wife helping herself to a drink and some food. Husband enters with very pleased look on his face. He

---

[6]Players must have thoroughly solved Where to get full benefit from this exercise. RELATING TO INCIDENT, p. 170, is a preliminary step to this problem.

lightly brushes off his jacket and smoothes his hair as he comes downstage to wife. Wife then starts action relating to where husband was and what he was doing.

EVALUATION

Did A assume what happened off stage, or did B show it? Did A find out by questioning? Did situation move into scene or simply end when A knew what B had done? Did actors stay with the Point of Concentration, or did they start acting?

POINTS OF OBSERVATION

1. This exercise, by expanding the reality off stage, will enrich on-stage work.
2. As the exercise is repeated at intervals throughout the training period, watch for growing subtlety of selection in student-actors. In the early sessions, if A comes on stage after having lost money in a gambling game, he might turn his pockets insied out and shake his head sadly. A later presentation of this same problem should communicate the same off-stage scene through a far more subtle level of action.
3. If communication has not been made, have the student-actors repeat the exercise after the evaluation has been given.

WHAT'S BEYOND? E

Two players.

Where, Who, and What agreed upon. Players are to pursue their What on stage. They have either done something (together) before they came on stage or are going to do something in the beyond when they leave. It is never brought out into the open.

POINT OF CONCENTRATION: on what has happened in the beyond or what will happen—while totally involved in an on-stage activity.

Evaluation and Side Coaching follow the same pattern of all the WHAT'S BEYOND. This can be played by a single player.

WHAT'S BEYOND? F

Two players.

Where, Who and What agreed upon. Players pursue on-stage

activity while something that involves both of them is taking place in the beyond.

POINT OF CONCENTRATION: on what is taking place in the beyond.

EXAMPLE I : Where—office. Who—co-workers. What—working at their respective jobs. What's beyond—meeting of the board of directors re: reducing staff.

EXAMPLE II: Where—bedroom. Who—husband and wife. What —in bed trying to get to sleep. What's beyond—young daughter is entertaining her date in the living room.
The scene is over the moment what's beyond is brought on stage. This happens if it is mentioned or played with at all. In the above example the turning, tossing rearranging of pillows, opening and closing windows, turning lights on and off, getting up to drink water, etc., developed into a delightful bit of comedy as mother and father waited for the boy to leave. These exercises are for advanced students only. Used too early in the training, WHAT'S BEYOND is brought on stage so fast that an improvisation takes but a few moments. If done by advanced players, however, the game can be kept going for a very long time, with the audience totally involved in the problem.

WHAT'S BEYOND? D, E, F and all the PREOCCUPATION exercises should not be given until using the Where and relating to another actor through an on-stage activity is second nature to the players. This can happen only after many hours work on refining awareness. Otherwise this dual problem of off-stage and on-stage becomes impossible to handle.

However, after all the early beyond exercises, CONVERSATION WITH INVOLVEMENT and ARGUMENT, for example, are solved (they are two-part problems), these can be tried. If the players become emotional, if WHAT'S BEYOND is brought on stage almost before the playing begins, simply stop the exercise and come back to it at a much later date.

WHAT'S BEYOND? F is a superlative problem for developing scene-improvisation.

PREOCCUPATION A

Two players.

Preferably seated in same immediate environment (such as in a restaurant, sharing seat on train, etc.). Each is totally preoccupied with his own train of thought. One player is verbal and garrulous about his preoccupation. The other player is silent. One is presumably listening to the other.

POINT OF CONCENTRATION: players to be totally preoccupied with their own thoughts, while using objects together in the immediate environment.

SIDE COACHING: Keep activity going between you. Keep relationship.

EXAMPLE: Where—restaurant. Who—two women friends. What —having lunch together.
A is preoccupied with a problem she is having with her boy friend and keeps up continuous verbalization of her problem. B is preoccupied with some personal problem that need never be mentioned. While concerned with their preoccupations, both are eating, asking to have things passed, having cigarettes, etc. B answers A only at the point where she actually hears what she is saying; however, B never enters into or becomes part of what A is saying, keeping her own preoccupation at all times.

POINTS OF OBSERVATION
1. Involvement with each other takes place only at the moments in which a "bridge" is made between them: at random moments when B hears A speaking or where the immediate environment brings them together (asking things to be passed to one another, etc.). Otherwise, each player is within himself.
2. Do not allow players to shut themselves off from each other. Even though they are preoccupied, they are still together in an activity and have relationship in the immediate environment.
3 . Variation of the exercise: while A is talking, B is preoccupied with an *object*, such as a book, TV, etc., instead of a personal thought.
4. PREOCCUPATION is closely linked to the exercise on chattiness

and CONTRAPUNTAL ARGUMENT, p. 180, and should be used in conjunction with this exercise.

POINTS OF OBSERVATION

1. If this problem is solved, the Where, Who, and What will come to total life and improvising is a fact. There will be no playwriting possible.
2. The scenes produced from this exercise will have incredible reality in detail. The audience will get to know everything about the characters and where they are without any telling. A fragment, with no beginning, middle, or end, this exercise produces an organic unfolding of the characters, their relationship, their background, and their attitudes without benefit of exposition, information, facts, or story.
3. While it follows CONTRAPUNTAL ARGUMENT procedures (p. 180), this exercise does not necessarily call for simultaneous talking by the players. Sometimes they will talk at the same time, and other times one will talk while the other is busy thinking and working at the activity.
4. The players are not in any conflict. There is agreement on what they will talk about and agreement on activity. Their preoccupation merely results from their points of view, not from a basis for argument.
5. This exercise builds rich scenes and is therefore valuable in developing material.
6. If conflict appears, stop the scene and have the players restate their agreed subject. If the original statement implied conflict, have them restate it toward a point of view.
7. Watch to see that the preoccupation during the scene does not become the players' involvement with each other.
8. Be certain the players have an activity (What) going on stage that keeps them completely occupied in doing physical things together that have no relation to the point of view each one is pursuing.
9. A resistance to the Point of Concentration will show itself by the players using the on-stage activity or each other in such a way that it displaces the preoccupation. This point is difficult to understand, particularly by players who consistently resist the Point of Concentration and rely on gags, jokes,

and playwriting to make a scene. They do not "trust the scheme."

10. If student-actors cannot solve this problem, they need more work on their preliminary steps. All the WHAT'S BEYOND exercises and CONTRAPUNTAL ARGUMENT should be solved first.
11. Players are not to answer one another unless it is a "jump" as in CONTRAPUNTAL ARGUMENT. Then such a response becomes a total organic one and not just intellectual and is very exciting to observe.
12. The moment the preoccupation replaces the activity (occupation) as the stage involvement, the scene is over, and in all cases this becomes an organic ending.

BEGIN AND END[7]

PART A

Single player.

Sets up a very simple Where, Who, and What. Plays it in usual manner.

EXAMPLE: Enters room. Looks around to make certain no one has seen him come in. Is obviously about to do something he shouldn't. Looks around room. Spots dresser. Goes to dresser. Opens a couple of the drawers and riffles the clothes. Runs back to door to make sure no one is coming. Returns to dresser. Goes through a couple more drawers. Finally finds what he is looking for. Quickly puts it in his coat pocket. Takes quick look in mirror to make sure he looks all right. Leaves through door.

PART B

Player must now break the little scene into a series of smaller scenes, or "beats." Each "beat" or smaller scene is to have its own beginning and end. Player is to call out "Begin!" at the beginning of each beat and "End!" when it ends. He is to build or intensify each beat/scene one upon the other. Using the image of "walking up stairs" should clarify this point.

---

[7]This exercise speeds up Where and develops scene material for performances.

EXAMPLE: Player enters (BEGIN). Stands looking around to make sure no one is there and finally closes door (END). (BEGIN) Stands and looks around room, spots dresser, and goes to it (END). (BEGIN) He opens a couple drawers, riffles the clothes, thinks he hears something, quickly closes the drawers, and goes back to the door to listen (END). (BEGIN) Looks back at dresser, goes to it again (END). (BEGIN) Opens more drawers, finds object he's looking for (END). (BEGIN) Looks at object in his hand and puts it in his pocket (END). (BEGIN) Looks in mirror and straightens coat, then walks out of room (END).

SIDE COACHING: *Give the new beat more energy! Build the next beat higher! Hit the BEGIN* (vocally) *harder!*

Part C

Player goes through scene as in Part A, without saying "Begin" and "End" but doing everything as fast as he can while keeping the details of the scene.

EVALUATION (on first and last scenes only)

To actor: which scene was the most real for you?

To audience: which scene came to life (existed in space) for you?

POINTS OF OBSERVATION

1. In almost every case, we will find that the final scene had life for both the actor and the audience. This is so because the first scene tended to be generalized, or the player was subjectively involved, using invention rather than creating. The "begin" and "end" forced the player into an outside (objective) detailing of his objects.[8] The speed-up scene, then, profited, by the detail created by "begin" and "end" and by the fact that the player did not have time to recall the details "begin" and "end" had brought up for him. He had immediate contact with W.W.W., present to the present moment.

2. The "begin" and "end" might be one moment on stage, like putting the object in the pocket, or it might be a series of activities, like closing the door, moving into the room, and walking to the dresser.

---

[8]As in BEGIN AND END WITH OBJECTS, p. 79, and NO MOTION, p. 189, the detail comes through because the static required in BEGIN AND END "holds time" momentarily so that we *see* an action.

3. This is a very valuable exercise for those interested in direction, for it gives the director a detailed breakdown of what
   must come out of the total scene—it gives him the single beats
   within the over-all scene, so that he too knows where he is
   going. It is equally valuable for the actors in improvisational
   theater, when scenes are being set for performance.
4. The process of speeding-up scenes without begin-and-end can
   be employed whenever the teacher-director wishes. It tends
   to remove the "generalizations" from a scene and brings the
   scene to more vivid life.
5. BEGIN-AND-END reveals an essence, without cerebral (left brain)
   interference.

RUMINATING

(For very advanced students. This exercise belongs in the group
of advanced WHAT'S BEYOND? and PREOCCUPATION.)
Single player.

As in WHAT'S BEYOND? the player sets up a double Where, Who,
and What. The first consists of the on-stage environment and activity; the second is the Where, Who, and What of a past incident in his life.

POINT OF CONCENTRATION: on the past incident.

EXAMPLE

> *On stage*
> Where: musty den
> Who: old man of 65
> What: working on his stamp collection.
> *Past Incident*
> Where: at work
> Who: fellow-employees
> What: farewell party retiring him.

SIDE COACHING: This should help the player in sensory concentration on the past incident. *Concentrate on the objects in
   the past incident! See the Where! What are the people around
   you wearing? Keep your on-stage activity going! Don't tell us
   the past incident—let it come forth!*

POINTS OF OBSERVATION

1. When what player is ruminating about comes to full view of the audience, the scene is over. This problem produces the most subtle and exciting material and acting.
2. If the scene becomes emotional or takes the form of talking about the past incident, the exercise has been given too early. Go back to earlier exercises.

Additional Exercises For Solving Problems Of Where

The following exercises are extra problems to be given throughout the Where period of training. During these sessions, students should continue to draw floorplans.

THE SPECIALIZED WHERE

Two or more players.

All teams are given the same general Where (e.g., a hotel room, an office, a schoolroom, etc.). They are each to develop the Where more specifically. Who and What agreed upon. Players do scene.

POINT OF CONCENTRATION: to show specialized Where through the use of physical objects

EXAMPLES: a Paris hotel room, a hospital office, a jungle schoolroom.

EVALUATION

Were there specially picked objects that made the setting distinctive and recognizable, or did they have to tell us where they were through talking? Is it possible to show different variations on a Where through objects alone?

POINTS OF OBSERVATION

1. If solved, the problem will result in different rhythms, depending upon the type of specialized Where chosen. A stock-

broker's office with constant ticker-tape bursts would be much different from the quiet rustle of a hospital office; a jungle schoolroom would be much different from a modern urban public-school classroom.
2. Encourage the actors to choose unusual, unrealistic settings (e.g., an office in Heaven, a hotel in the jungle). If they have had WORD GAME this will be no problem for them.
3. Use WHERE WITH HELP and WHERE WITH OBSTACLES whenever the playing needs an assist from the teacher.

ART GALLERY

Two players.

Where: art gallery or museum. Who: to be developed within exercise. What: visiting the art gallery or museum.

A is seated on stage. B makes entrance, walks around viewing exhibit. B decides what A looks like and must in some way show this to A. When A knows what he looks like, he gets up with the character qualities B has given him, walks around the gallery, and exits.

POINT OF CONCENTRATION: to show physical characteristics.

EXAMPLES: tall, fat, midget.

POINTS OF OBSERVATION
1. This may be too difficult and will not be solved by many students in the early sessions. They will, however, find it most interesting. Most important, it creates an intense observation of each other.
2. The teacher might suggest that the players can get fanciful about the other character (e.g., ten feet tall, big feet, light as a balloon, etc.). But the teacher should not give students samples beforehand.

SHOWING WHO THROUGH THE USE OF AN OBJECT

Two players.

Players agree upon one object that will show Who they are. They use that object within an activity.

POINT OF CONCENTRATION: to show Who through the use of an
object.

EXAMPLE: Who—two physicists. Object—blackboard.

A and B are sitting quietly looking at something a short distance
in front of them. A gets up and walks to the object. He picks up
a piece of chalk and writes down a series of numbers—obviously
an equation—on it. B watches him write, mumbles some indistinct
sounds, shakes his head, mumbles some more. A looks inquiringly
at B. B concentrates on blackboard and then gets up, moves
toward it, and writes another equation on it. B turns to A inquiringly. A: "You're right. That's the solution!"

EVALUATION

Did they show us or tell us?

POINT OF OBSERVATION

Continue to caution: *Show, don't tell! Act, don't react!*

WHERE WITH SET PIECES

Two or more players.

All teams are given a list of identical props and furniture.
Where, Who, and What agreed upon. Players do scene.

POINT OF CONCENTRATION: to let the objects (set pieces) create
the scene.

EXAMPLE

A typical list of furniture and props might be:

> window to a fire escape
> door to a clothes closet
> door to a bathroom
> door to the outside
> window to the street
> pull-down bed
> small refrigerator
> glasses, cigarettes, miscellaneous hand props
> bookcase
> dresser or chest
> easy chair or two
> photographs

EVALUATION

Did they write a scenario around the objects, or did the objects create a scene? How different were the scenes from one another? Did the fire escape bring up a new view, or was it just a prop?

POINTS OF OBSERVATION

1. Do not evaluate until all the teams have worked on the exercise.
2. This exercise should help the teacher-director to determine whether actors are beginning to understand the phrase "let the Where create the scene." If they imposed a scene upon the objects instead of letting the objects create the scene, then the way Point of Concentration works is not yet fully understood.

WHERE HOMEWORK EXERCISE

Each student fills out floorplan at home, concentrating on Where, and studies how it might be used by characters. The student plans for two characters, setting up about a three-minute scene. He then writes a script setting up characters and action in relation to Where. Students come to class with their floorplans and scripts, and members of the group follow these and go through the exercise.

POINT OF CONCENTRATION: all dialogue and action must come out of contact with the physical objects.

EXAMPLE: Where—living room. Who—boy and girl. What—studying.
Boy (focusing on desk) sits at desk writing (uses desk, pen, etc.). Girl (focusing on door) knocks on door (handles door). Boy (focusing on door) goes to door and opens it (handles door). Etc.

EVALUATION

Did each action come out of Where, or was the action imposed upon it?

POINTS OF OBSERVATION

1. Player must focus on objects first. This focus will generate an action toward it.
2. This exercise can be done within a workshop session. Teams of two can first work it out on paper and then go on stage and do scene.

THE ABSTRACT WHERE A[9]

Some of the students arrange the stage behind a closed curtain. The intent is to create a setting which is not a literal representation of any particular place. They may use stage blocks, pieces of cloth, strange props, and unusual lighting effects. When they have finished, the curtain is opened, and another player must go up into the setting and remain quietly within it. He is not to perform any activity until the setting moves (inspires) him to do so.

SIDE COACHING: *Do not force! Take all the time you need! Remain quiet!*

EVALUATION

Did the setting generate the W.W.W., or did the actor impose the W.W.W.?

POINTS OF OBSERVATION

1. Genuine set pieces and lighting are essential to the success of this exercise, since they stimulate mood, perception, and action.
2. Urgency for activity often moves an actor into a scene before it emerges. Watch for this.
3. Another actor may be sent on stage after the scene begins to move. He is not to impose any outside mood on the scene, however, but simply to come on stage waiting for the initiator of the scene to put him to use. The actor on stage may call for other actors—within the mood of the scene, of course.

---

[9] EXCURSION INTO THE INTUITIVE, p. 191, is a similar exercise.

THE ABSTRACT WHERE B

Player A sets up a grouping of furniture such as chairs, com-·bination of chairs, tables, window frames, etc. that suggests some human activity. The student audience observes the set-up, and any one then enters into a scene suggested by the groupings.

POINT OF CONCENTRATION: on the grouping of the props and set pieces and letting them work for the player.

EVALUATION

Did the players allow the "set" to work for them or did they impose a story upon it? Did the one who set up the stage have a story in mind? A scene? A definite goal?

POINT OF OBSERVATION

This problem requires set pieces and props and lighting to be fully utilized. The one who sets up should let the props work for him. Also, he need not have a story in mind but can let the "life in the object" suggest ways of grouping.

SHOWING WHERE WITHOUT OBJECTS

Two players.

Players must show Where by any one of the following:
1. by looking at something (seeing)
2. by hearing (listening)
3. by relationship (who you are)
4. by sound effects
5. by lighting effects
6. through an activity

POINT OF CONCENTRATION: on using sensory equipment and/or relationships to show Where.

EVALUATION

Did they use an object to show us? Did they just do an exercise in seeing, listening, or whatever (as in Orientation), or did they show us Where?

POINTS OF OBSERVATION

1. This exercise will help to remove the fearful student's

"crutch": using physical objects only by handling to show Where.

2. While this may appear similar to the kind of exercise given in early Orientation, the Point of Concentration here is on Where—a subtle difference, but an important one.

3. Do not use this exercise until SHOWING WHERE THROUGH PHYSICAL OBJECTS has been covered thoroughly and is automatic with students.

4. Character relationships grow in great intensity throughout this exercise.

5. Advanced students find this problem most challenging; and many sessions can be spent on it, using all the methods for showing Where.

SENDING SOMEONE ON STAGE

Two players.

Where, Who, and What agreed upon. Other players enter scene during the playing if they feel they can help develop it.

POINT OF CONCENTRATION: to enter the scene and help develop it and/or end it.

EVALUATION

Did player or players who entered the scene develop the scene? Did the player come in at a time of emergency?

POINTS OF OBSERVATION

1. This exercise is useful when a performing group is doing suggestions from the audience. It alerts all players to help end the scene on stage when it becomes bogged down. Though "One minute!" cannot be called out during performance, this serves the same purpose.

2. This exercise is similar to the WHERE GAME but more advanced in that the players who enter the scene do so only if they can help develop it and/or end it.

THE THUMBNAIL SKETCH

Single player.

Decides on Where, Who, and What. Plays scene.

POINT OF CONCENTRATION: to show Who he is and What is going on through the use of the Where.

POINT OF OBSERVATION

A variation of this exercise adds a point of decision to the person's life. Examples: whether or not to go to poorhouse; whether or not to give up son; whether or not to commit suicide.

SHOWING WHERE THROUGH WHO AND WHAT

Two or more players. Where, Who, and What agreed upon.

POINT OF CONCENTRATION: use Who to show Where.

EXAMPLE: Where—an orphanage. Who—a little girl and a man. What—new parent picking up girl. In this case, the whole sense of the orphanage came through.

EVALUATION

Did trying to show Where through Who intensify relationship? Is it possible to show Where through Who?

POINTS OF OBSERVATION:

1. The student-actor must never tell Where he is.
2. This exercise serves the purpose of intensifying relationships.

WHERE WITHOUT HANDS

Played the same way as INVOLVEMENT WITHOUT HANDS, p. 65.

Watch to see which players are breaking dependency upon the teacher-director and without being told integrate using no hands. In a bedroom scene, for instance, the player may have fresh nail polish on her fingers, making it necessary to open and shut drawers and closets with feet, elbows and shoulders. A player enjoying a walk in the park might keep his hands in his pockets as he kicks rocks, lets trees brush his shoulders and buries his face in a bed of flowers. Players who do not integrate use of no hands will keep POC on hands instead of using objects to show Where, which completely alters the problem. Let players discover this for themselves.

V. Acting With the Whole Body

The actor must know that he is one unified organism, that his whole body, from head to toe, functions as one unit in a life response. (See Chapter XI). His whole body must be a vehicle of expression and must develop as a sensitive instrument for perceiving, making contact, and communicating. The phrase "See it with your elbow!" is a way to help the student-actor transcend his cerebral concept of a feeling and restore it where it belongs—within his total organism. He must, in fact, cry with his stomach and digest with his eyes.

This chapter contains exercises which help the student-actor physicalize for himself the side coaching used throughout the workshop: *Feel your anger in the small of your back! Hear that sound in your fingertips! Taste the food all the way down to your toes!*

Ideally, however, all acting workshops should be implemented with regular bodywork by a specialist in the field. It is the avant-garde teachers who are sought, those who are also investigating the problems of movement as it relates to the environment. Those have come to realize that body release, not body control, is what is needed for natural grace to emerge, as opposed to artificial movement.

146

Exercises For Parts Of The Body

These exercises are designed to develop more organic use of the feet and legs and to awaken the student to the realization that his feet and legs are integral parts of his body.

A stage curtain is needed for these exercises, a curtain raised just high enough to show the feet and legs of the actors. If the stage curtain cannot be raised up and down, a cloth can easily be hung at knee-height. Just be certain the upper part of the body is concealed.

FEET AND LEGS ALONE

EXERCISE 1

Single players.

Each player is to show one of the following through the use of his feet and legs alone: Who you are? What you are doing? A state of being (impatience, grief, etc.).

POINT OF CONCENTRATION: on showing Who, What, or a state of being with the feet alone.

EVALUATION

See Evaluation used in the EXERCISE FOR BACK, p. 150.

EXERCISE 2

Two players.

Where, Who, and What agreed upon. No dialogue is to be used.

POINT OF CONCENTRATION: all focus on legs and feet alone. Relationships, laughter, sadness, etc., are to be communicated by the feet alone.

EXAMPLE I: A boy's feet approached a door—they hesitated. Did they dare go farther? After a moment of indecision, they screwed up their courage and stepped onto the door mat. The nervous feet wiped themselves too zealously on the mat—obviously, a bell was ringing inside the house.

A girl's sandaled feet appeared at the door. It seems they too were shy. They came out; and there ensued a walk in the garden,

147

with the shy young lovers side by side. The feet easily told the story of love overcoming embarrassment.

EXAMPLE II: Where—a theater. Who—two strangers. What—watching a movie.

We first saw two pairs of feet inching along the aisle, finally coming to rest as their owners sat down. The scene soon revealed that they were watching an exciting western. In the course of the excitement, each player took off his shoes, the better to relax. And when they stood up to leave, the shoes became confused; and the two pairs of feet inched out along the aisles, each shod with the other's brogans.

POINTS OF OBSERVATION

1. Once the problem is solved with twos, any number of players can be used effectively.
2. Actors should also do this exercise barefooted. Knowing their feet are exposed, they will work with greater understanding of the problem to show the audience how they feel.
3. Note students' later work to see how much has been absorbed by them. Are their feet brought more into action? Are doors shut by feet? Are feet used more for contemplation, for anger, within a scene? Do the feet come alive? Do the actors show more head-to-toe energy in their work? Did the feet tell a story, or did the scene evolve?

HANDS ALONE

Many actors who do use their hands along with their faces and voices are oblivious to their full value. Others wave them about as if they were gunny sacks, gesture like French chefs, or use them only to hold cigarettes. And, of course, some immature actors use their hands to accent every word spoken—uninteresting usage of some very important energy. In the following exercise, the student-actor learns to show relationship through the use of his hands.

In preparation for the exercise, the teacher-director must see that a small, puppet-like stage is available, a stage which hides the students' bodies from view. An oblong table, curtained off, might be used. A light may be needed to illuminate the miniature playing area. Hand props are useful but not essential.

Teams of two. Players agree on Where, Who, and What. Speech is not to be used, nor are the players to use any part of their bodies except their hands and forearms.

POINT OF CONCENTRATION: to show Where, Who, and What, by means of the hands alone.

EXAMPLE I: At first we saw the hands of someone writing on a piece of paper. They laid the paper aside and made a gesture for someone off stage to come in and sit down on the other side of the desk. The second pair of hands entered. They were tense and seemed gnarled and twisted, as if they belonged to a paralytic. They tried to hide themselves, to become composed. The first hands smoothly reassured them and proferred the paper for the paralyzed hands to sign. They pushed over a pen, which the latter picked up with great difficulty. While the paralyzed ones struggled to sign the paper, the first ones made smoothing, confident, friendly gestures. The scene went on for some time; with all our attention focused on these hands alone, the scene became intensely emotional and exciting.

EXAMPLE II: Where—priest's study. Who—priest and criminal. What—criminal is confessing to the priest.

SIDE COACHING: *Laugh with your fingers! Shrug your hands, not your shoulders! Remember, we can't see your face! Put all that energy into your fingertips!*

EVALUATION

See Evaluation used in EXERCISE FOR BACK. Emphasize, to audience: did they communicate relationship? To players: did you plan a story?

POINTS OF OBSERVATION

1. Exercise can also be done as FEET AND LEGS ALONE, with single players. They are to show: who they are; what they are doing; state of being such as grieving.
2. At first, students will have a strong tendency to use their faces or other parts of their bodies, which are, of course, invisible to the audience. If they solve the problem of showing

Where, Who, and What with their hands, they will soon develop articulate fingers.
3. At all times avoid discussing over-use of hands. If students begin to think in terms of energy, using this terminology is useful, because instead of telling them *not* to use their hands, the teacher can suggest that their energy be shifted to a more suitable location. In most cases it need never be mentioned.
4. Finger exercises are useful for hand development.
5. The tendency to plan a story is strong in this exercise. Players may have to be reminded again to let the POC work for them.

EXERCISE FOR BACK

Any number of players.

Through this exercise, student-actors should be made aware that "no backs to the audience" is merely employed as insurance against loss of communication with the audience. The actor learns to communicate to his audience without the aid of dialogue or facial expression—in short, to communicate with his body.

Preliminary Work

Ask two students to come up in front of the class. One is to face the audience, and the other is to stand with his back to them. Have the audience list the parts of each person's body which can be used for communication, having the student move the parts as mentioned.

Front View

1.	Movable forehead	9.	Teeth
2.	Movable eyebrows	10.	Shoulders
3.	Movable eyes	11.	Expandable chest
4.	Pliable cheeks	12.	Hands and arms
5.	Wrinkling nose	13.	Movable stomach
6.	Movable mouth	14.	Knees
7.	Working jaw	15.	Ankles and feet
8.	Movable tongue	16.	Curling toes

Back View

1. Head (no moving parts)
2. Shoulders (same as front)

3. Torso (solid mass)
4. Arms and hands (limited movement)
5. Buttocks
6. Heels, ankles, and backs of legs
   (comparatively immobile)

Now have individual students sit at a piano with their backs to the audience. They are to show how they feel through their manner of playing. Let them find their own attitudes. Some examples of attitudes might be: practicing unwillingly, concertizing, playing with nostalgia,

Following this, students agree on Where, Who, and What. Scene must be played with their backs to audience. They should choose a setting where dialogue is not usable (e.g., a church, around a mine disaster, a place where strangers gather). Point of Concentration is in using their backs to show the audience their inner action—what they are feeling. They should take something which has a focus of interest (e.g., people watching a man threatening to jump from window ledge, people watching gang fight, people watching football game).

EXAMPLE I: Where—Bare waiting room with benches. Who—Refugees, doctors, nurses, etc. What—Flood. Time—Four A.M. Weather—Thunder and lightning. Problem—Trying to sleep and ease discomfort.

SIDE COACHING: *Don't show it in your face, show it in your back!*

EXAMPLE II: A play in which an eight-year-old played a nasty little princess required her to shove her prime minister off the stage. In the side coaching, she was asked to show her anger and nastiness in her shoulder blades. The resultant action was not only body-wide, but her voice rose to great rage; and interesting stage business appeared as she shoved the minister out of the room. She was told to keep the anger in her shoulder blades as she came prancing down to her desk. She literally filled the stage with her feeling and had no trouble solving the problem. It was understandable and amusing to her to be "mad with your shoulder blades."

EVALUATION

Did they show us with their backs? Could they have found

more variety of movement? Did they diffuse or concentrate expression? How old were they?

POINTS OF OBSERVATION

1. Variations of this exercise can be done using single players.
2. Do not expect too much at first. Only the more naturally skilled will be able to give a complete expression in the beginning.
3. The teacher-director may have to use this exercise early in the work, when the "backs or no backs" argument first comes up.
4. This exercise is useful for the formal theater in rehearsal for such things as a crowd scene.

PARTS OF THE BODY: FULL SCENE

After each individual exercise or series of exercises concentrating on parts of the body, divide the group into teams. Where, Who, and What agreed upon. Scene is done in regular way, with student-actors in full view of audience.

POINT OF CONCENTRATION: on the specific part of the body previously covered.

POINT OF OBSERVATION

1. Note that many mannerisms have disappeared. For instance, ·student-actors who previously relied on facial grimaces will in many cases have lost this crutch as a result of these exercises.

Exercises For Total Body Involvement

TOTAL BODY INVOLVEMENT

Two or more players. For advanced students.

Where, Who, and What agreed upon. Must choose scene which involves head-to-toe action.

POINT OF CONCENTRATION: head-to-toe involvement.

EXAMPLE: revival meeting; pilgrims crawling to shrine; deep-sea divers hunting treasures underwater; removing boulder from mouth of a cave; non-gravity space ship.

RHYTHMIC MOVEMENT[1]

Full group.

Have players sit or stand in large area. Teacher-director calls out an object (train, airplane, space ship, washing machine, etc.). Players are instantly, without reflection, to make some motion that the object suggests to them.

Have them continue the movements until they become rhythmical and easy. When this has occurred, side-coach the group to move around the area, keeping their movements going. Put on a record or have a pianist play and have them keep the same movements, now accompanied by music.

Set up a scene for the students as they are moving around.

EXAMPLE: The characters were quickly cast without halting their movements. A student who had developed an interesting dipping movement, using his full torso, became a barker. Two girls who used hand-propeller movements became side-show dancers. One girl, darting speedily from one end of the stage to the other, became a mother looking for her child, and so on. The whole stage became an animated, exciting carnival.

TENSE MUSCLE

Two or more players.

Where, Who, and What agreed upon. Each player is to tense up some part of his body and is to keep it tense throughout the scene. However, this is not to be a part of the scene—it is to be a purely personal thing. Although the tenseness will almost always be noticed by the audience, the actor should not attempt to show it to the audience or to justify it in any way. If one player takes a stiff leg, for example, he is not to justify it by being lame but is to play the scene as if the stiffness did not exist.

POINT OF CONCENTRATION: on tensing up some part of the body.

EVALUATION

Did the actors try to justify their tenseness, or did they simply work with it? Did their concentration on tense muscle give more

---

[1] See also RANDOM WALK, p. 221.

spontaneity to the actors' work? To actors: Did your concentration on tense muscle give you a freedom of response?

POINTS OF OBSERVATION

1. On the initial presentation of this exercise, note that many players will tense up what is already a personal muscular problem for them (i.e., the stiff-necked person will take a stiff neck; the student who over-uses mouth and face will concentrate on a facial muscle). Do not point this out to the student-actors until the full group has completed the exercise the first time. Then, after bringing this out into the open through an evaluation, have them re-do the scene, taking another tense muscle. Needless to say, this may necessitate two or more sessions.

2. The resistance to Point of Concentration which comes up in all the exercises will be very evident here. Choosing to tense up what is already a tense muscle constitutes resistance to working on the problem.

3. This exercise keeps the actor intensely preoccupied as he moves through the scene. In one case, a student-actor who resisted almost all the problems had a dramatic breakthrough on this one.

PUPPETS AND/OR AUTOMATION

(Can be used for development material for scenes.)

Discuss with the student-actors the movements of string puppets. If possible, bring a string puppet and toys and dolls to class for them to observe.

EXERCISE 1

Two or more players.

Where, Who, and What agreed upon.

POINT OF CONCENTRATION: characters are to move like puppets.

EXERCISE 2

Same as #1, except that we now have a combination of both puppets and humans.

EXAMPLES: One man, in power, manipulates a large group of people who respond as puppets. Or, a puppet-maker puts on a show.

EXERCISE 3

(The following exercise, intended for young children, is a variation of the above).

The teacher-director gives the scene to class: Where—toy shop. Who—toys, shop-owner, customers. What—toys are being repaired, cleaned, and sold. Suggested toys—talking dolls, walking dolls, dancing bear, jack-in-the-box, puppets, pirouetting doll, wind-up toys.

EXERCISE 4

Vary the preceding scenes by concentrating on things that work mechanically, such as a computer, a mechanical clock, a gum machine.

VI. Non-Directional Blocking

Fundamentals

One of the marks of the seasoned actor is his natural, purposeful stage movement. Stage movement, or blocking, must be understood for what it is. The teacher-director should not influence exactly where an actor stands or how he gets on and off the stage except where position strengthens or weakens relationships, mood, or characterization.

Blocking should facilitate movement, emphasize and heighten thought and action, and strengthen relationships. It can be used symbolically or visually to underline conflict relationship and mood. It is mass balancing mass, mass balancing action, mass balancing design. It is the actor inside the set moving within the color and background of set and costumes. *It is the integration of the stage picture.*

Blocking must be understood in this way. The actor must learn to consider the demands of the scene. Like a lithe ball player, he must always be alerted to where the ball may land and should as he moves around the stage be aware of his fellow players as well as of his place and his part within the total environment. The actor must become so sensitive to blocking that he keeps the stage picture interesting and the sight-lines clear in every moment of his work.

For the formal play, blocking should never intrude or appear to be a learned response. The actor must not move from sofa to chair to door like an awkward dancer who has learned his steps by count. Premature blocking arbitrarily put upon unseasoned actors not only creates this unpleasant rigidity but also renders the players unable to meet crises during performances. The student-actor who has been trained in non-directional blocking greatly implements the work of the director as he moves around the stage, always aware of his place within the total picture. Non-directional blocking achieves spontaneous selection and the ability to meet all crises.

For improvisational theater, the necessity to understand this point is apparent. And, as with other stage conventions, student-actors must absorb this awareness until it becomes intuitive or second nature to them. Spontaneous blocking appears to be carefully rehearsed when players are *truly* improvising.

Non-directional blocking gives the actor and director the same relationship that they must have when developing scenes for improvisational theater presentation. It is give and take between actor and director. Because the director has a different look-in and is seeing the canvas from the viewer's standpoint, he can (by observing what has been achieved spontaneously by the actor) take from the actor what is best needed for the scene and give it back to him. The director thus selects, rejects, or adds to what is being done on stage, plus the playwright's suggestions. In this way the actors and director work as one unit, strengthening the finished play with the totality of their individual creative energy.

The growing ability to see the stage from the audience's point of view while on stage gives the player awareness of action in relation to others and so becomes a great step towards self-identity, ridding him of the crippling effects of egocentricity and exhibitionism.

Stage Business

Stage business is closely tied in with blocking; and the two will grow hand in hand. The most skilled director or actor cannot always intellectually find interesting stage business, Like blocking, business should be unobtrusive and spontaneous in appearance. This can only happen when it grows out of the stage relationship. Stage business should not be an activity just to keep actors occupied. Aside from the obvious method of adopting the business suggested in the script itself, the director of formal plays will find that using the following acting exercises will create more business than the director or actor could find in many hours of work on the script.

Share With Your Audience

The phrases "Share with your audience" and "You're rocking the boat" will give the students a sensitivity towards the problem of blocking. The word "blocking" itself is deliberately avoided in the workshops, since it is a label. "Share with your audience" should become a personal problem to the student-actor. When it is thoroughly understood, then the word "blocking" can be introduced; although, even with professional actors, "Share with your audience" brings out a more natural response than a comment on their poor blocking. For sometimes professional actors need to be reminded that they are on stage for a reason.

Many interesting moments occur on stage when actors, in trying to share the stage picture, must move other actors. When the director coaches, "Share the stage picture," he should never call the name of any particular actor. *Every* actor on stage is responsible for everything that happens. If some actors are not aware of the stage picture, other actors must move them. If this cannot be done, then all must move into a new stage picture around the unaware actor. This awareness of each other creates continually flexible, moving stage. In a sense, whenever necessary each actor fills the role of director or prompter.

When actors work for the total scene, they can only be grateful for such help. For instance, the situation is an office. Howard is standing in front of the secretary, and so we cannot see her. Howard is oblivious to the fact that he is "blocking" and does not respond to the coaching: "Share the stage picture!" The secretary simply says, "Will you please be seated?" Or, "Would you please come here?" Or, if there is still no response, she may physically move him to a more satisfactory position; or, if this is not possible, she will re-block herself in relation to him.

When student-actors thoroughly understand "Share with your audience," then they are indeed free! There is no one to blame.

Exercises

PREOCCUPATION B

Two advanced players (Superlative for developing scenes for performance but wasted if players do not know how to use POC.)

Where, Who, and What agreed upon. What should be an activity totally involving both players, such as preparing for a picnic, dressing to go out, etc. Players also agree on a subject or point of view to be discussed during this activity. They must have total occupation (physical) together and total preoccupation of thought at the same time (see NO MOTION, p. 189).

POINT OF CONCENTRATION: Each player is to verbalize and become totally preoccupied with his own point of view on the subject they have agreed upon. At the same time each player is to remain completely occupied with an interrelated activity so that all through the scene they consistently need each other's help —as in the case of the picnic, the preparation of food, helping each other find things, etc.—keeping a flow of dialogue on their preoccupation while relating to each other with action and dialogue in the activity going on at present (on stage).

SIDE COACHING: *Hand each other things! Keep your own point of view! Keep the activity going between you! Meet each other only because of the on-stage activity!*

EXAMPLES: Where—kitchen. Who—two sisters. What—helping each other prepare for a picnic. Agreed subject—right of divorce. Where—lawn. Who—sweethearts. What—playing croquet. Agreed subject—kissing in public. Where—bowling alley. Who—husband and wife. What—playing and scoring. Agreed subject—what to do with his mother. (Once when this sample situation produced conflict in actual use, it was stopped and restated. The restatement, "what to do about old people," was more appropriate. And "what to do with mother" appeared out of it naturally.)

EVALUATION

Did they have total preoccupation with their points of view? Did they work together on the activity? Did they use the Where

159

continuously? Was their preoccupation with their points of view separate in that they did not build on each other's? Did their preoccupations keep them from each other on one level, while the Where, Who, and What kept them fully involved and relating in the stage present? Did they verbalize things in the immediate environment without displacing the preoccupation?

TWO SCENES (GIVE AND TAKE)

TWO SCENES, requiring give and take, is also closely related to problems of listening and speech and should be exploited for these purposes. The first four parts of this exercise, A through D, should be used in problems of listening and speech. Although subsequent exercises are directly related to self-blocking, A through D ought to precede them for clarification.

Without listening, a team can neither give nor take. And when a team is taking, the other team cannot give unless the voice cuts into their scene with sharpness, resonance, and clarity. For this reason give and take (players' choice) is especially valuable for speech resonance. The exercise can be played with both teams so attentive to giving and taking that dialogue comes through with depth and resonance. To give or take, a voice must, like an instrument, make its tone felt. Players can develop this ability to give and take so sharply that sometimes teams can give or take the scene with only a single word. TWO-SCENES originated when it was noted that actors had difficulty relating when they were in a scene with four or more on stage at once and where there was more than one center of attention, such as a restaurant, a party scene, etc.

A. GIVE AND TAKE (with direction)

Divide into teams of four. Teams sub-divide into teams of two. Set up two tables on stage, with a sub-team at each table. The members of each sub-team set up a relationship between themselves (e.g., sub-team A, a husband and wife deciding on a separation; sub-team B, two businessmen trying to agree on a contract). At no time during the exercise do the sub-teams have any interchange with one another. Each sub-team works as an independent scene.

Both sub-teams start their scenes at the same time. Once they've begun, the teacher-director steps in and calls out the name of one sub-team, say subteam A. Sub-team B must then fade out of the focus and give the frame or focus to sub-team A. In other words, when sub-team A is called, their scene becomes the focus on stage (much like a camera closeup), and they must share their voices and their problem of relationship with the audience. At the same time, sub-team B must stop all visual and sound activity. Sub-team B is not to freeze, however, but is to continue relationship and problem even though they have moved out of focus. When the teacher-director calls sub-team B, they are to move back into focus and share their voices and problem with the audience, with sub-team A moving out of focus and stopping all sound and visual activity.

The problem to be solved here lies in the student-actors' ability to continue relationship and problem while stopping all physical movement . . . in *not freezing* when their sub-teams moves out of the focus.

EXAMPLES: When sub-team A is called, sub-team B (the businessmen trying to agree on a contract) might, though stopping all sound and visual action stay with their relationship by reading over the contract, leaning head on hand contemplatively, eyeing each other speculatively.

When sub-team B is called, sub-team A (husband and wife deciding on separation) might turn their backs on each other in anger, weep or mope, embrace.

These techniques serve to keep the sub-teams out of the focus and yet still relating to each other and their problem.

POINTS OF OBSERVAITION

1. If either of the sub-teams is obviously waiting for their "turn," if they freeze, then they have not solved the problem. Many student-actors find it difficult to maintain relationship and tension in stillness. They will manage to keep themselves in constant activity no matter how minute. If this becomes a problem with your group, give them the exercise called SILENT-TENSION SCENE (p. 188) along with the present one.
2. Watch for spontaneous breakthrough in players struggling

with the problem of retiring without freezing and without depending on the teacher for examples. If this exercise is to be used for public performance, then verbalizing all possibilities of retiring from scene would be explored.

3. Examples are given in this handbook to clarify and demonstrate, but the teacher is never to give examples to the students in workshop sessions. Those who resist an exercise may say that it is "silly," "impossible," etc. Just encourage them to work on the problem, to try to solve it even though they may not succeed.

4. Give TWO-SCENES for the first time during a Where session when five or more players are on stage and all move and talk at once.

B. USING "GIVE"

Sub-teams follow the same patterns as in Part A except that instead of the director calling on them, the sub-teams must now give the focus (frame) to each other. When and how this is done can only be determined by the sub-teams themselves.

C. USING "TAKE"

Follow the same patterns. However, the sub-teams must now take the focus from each other. This will often turn into shouting and confusion, but keep with it. When spontaneous selection is thus forced up by the problems of the scenes, the student-actors will sing, jump on chairs, stand on their heads, etc. if such tactics are necessary to take the focus. Note an extraordinary heightening of energy and impact as the student-actors seeks to solve the problem of taking the focus from one another.

D. PLAYERS' CHOICE

Repeat same exercise, but this time the sub-teams are to give to and take from each other as the situations arise.

EVALUATION

Was there a problem in giving the focus? The answer in almost every instance is "yes." Why? We couldn't hear the other sub-team, and so didn't know when to give it.

When were you able to give the focus? When the other sub-team came in strong.

162

Did you have a problem taking the focus? Yes. Why? Because we couldn't come in strong enough to take it from them.

The evaluation will cause most of the actors to realize that whether they give or take, relationship is implicit in either one and must take place before a play can come into focus. The student-actor in improvisational theater must know when to give the focus and when to take the focus. In either case, the same result will be apparent: heightened stage energy and a clearer stage picture.

POINTS OF OBSERVATION

1. When stages get cluttered with everyone talking at once, side-coach "TWO-SCENES!" and actors will give or take as necessary.
2. This exercise should be repeated continuously throughout training. Frame can be used interchangeably with focus.
3. This exercise has value for the student director.

CONVERGE AND RE-DIVIDE

If possible, this exercise should be used immediately following TWO SCENES. It is very exciting when used with students advanced in gibberish.

Group divides into teams of four, six, or eight. A team agrees on Where, Who, and What and then divides into sub-teams. They move through their scenes, giving and taking the focus from each other as in TWO SCENES.

When the scene is moving, the director calls "Converge!" Sub-teams must then begin action with other sub-teams. When the director calls "Re-divide," the sub-teams must split, and the players continue their scenes with new partners, again using the give and take technique.

The director may call Converge and Re-divide as often as he wishes. However, towards the end of the exercise, the director should call, "As you were!" so that the players end the scene by getting back into the relationships of their original sub-team.

EXAMPLES

Where—park. Who—photographer and customer (sub-team A). nursemaid and a maintenance man (sub-team B).

Where—separate booths in a dance studio. Who—teacher and teen-age girl (sub-team A), teacher and elderly man (sub-team B), interviewer and new customer (sub-team C).

EVALUATION

Did the sub-teams give and take? If sub-team A had the focus, did sub-teams B and C use interesting ways of fading out? Did they integrate converging and re-dividing? Did they give and take for the enrichment of the total scene?

LONE WOLF

Uneven sub-teams

This is much the same as CONVERGE AND RE-DIVIDE. However, instead of splitting entirely into sub-teams of two people each, the group includes one sub-team with only a single player. In other words, if there are five people on a team, then the sub-teams will consist of two, two, and one.

This becomes an interesting problem for the single player as he strives to gain the focus or frame without having a player to work with. Converging and redividing need not be called in this.

EXAMPLES: Two and one. Where—Old Peoples' Home, in the garden. Who—two elderly men (sub-team A). An old lady (sub-team B).

Two, two, and one. Where—newspaper office. Who—two reporters (sub-team A), city editor and photographer (sub-team B), copy boy (sub-team C).

POINTS OF OBSERVATION

1 . Until "Converge!" is called, teams remain preoccupied with their own involvement and relationship. During the converging, the dialogue and action of all players intermingle. When they re-divide, the teams again relate to new player.

2. This exercise could be done with teams of four or more players as one unit (e.g., groups of people gathered around an accident, at a political meeting, on a picnic, etc.).

3. When teams agree on Where, Who, and What, they remain separate from the others on Who and What, but all the sub-

teams must be in the same place (Where), under the same roof, so to speak.

CHANGING PLACES

Any number of players.

During playing, actors must be in constant re-formation. Any one of the actors may initiate movement. If any one actor moves, the other actors must instantly do likewise. If an actor goes down stage for instance, the other actors find a reason for moving up (or right and left).

In a version for two players, a player must move into the exact stage position the other player has just left.

Another version calls for one large team with a series of sub-teams. Teams of two are placed within a larger grouping of people as at a cocktail party. If there are ten people on one team, for instance, five sub-teams (two each) are to be set up, and these sub-teams are to change places with one another whenever one moves, while all players stay within the Where, Who, and What (at the same time).

POINT OF CONCENTRATION: constant observation of fellow players.

EVALUATION

To audience: was movement integrated? Did players find ways to move into opposite players' position that were non-pedestrian?

POINTS OF OBSERVATION

1. Players may or may not know each other within the situation. In a party scene, for instance, the characters are assumed to know one another, but this would not necessarily be true of a scene laid in train station.
2. The concentration required in observing one's partner's movements, while at the same time initiating movement, brings an interesting sparkle to the stage as the players are alerted to each other.
3. Do not allow teams to select a "built-in" movement situation as in an art gallery. Remind student-actors to keep the problems challenging.

4. All exchange of position and rhythm of movement must be determined by the limitation of the agreed structure.

SIGHT-LINES (TRANSFORMATION OF STAGE PICTURE)

Sharing the stage picture will eventually become an organic process for the student-actor. However, this exercise is especially helpful in emphasizing the visual tie between the actor and the audience. It also has value in stimulating unusual design and movement within the stage picture.

Stage blocks, risers, and ramps are particularly useful in helping to find interesting and different uses of stage levels.

1. Using a blackboard, sketch out a diagram of the line of sight from the individual actor on stage to the individual in the audience.

2. To increase awareness of perspectives, have student place his hand a few inches in front of his face and note how the objects beyond his hand, although larger, are almost obliterated from view.

3. Discuss the uses of the blocks and risers in clearing sight lines and creating an interesting stage picture through the use of levels.

4. Have the teams do scenes in the usual way, keeping in mind the actor-to-audience sight-lines and utilizing the stage levels.

5. Through a series of commands to "Change!" players continuously transform the stage picture; (b) players initiate change. In either case, there is to be no forethought as to the changes.

POINT OF OBSERVATION

Professional actors can use this exercise as a freshener and reminder that they, too, should strive for interesting and exciting stage pictures to share with the audience.

MOB SCENES

To give life and vitality to mob scenes, each individual within the mob should have a personal reality. Improvisations around such characters' lives prior to joining the scene can give substance to their mob participation. It is important in mob scenes that the sight-lines to individuals or groupings are kept clear. Mob scenes can often be very refreshing to the eye if broken lines are used. Use of backs creates broken lines (see Chapter V).

EXAMPLE: To create a mob scene in which many people hovered around a disaster area, improvisation was used in the following manner. Prior to going on stage, each family group or individual who was to be in the scene was put into a "house" of his or their own. Each group established a Where, Who, and What. A large room off stage was used for this, and about fifteen of these units were set up simultaneously. All were busy with their own private lives. Some visited others, some talked over the fence to their neighbors, etc. The director moved down the "street," calling "Focus!" at different houses. Each group called, then played its relationships. When the disaster whistle blew, bedlam broke loose, and there were some truly interesting scenes: dashing from house to house, collecting children who were playing, etc. Then, en masse, the players rushed to the scene of the disaster—to the stage. Thus the mob became a real lively excited group of people.

EVALUATION

This exercise has extra value, since the actors very often need to feel they are more than a mob—as indeed they are. By individualizing them and making them realize they are an essential part of the play, the stage gains depth.

POINT OF OBSERVATION

The director of formal plays should never have individuals in mobs make incoherent sounds. They should all speak and shout full meaningful remarks. To achieve this, the director can have each one speak a line individually. Then, like a conductor, he can bring up or lower individual voices to create the mob composition.

EXITS AND ENTRANCES[1]

An actor must not only integrate entering the stage but also upon leaving it. There must be sharp focus upon him, if only

---

[1]Cf. WHAT'S BEYOND?, p. 102.

for a fleeting moment. It is sharpness in framing such details that gives stages clarity and brilliance.

In formal plays, the playwright and director usually take care of this focusing; but many actors neglect this fine point. In improvisational theater, details are often neglected, and exits and entrances become fuzzy for the actor. This exercise, then, is designed to make sharp exits and entrances automatic with student-actors.

EXERCISE A

First Scene

Two or more players.

Where, Who, and What are agreed upon. Ask the teams to choose a Where that necessitates many exits and entrances—as at a party or in a waiting room. Every actor in the scene must, at one time or another while playing, make at least one exit and one entrance—more if the scene permits. Actors may couple up for this if they wish.

POINT OF CONCENTRATION: the actor is to frame his exit and entrance in any way that he chooses. He is, of course, as in all the exercises, limited only by Where, Who, and What. He may fly in, walk in, dance in, fall in, sing his way in, laugh or scream or talk. "Enter on your upstage foot," commonly given to drama students as a necessary rule, is simply used to keep a player from "hiding" as he comes on stage. This exercise suggests that there are many more exciting and challenging ways to meet an audience.

EXERCISE B

Second Scene

Reverse the emphasis. Now the other onstage players must frame the actor as he exits or enters.

BEGIN AND END

This is the time in workshop development to repeat BEGIN AND END from the Where sessions (p. 135). The exercise sharply delineates off stage from on stage and marks the *moment* of entrance and exit.

VII. Refining Awareness

The actor in improvisational theater must listen to his fellow actor and hear everything he says if he is to improvise a scene. He must look and *see* everything that is going on. This is the only way players can play the same game together.

The exercises that follow serve as tools for actors in the formal theater as well. They will, if pursued, relieve the actor of rigidity and posed movements; for when an actor sees another actor and listens to another's dialogue rather than mouthing or sub-vocally reading the other actor's lines as memorized along with his own, his work has a naturalness on stage. If actors in formal theater would see a fellow player opposite them, not a character, their work too would be free of "acting."

That exercises in verbal agility are necessary to the improvisational actor should be self-evident. Moreover, learning to communicate within silences can lead to heightened moments on stage.

Listening and seeing games should be used throughout workshops. Some good ones are: THROWING LIGHT, NUMBERS CHANGE, SINGING SYLLABLES, RING ON A STRING, WHO STARTED THE MOTION—all to be found in Neva Boyd, *Handbook of Games* (Chicago: H. T. Fitzsimons Co., 1945).

Listening

RELATING AN INCIDENT

A warm-up exercise. Two players.

Players are on stage. A relates a story to B, who then repeats the same story, this time putting color into it.

EXAMPLE: A narrates. I was walking down the street; and there seemed to be a car accident. There was a group of people around the car. I wanted to see what had happened; so I used my hands to push through the crowd.

B narrates. I was walking along the grey street; and there seemed to be an accident involving a green and black car. There was a group of people wearing pink and blue dresses and dark suits around the car. I used my flesh-colored hands with the gold ring to push through the crowd of blonde and black-haired men and women.

Narration reversed. Now B tells a story to A, and A repeats, with color.

POINTS OF OBSERVATION

1. The teacher-director may have to stress eye-contact to the players, who, to concentrate on color, turn away from the speaker while listening. It may sometimes be best to have players jot down colors as they listen, to prevent them from postponing colors until the time for re-telling. The purpose of this exercise is for the listener to see the incident in full color at the *moment* of listening to it.
2. The same exercise can be done with concentration on another visual aspect (e.g., various shapes of objects) while listening.
3. This exercise can be a preliminary step to VERBALIZING THE WHERE, p. 128.
4. Players are not to embellish the re-telling of the story. They simply relate what they have heard, bringing color into it.

TWO SCENES

Repeat this exercise from the previous chapter (p. 160). It is invaluable for getting student-actors to hear one another.

BASIC BLIND

Teams of two or more. Materials needed: blindfolds, an abundance of real props and set pieces, and a telephone.

After preparing a simple Where, Who, and What, the members of a team should be blindfolded. They must devise a What in which many things will be handed from one person to another —a tea party, for example. The playing must be done with real props and set pieces. A scene in which "not seeing" is implicit (such as with blind characters or in a dark room) cannot be used.

POINT OF CONCENTRATION: The blindfolded players are to move about the stage as if they can see.

SIDE COACHING: *Integrate that groping! Follow through on that action! Find the chair you were looking for! Hang up your hat! Be adventurous!*

EVALUATION

Did they move naturally? Were all gropings and movements integrated by their Where, Who, and What? Was such integration interesting? (If a player were looking for a chair, he might use a swinging hand or rolling body motion as part of his character, to avoid what might otherwise by groping.) Were they adventurous?

POINTS OF OBSERVATION

1. Any groping while hunting for seats, props, etc. must be integrated through Who (a physical quality of the characters they are playing) or What (part of the activity of the scene). If, for any reason, a player leaves the playing area, he is to remain blindfolded until the end of the scene.

2. In the beginning, the loss of sight produces great anxiety in some players. Often student-actors will not dare venture out into the exercise but will sit glued to a seat, hang onto another person, or stand immobile in one spot. Side coaching and the use of the telephone will help. The telephone will move the frightened, clinging student away from his "straw." The teacher simply rings the bell and asks the student who answers to call the student who needs helping to the phone. It has also the opposite effect upon some. One student remarked

after a blind session: "I feel so much freer doing blind." This showed the teacher that this student was still not part of he game and still fearful of exposure on stage. When one student articulates a feeling, it is certain he speaks for others as well.

3. Unless children younger than ten are doing this exercise, keep opposite sexes on separate teams. Because they are unable to see, fear of body contact keeps actors tense and not free to solve the problem. Contact such as handing things to each other is necessary to the success of this exercise.

4. If possible, do this exercise in a flat area where there is no danger of student-actors falling off stage. This will remove a very real fear of doing so. Be sure to avoid using sharp, pointed, or breakable props.

5. Watch for players who might be peeking, so expertly do they move from place to place. Go on stage and alter a few things here and there and check that blindfolds are secure.[1]

BLIND FOR ADVANCED STUDENTS A

Students play BASIC BLIND in the regular way. However, they must state what they are going to do before following through with actions. For example, "I think I'll have some candy" must be stated; and then the candy must be sought. A group will have to be fairly skilled to do this.

BLIND FOR ADVANCED STUDENTS B

Two or more players.

This exercise puts the audience back into the picture. It is set up as was the first Where exercise.

Two or more blindfolded students assemble on a bare stage without props. The floorplan has been drawn on a board that is visible to the audience, with words (written large enough for them to read) instead of the usual symbols.

POINT OF CONCENTRATION: The actors must use all the objects on the board and proceed as if they could see—and they must

---

[1]See comments on the uncertain child, p. 289.

share with the audience. If an actor achieves close communion with the audience, he will know when he has lost his way.

SIDE COACHING: *Share the stage picture! Share your face!*

Summary On Blind Exercise

By breaking the student-actor's dependency on his sense of sight, energy is released into new areas—the most important of which are hearing and listening. This exercise forces the student-actor to develop *physical* head-to-foot attentiveness to what is happening on stage and creates a total bodily awareness of objects and fellow players. Because of the total involvement with the Point of Concentration in this exercise, BLIND develops an awareness of space and sound in space and makes this space a living, palpable substance for the player.

Players must follow through on every action, utilizing contact and interchange between people. If one character offers tea to another, he must then locate that actor and give him the teacup; the other actor must, in turn, find the teacup that is being handed to him. Or, should an actor make an entrance into a scene as a guest and be greeted by his hostess, extended hands must be shaken and wraps received and hung up.

If the scene is a cocktail party, one of the actors may "get drunk" and integrate his groping or bumping into things this way; however, if he thinks of this before going into the scene, it will have lost its spontaneity and, therefore, its usefulness. For the student's development, it then becomes a rehearsed bit (performance) rather than a working on solving-the-problem during action.[2] Another actor, searching for the art-object his hostess is handing to him, may take a few steps at a time as if viewing the art-object critically from a distance. This stopping and starting and continuing dialogue around the object will help him to locate both the hostess and the object he is to handle and will integrate his "searching." Or, an actor who is having trouble locating things may develop a physical (character) quality such as mincing steps or a rolling body and swinging arms.

---

[2]For using BLIND during rehearsal of a formal play, see p. 348. Players who continue to grope with their hands have little or no body awareness. Repeat SPACE SUBSTANCE EXERCISE (p. 81) as a warm-up for BLIND.

Any failures to integrate connections to one another should be watched for. If A enters the scene saying "Hello!" and holding out his hand, B quite naturally will not see it. A must then follow through on his action—he must let B know his hand is extended to him for a handshake; and B, in turn, if he fails to shake hands, must physicalize not seeing or accepting the extended hand immediately. An excess of real props and set pieces should be used; and players should wear lots of extra hats, bags, etc., to make the problem of handing things around more challenging.

Seeing And Not Staring

The following exercises emphasize visual involvement with fellow players. A student must not only look. He must *see* if he is to "solve the problem." These exercises can be used throughout the workshops to precede exercises in relationships of a more complex nature. For the director of formal theater, they can be interjected throughout rehearsals, using the dialogue and actions of the script.

Staring is a curtain in front of the eyes as surely as though the eyes were closed. It is a mirror reflecting the actor to himself. It is isolation. Student-actors who *stare* but do not *see* prevent themselves from directly experiencing their environment and entering into relationships.

Staring is easily detected by watching for certain physical characteristics: namely, a flat look to the eyes and a rigidity to the body. Gibberish will quickly show the teacher-director the degree to which this problem exists in his student-actors. One adult player who consistently resisted the POC and avoided contact with his fellow players in every way by playing "characters" had a breakthrough on this problem.[3] When it was pointed out that he was working on a character and not on the problem of seeing, he replied, "How can I see if I am not a character?" "Well, how can you?" he was asked. He thought this through seriously and was most perplexed. A further question was asked: "What do you do when you see?" He could think of no answer but, "You just

---

[3]See Chapter XII.

look." That was the answer. "That is all the problem is asking you to do, to see."

When the teacher-director can induce the actor to *see*, even momentarily, he will observe how the face and body become more pliant and more natural as muscle holds and fear of contact disappear. When an actor sees another, direct contact without attitudes is the result. Recognition of a fellow player gives one a compassionate glimpse of oneself as well.

MIRROR EXERCISE #4

This exercise is ordinarily to be used some time after WORD GAME. It can be used earlier, however, if the teacher-director feels students have a good understanding of Where, Who and What.

By this time, students have learned and now respond to the meaning of sharing with the audience. The audience has now lost the role of "judge" for them and has become part of the experience. However there still may be a strong resistance to involvement on the part of some students, evidenced by the editing, judging, joking, and playwriting that persists in their work. In such a case, it may well be that the actor is being his own audience in the most subtle sense. This exercise will help eliminate the "last judge"—the actor himself.

The exercise is done exactly as MIRROR EXERCISE #2 (p. 66), except that where that lesson emphasized simple activity, the actors must now strive to mirror the feelings of the other actors. Have teams add Where, Who, and What (or problem) to a scene between two people. Suggest a W.W.W. of intimate or personal nature where there will not be too much moving around (e.g., sweethearts at a drive-in movie, husband and wife working on budget late at night). Since the actors are after a more complex observation of relationships, too much movement can defeat the purpose of the exercise.

POINT OF OBSERVATION

After this exercise, there should be greater intensity and involvement with the total stage picture in the student-actor's work. If not, repeat the exercise at a later date; it has probably been used too soon.

ERISH #1

GIBBERISH #1, outlined on p. 123 (selling or demonstrating something to audience) can be used very successfully to emphasize seeing and not staring. This exercise has probably already been done in the ninth or tenth session of Where.

For the director of formal theater whose actors are staring, GIBBERISH #1 will be a great assist.

EYE CONTACT #1

Single player.

Each student-actor must sell, demonstrate, or teach something to the audience. His Point of Concentration is on making physical, prop, or eye contact with every member of the audience during the course of his speech.

EVALUATION

Did the actor make physical contact as well as eye contact with the audience? Did he contact every member of the audience in some way?

PITCHMAN

Single player.

Each student-actor must sell or demonstrate something to the audience. After he has gone through his speech once, have him repeat it again—but this time, he must make himself a pitchman.

EVALUATION

Discuss the difference between the two speeches. Why did the pitching make the scene come to life? The student audience will recognize that a pitchman has to communicate with his audience and must therefore keep himself closely involved with them.

POINT OF OBSERVATION

PITCHMAN is also done with GIBBERISH #1

EYE CONTACT #2

Two or more players, Where, Who, and What are agreed upon.

This exercise should follow CONTACT (p. 184) and should be repeated at intervals throughout training.

POINT OF CONCENTRATION: actor must make direct eye contact with other players and direct his eyes to the prop or stage area to which he is referring.

EXAMPLE: Mary enters the room to visit John.
John: "Hello, Mary" (Eye contact to Mary). "Won't you come into the room?" (Eye contact to room).

Mary: "Hello, John" (Eye contact to John). "Here's the book I said I'd bring" (Eye contact directly to book). "Do you want it?" (Eye contact to John).

EVALUATION

Did they solve the problem? Was extra focus (energy) given at the time of eye contact?

POINT OF OBSERVATION

To get the heightened energy or extra focus, the teacher-director should suggest that their eyes take a closeup as with a camera. It is good to get this heightened focus at the time of eye contact, even though it may be exaggerated. In time, student-actors will learn to integrate eye contact with all their work (subtly).

SHADOWING[4]

Four or more players.

(This exercise should not be done before the fifth or sixth month of training and should be repeated at varying intervals.)

Teams sub-divide. Where, Who, and What agreed upon. Sub-team A plays the scene and sub-team B shadows them. Floorplan is known by all, actors and shadows alike. Shadows make continuous comment to the actors they are shadowing.

POINT OF CONCENTRATION: on the Where, Who, and What.

---

[4]See DUBBING, p. 227, and VERBALIZING THE WHERE, p. 128, for material to be used in conjunction with this exercise.

EXAMPLE: Where—bedroom. Who—husband and wife. What—getting dressed to go out.

As sub-team A goes through the scene, one member of sub-team B shadows the husband, and the other shadows the wife. The shadows should stay close to the actor and speak quietly so that the other actor and shadow do not hear.

Why does she always hog the mirror? Do you see the brown flecks in her eyes? Are you going to let him wear that tie? The picture of your mother on the wall is crooked. Why don't you help her zip up her dress?

POINTS OF OBSERVATION

1. Shadows are not to direct, to take over the action, but merely implement and strengthen the actor's physical reality at his own (the shadow's) discretion.
2. Caution: this is a fairly advanced problem and should not be given until the group members have already shown some degree of breakthrough and insight into former problems.
3. Shadows can comment on inner action if desired. If scene becomes "soap opera," however, stop exercise and keep shadows commenting on the physical objects in the environment. It can be deliberately used this way, however, if a soap-opera scene for performance is wanted.

Verbal Agility

The following exercises are designed to help the student-actors toss dialogue, as a ball, back and forth among themselves, so as to constantly keep building the scene. As the actor in improvisational theater must verbalize on the run, so to speak, the following problems should facilitate verbal agility and the place of dialogue within a scene.

Dialogue must be used to further flow between players, not to impede it. Building dialogue goes hand in hand with building action.

THROWING LIGHT GAME⁵

Four or more players.

Two players secretly decide upon a topic of conversation. They then begin discussing the topic in the presence of the other players. Their Point of Concentration is to mislead the others as to the identity of the topic they are discussing. They may not use any false statements during their discussion.

The other players may not ask questions nor guess the topic aloud. But when a player thinks he knows what the topic is, he is to join in the conversation. At any time after he has joined in the conversation, he may be challenged. When this occurs, he must whisper what he thinks the topic is to one of the two conversation leaders. If he has guessed correctly, he continues to participate in the conversation. If he is incorrect, he is one-third out of the game and must become an observer again until he has a new guess and rejoins the conversation. A player may join in the conversation for some time without arousing suspicion and being challenged.

The game goes on until all the players have either guessed correctly and joined the conversation or have made three wrong guesses and are out of the game.

STORY-TELLING

Here use the exercise outlined on p. 312.

STORY-BUILDING

Four or more players.

YARN

The first player starts a story about anything he wishes. As the game progresses, the leader points out various players who must immediately step in and continue the story from the point where the last player left off. This is continued until the story has been completed or until the leader calls a halt.

---

⁵Adapted from Neva L. Boyd, *Handbook of Games* (Chicago: H. T. Fitzsimons Co., 1945), p. 87.

RHYME

First player gives one line, second player adds a line, and so on. All lines must rhyme. Leader can point out at random a player to supply the next line to add an extra challenge to the exercise. The game can also be played so that every player missing the rhyme drops out.

SONG

Using rhyme as a singing vehicle was charmingly done in Chicago during the Christmas holidays with the madrigal form. The audience was asked to name an object or an event. And this object or event was sung by each person in line and picked up in a tra-la-la chorus by the whole group. The cantata or oratorio form can be used similarly.

POETRY-BUILDING

Teams of four or more.

Each person in the group writes out the following on individual slips of paper: an adjective, a noun, a pronoun, a verb, an adverb.

Then the slips of paper are placed in separate piles according to their classification, and these piles are jumbled up. They must then pick up five slips and construct a poem from the five words they have chosen, adding prepositions and other parts of speech if necessary.

When ready, the groups compare their poems.

CONTRAPUNTAL ARGUMENT A

Two players and a timekeeper and a scorer.

The players begin an argument involving both of them, with each developing and unfolding his own theme. They are to talk simultaneously and without pause. The object is for each player to avoid letting the other interrupt his argument. Scoring should be set up on the basis of how often each player is stopped; points are lost with hemming and hawing, saying yes or no, with repeats of other players' lines, with stoppages of any sort, with any "dribbling of the ball" or just "treading water" and not continuing unfolding of point of view. Example: husband and wife discussing last night's party. Time limit of from one to two minutes must be decided upon.

CONTRAPUNTAL ARGUMENT B
Two players.

The players simultaneously carry on a discussion or argument in which each keeps his own point of view.

Scoring should be set up on the basis of how many times each player succeeds in getting the other player to pick up on his point of view.

POINT OF CONCENTRATION: each player avoids picking up and repeating any subject matter from the other player, while at the same time trying to get the other player to pick up content from his point of view.

CONTRAPUNTAL ARGUMENT C (TRANSFORMATION)
Two players.

In this exercise (which calls for transformation of the point of view) players keep to their own points of view as in the previous contrapuntal arguments but at the same time pick up from each other. They are to "explore and heighten" (as in the exercise with that title, p. 235) what they have received. They are to talk simultaneously. No time limit is necessary.

SIDE COACHING: *Talk to each other! Keep your own point of view! You're together!* (In trying to concentrate, some players work "alone," which forestalls the solving of the problem.) *Penetrate his point of view! Expand your point of view! Expand your partner's point of view!*

POINTS OF OBSERVATION

1. Argument as used here relates to discourse or point of view and not to debate or conflict. It is sometimes difficult for student-actors to realize that people might hold different points of view without imposing or being in conflict (and have a right to it).
2. Players must talk *to* each other and not *at* each other.
3. As in all transformation exercises, this is not to become a workout in association or inventiveness springing from a limited

or prejudiced view of something. Suggest that players avoid all words that bring in subject, whether it be "I," "you," or mention of the "subject" itself. This will prevent agreement or disagreement from sliding into mere back-and-forth chit-chat. When keen penetration of each other's points of view is made and both players' points of view expand, "I," "you," and "subject" are brought in as part of the content rather than as a "hanging on" point, and the players transcend their points of view. An intuitive jump between players seems to take place (see Points of Observation in USING OBJECTS TO EVOLVE SCENES, p. 212).

4. If players do not solve this problem, come back to it after using TRANSFORMATION OF RELATIONSHIP (p. 272). In that exercise "transforming" becomes more understandable because it is on a physical level. Interestingly enough, when CONTRAPUNTAL ARGUMENT exercises succeed, players physicalize, for it becomes impossible just to sit and verbalize. The point of view takes over the player from head to foot, and he is *there*, so to speak.

5. It is interesting to try this exercise in singles, wherein each player transforms his own material. This would be for advanced students.

6. Suggested homework: have student-actors write out a series of transformations. This should clarify the point that action or change can come only from apprehending and exhausting each present moment.

WANDERING SPEECH A

Two players.

Where and Who agreed upon. One person is delayed from getting information or completing an activity because of the chattiness of the other person, who keeps talking, changing subject, and digressing into different areas of conversation.

Reverse so that both players have chance at chatty role. They may change the Where and Who at this time if they wish.

POINT OF CONCENTRATION: to unintentionally digress from completing the desired activity through random speech.

EXAMPLES: Who—chatty customer and salesman. Where—department store. What—customer has come to buy something for his wife's Christmas present.
Customer is chatty. Salesman tries to make a sale, but customer keeps digressing.
Who—chatty nurse's aide and hospital visitor. Where—information desk in hospital. What—visitor needs admission card to get on elevator.
Nurse's aide uses telephone, gives directions to others, etc., while visitor stands by trying to get card from her.

POINTS OF OBSERVATION

1. Hostility is *not* a part of this exercise. The chatty person is not to deliberately set up an obstacle. The digression is to be a purely innocent, friendly one.
2. If the Point of Concentration is held, a great deal of humor will develop, and the result will be many charming vignettes. The exercise is very helpful for development of scene material.

WANDERING SPEECH B

Three players.

One player (A) is the center. The other two players (B and C) are each absorbed with their own trend of thought and/or activity. They come to the center player for comment, advice, etc. while completely ignoring each other.

EXAMPLE: Where—living room. Who—hostess, two guests. What—visiting.
Guest B is examining the family album and making comments and asking questions of the hostess A. Guest C is talking about the problems of a mutual friend.

POINTS OF OBSERVATION

1. The center player (A) must be equally attentive and responsive to both B and C.
2. This can be played with many more players. Avoid situations where multiple demands for attention are built in and therefore not challenging (as teacher and pupils). Change around and allow each member of team to be the center player.

Contact

Contact can provoke many highly dramatic scenes. Since the actors cannot verbalize everything, they must stand and think. And so, the schism between expression and thought begins to dissolve, and the student-actors begin to find more economy in dialogue and movement.

While it is probably true that the fear of making physical contact may be tied up with psychological problems, it is not our role to deal with this. If we present only objective problems which are solvable, however, many subjective resistances such as these may be washed away.

The complex CONTACT EXERCISE has been a dramatic turning point for many student-actors. It develops a closer communication and a deeper relationship with fellow actors because of the necessity of physical touch.

In CONTACT, the nature of the focus makes an absolute necessity of staying with the Point of Concentration, thus creating a great stage intensity. The players are put directly on their inner resources (X-area), and stage business is given infinite variety as more subtlety and nuances are brought into the work.

CONTACT also intensifies scenes for the written script and is extremely useful to the director rehearsing a formal play. It teaches the student-actor that he can be a part of a scene even if he is not the center of action. The overly verbal student-actor is forced to stop idle chatter in order to solve the problem: no contact, no dialogue.

CONTACT EXERCISE

Two players.

Who, What, and Where are agreed upon. The student-actor is to make a direct physical contact (touch) as each new thought or phrase of dialogue is introduced. With each change of dialogue, a different physical contact must be made.

Actor who originates the dialogue is to make the contact; each actor is responsible for his own dialogue and contact. Non-verbal communication (nods, whistles, shoulder shrugs, etc.) is acceptable without contact. If contact cannot be made, there is to be no dialogue. The teacher-director tells student actors that when he calls "Contact!" they have used dialogue without physically touching the other player. (A demonstration of this exercise might be a useful preliminary for student-actors.)

POINT OF CONCENTRATION: to make a new direct physical contact with each new thought or phrase of dialogue.

EXAMPLE: The doorbell rings, and John opens the door for his friend, Jim.

"Hello, Jim. Nice to see you" (contact by shaking hands).

That was one phrase, one whole thought. If John wants to say more, such as "Come in and sit down," he must make a fresh contact (e.g., he might put his arm around Jim and lead him to the chair).

"Nice shirt you're wearing" says Jim (contact by touching the chest or shoulders, not the shirt).

Jim sits down, and John goes to the table, half a stage away. It looks as if they are immersed in a great deal of concentration and thought. There is even a faint suggestion of some intense emotion in the air—actually, they are merely thinking of how to make the next contact.

Jim gets up from his chair, book in hand, and goes to John poking him with his knee to make him turn around.

"Say, have you seen this story?"

John takes the book (this is not contact, unless the hands touch). He leafs through a few pages, and Jim walks back to chair. How can John answer Jim, who is on the other side of the stage, and still be a part of the reality of the scene? John continues to thumb the pages of the book as he works on the problem of contact. He gives himself over to the POC, looks up from the book, let out a long whistle, and laughs and clicks his tongue as he communicates his response to the book Jim has given him, because he has no way of making physical contact.

Actors not yet adept at contact suddenly realize that a good fight would solve all their problems—as indeed it does. So, what they have now discovered as they throw each other around the stage, is that a conflict will strengthen any contact situation. However, a fight, like any huddle scene, is the easy way out.

Actors should work toward the less obvious ways of making contact.

SIDE COACHING: *Use your full stage! Move around stage! More variety of contact! Contact! Be quiet if you can't find a contact—there's no need to talk. Keep your point of concentration!*

The following exercises increase the energy level and bring great variety to the playing.

CONTACT, PART II, No contact twice in the same spot!

CONTACT, PART III, No contact with hands!

CONTACT, PART IV, No contact with feet!

EVALUATION

In addition to the regular questions involving the scene, some questions related specifically to CONTACT might be: Did you keep asking yourself, "How can I make contact"? Was all contact organic? Was contact "stuck on" after dialogue? Did you work upon the Point of Concentration, or was the scene imposed upon the problem? Were you concerned with the activity or the problem? Did you create dialogue and action?

Was new contact made at every new thought grouping or phrase of dialogue? What could they have done to make their contact fresher? Was involvement between players greater because of contact?

POINTS OF OBSERVATION

1. Contact should be subtle and related to the character relationships, not to the dialogue alone. It should be natural and spontaneous, not forced.
2. Keep the problem challenging. Have the actors avoid scenes where they are all huddled together.
3. Let the student-actor find his own ways of putting variety into make contact. Fingers can rumple hair, feet can kick, there can be jostling, bumping, pushing with the hips, falling into one another's arms, etc.

4. If the student-actors complain that they cannot find ways of making variety in contact, remind them that there are other ways of communicating besides dialogue (see Chapter V).
5. No contact is necessary if there is no dialogue, but do not allow actors to avoid the problem by doing a completely silent scene. Remind them (only if absolutely necessary) that they may communicate through singing, laughing, crying, coughing—in fact, any sound without making contact.
6. Keep student-actors from planning contact during preparation of scene ("When I tap you on the shoulder, you . . . .").
7. Student-actors who resist contact usually have a personal fear of touching another person. Going back and doing more intense work in the earlier problems of relationships, body work, and space substance should help student-actors break through this fear. Such resistances show themselves in the following manner:
   A. General irritation at having to find variety. They will continue to use hands and poke at each other for contact. This constitutes pushing others away from them, which is the exact opposite of what we are trying to achieve.
   B. Trying to make contact through props.
   C. Using only the most casual, socially restricted contact (tapping on shoulders, etc.).
8. A homework assignment is of definite value here. Ask student-actors to spend five minutes a day consciously making contact with whomever they may be with. They should not tell this person what they are doing. The class period following this assignment should devote some time to a discussion of what they observed.
9. If student-actors will not wait for the Point of Concentration to work for them and still feel urgent about making something happen themselves, they will fall into irrelevant ad-libbing, poke at each other instead of making real contact, and invent useless activity. When this happens, it is an indication that they are not ready for contact. Go to the next exercise, on silence, and return to contact at another time.
10. When student-actors can solve the contact problem by making their physical contact an integrated, organic part of the

scene and not something "stuck on," their work will develop subtlety of relationship and will provide enriched content for the scene.

11. When the actors work fully on the Point of Concentration, laughter, crying, singing, coughing, etc., come into very unique use as means to solve the problem. Then we will have an advanced group of competent actors.

12. CONTACT is an excellent problem from which to observe your student-actors who are still resisting involvement and relationship.

Silence

In the silence exercises the student-actor is not to substitute sub-vocal or unspoken words but is to concentrate on the silence itself and learn to communicate through it. True silence creates an openness between players and a flow of very evident energy, making it possible for them to reach into deeper personal resources. These exercises done with an advanced group of players often result in uncanny clarity on a non-verbal level of communication.

SILENT TENSION #1

Two or more players (two preferred).

Where, Who, and What agreed upon. Scene is played. Tension between players is so strong they are unable to speak. There will be no dialogue during this scene as a result. Where, Who, and What must be communicated through the silence.

POINT OF CONCENTRATION: a moment of intense involvement with fellow players where communication is made with the silence.

EXAMPLES: Two players. Where—restaurant. Who—two sweethearts. What—have just broken their engagement. Three players. Where—bedroom. Who—old man who is dying, son, daughter-in-law. What—couple are waiting for his death, and he knows it. Four or more players. Where—mining area. Who—men, women, and children. What—waiting for news of missing men.

EVALUATION

Did they have a *silent* scene or one without words?

POINTS OF OBSERVATION

1. This exercise usually produces highly dramatic scenes, for it necessitates intensely close visual contact with fellow players.
2. Often these scenes end in a single scream, a laugh, or some sound. *Do not tell this* to students, however. If they solve the problem, it will come spontaneously. If an actor says, "I wanted to scream but thought you didn't want us to," he was working not on the problem but on the teacher for approval.

SILENT TENSION # 2

Two players at a real table. *No* W.W.W. The focus is openness to one another.

SIDE COACHING: (gently) *Keep silence between you! Silence above, around, within!*

The following NO MOTION exercises offer another means of stopping compulsive cerebral activity, expressed in questions and wordiness that keep players out on contact and relationship. No Motion is the static used dynamically to punctuate scenes and increase stage tension. It is a way of communicating process and suspense to actors and audience alike. It is the preoccupation that holds the energy content of a scene.

It should be preceded by a warm-up with SPACE SUBSTANCE (p. 81), dwelling upon the No Motion Warm-Up (p. 85) in particular. This will remind the players once again that out of concentrating on No Motion all necessary movement evolves.

NO MOTION #1

Two players.

Players agree on an immediate environment, such as a restaurant, car, in bed, etc., and decide on a Who in which relationship between them exists in two areas: the one onstage where we meet and see them, and another about which we (the audience) know nothing; the What or stage occupation is also planned. They then work out in the usual manner, using dialogue, and as the action progresses, they use No Motion to accent their communication and reveal their relationship. The audience is to learn everything about them through this non-verbal communication.

POINT OF CONCENTRATION: Players are to send a message of No Motion to their total organism as in HOW OLD AM I? REPEAT and EXCURSIONS INTO THE INTUITIVE.

POINTS OF OBSERVATION

1. No Motion is not a freeze. Its purpose is to create a resting or non-thinking area between people precisely when they are busy with on-stage dialogue and activity. If done with understanding, out of the resting or non-thinking area energy bursts through and expresses itself in unique use of props, dialogue, intensifies character relationship and builds rising tensions within the on-stage scene.
2. Some players find the words "silence" or "quiet" or "wait" more useful to them in achieving the physical feeling necessary for the exercise.
3. As the purpose of the exercise is to stop conceptual thinking, and verbalization of the relationship, avoid over-presentation. Your players, who by now have had WHAT'S BEYOND, and in some instances PREOCCUPATION, will know how to handle it. An experiment in using this exercise with a group who had little if any theater background and only six workshop sessions was tried. They had been given intense work on all aspects of SPACE SUBSTANCE, and repeated work on WHAT DO I DO FOR A LIVING? REPEAT, HOW OLD AM I? REPEAT and MIRROR EXERCISE #3. They were asked simply to think No Motion or Rest. The result was astonishing. The objects in the immediate environment came to life to the minutest detail, whether it was reaching for an ash tray to drop an ash, or picking up and nibbling the crumbs from the table cloth. There were great stretches of true improvisation which is rare so early in training. Animation, excitement, and energy abounded in the workshop. At first the players found it difficult to look at each other and did a lot of giggling as well. In this instance, however, it constituted shyness rather than withdrawal, for contact and recognition had been made between them. It is

interesting to note that when this problem was done with professional improvisational actors their "shyness" was also evident.

4. No Motion does not mean holding back or inhibiting an emotion or a verbalization, nor is it a censoring mechanism. This, then, would make every scene an "acting" scene. By keeping complete occupation on stage, the preoccupation of No Motion unfolds the scene step by step. The players are walking "the ledge of the cliff" and student-audience and players alike are breathlessly involved in the problem. This element of suspense should exist in all two-way problems.

NO MOTION #2

Single player.

Where, Who, and What set up. Player is at a point of decision.

POINT OF CONCENTRATION: No Motion to what player is thinking and deciding.

NO MOTION #3

Two players.

Where, Who, and What agreed upon. Use of general environment. Play scene as usual.

POINT OF CONCENTRATION: No Motion to heighten relationship.

NO MOTION #4

Large group of players.

Where, Who, and What agreed upon.

POINT OF CONCENTRATION: No Motion to heighten relationship, as in NO MOTION #3.

EXCURSIONS INTO THE INTUITIVE

An experiment in dramatic tension without benefit of content.

Students sit on chairs. Instruct them to sit as if their legs grew straight down from their buttocks. This will give a released, straight line to the spine. Their shoulders should be free of tensions, and their hands should rest on their thighs. Everyone is to concentrate on a slight hissing sound on the exhalation.[6] Eyes open, they sit looking on the stage. They are to force nothing and to think of nothing. When and if anyone feels the urge to go up on stage and do something, he is to do so.

POINT OF CONCENTRATION: on hissing from the back of the throat.

SIDE COACHING: *Release your shoulders; Concentrate on exhalation! Look at the stage! Trust yourself! Stop thinking what to do!*

EXAMPLE: Player A goes on stage, walks around, looks over edge as if he is up high. He grabs a chair, climbs onto it. Player B walks up to him: "Here, buddy, have a cigarette." Player A stops and looks at him: "Thanks." Player B waves as he leaves; player C enters and walks slowly back and forth as if in great contemplation. Player A mirrors him . . . etc.

POINTS OF OBSERVATION

1. With an advanced group, this exercise can be extraordinarily interesting, since it invariably leads to an avant-garde type of scene. There is often little dialogue as the stage, full of tensions, comes to life.
2. Make it clear that students are not to think of something literal, nor should they "do something" just for the sake of doing something.
3. After a scene, it is interesting to read into it a literal thread or story which can be given to the random stage activity. Repeat some scene with the "story."
4. HOW OLD AM I? REPEAT and similar exercises are preliminary steps to this one.
5. This exercise should not be used until student-actors are a *group* and therefore will not feel "silly" (exposed).

Silence Before Scenes

If students are urgent, rushed, over-active, throwing them-

---

[6]"In the expiratory phase lies renewal of vigor through some hidden form of muscular release" (*The Thinking Body,* p. 261).

selves into scenes without thought, have them sit quietly on stage before they begin to play. They are to concentrate on exhalation, to blank out imagery, and are to sit quietly as long as necessary. The action will begin whenever one of the students gets up and starts it.

VIII. Speech, Broadcasting, and Technical Effects

Speech

Students should not be made overly conscious of their speech variances. As they move alone into their stage problems, their speech will be cleaned up organically, and this clarity will usually carry over into their daily speech patterns. To quote Marguerite Hermann, co-author with her husband Lewis of manuals on dialect, "Unless a student has basic speech problems, no great change in pronunciation should be forced upon him. A 'cleaning up' and 'toning up' should be all that is necessary."

CALLING-OUT EXERCISE

Two or more players.

Where, Who, and What agreed upon.

Where should be a setting in which the players must, of necessity, call to each other across a wide distance.

EXAMPLE: Where—cave. Who—guide and tourists. What—tourists are separated from guides. Where—mountain top. Who—mountain climbers.—What—climbers, connected by a long rope, are scaling mountain.

POINT OF CONCENTRATION: keeping vocal contacts at long distances.

EVALUATION

Was the vocal contact realistic within the situation?

POINT OF OBSERVATION

See that students give a reality to the alleged distance through the use of their voices.

STAGE WHISPER

Play this exercise the same as CALLING-OUT, only this time the actors agree upon a Where in which they are forced to whisper to each other, such as a schoolroom, hiding from someone, etc.

EVALUATION

Did they talk low or whisper?
Did the actors share their stage whisper with audience?

POINT OF OBSERVATION

Use this exercise at a time during workshop when whispering occurs and the actors cannot be heard. Teacher-director need only side-coach "*Stage whisper!*" from then on to get players to respond.

CHORAL READING

Two large teams. (This should be given after the students have had some elementary introduction to choral reading.)

Where, Who, and What agreed upon. Divide workshop into two large groups. Each group or team breaks down into two players and a large choral group (with one person as "conductor"). Choral group sits or stands on stage right and left, or on risers if available. Two players play scene out with choral group supplying background music, sound effects, etc.

POINT OF CONCENTRATION: choral group is to watch their conductor for cues.

POINT OF OBSERVATION: Useful for public performance.

195

GREEK CHORUS

Two large teams. (This exercise is used primarily with very young actors.)

Same set-up as CHORAL READING. Choose a children's game and have the chorus sing the verses as the actors act them out. Chorus can also do sound effects, such as wind, birds, etc.

EXAMPLES: Thorne Rosa. All Around the Mulberry Bush.

POINT OF OBSERVATION

Useful for public performance.

A variation: Set up a structure in the usual way using a Greek Chorus for underlining (through chanting) the stage action—similar to SHADOWING and STORY-TELLING.

TWO SCENES

Repeat TWO SCENES, p. 160. Excellent for developing clarity and resonance in the student-actors' speech.

WHISPER-SHOUT EXERCISE

Two or more players.

Where, Who, and What agreed upon. Players do same scene three times. The first time, they *whisper;* the second time, they *shout;* and the third time, they speak in their normal voices. A variation is to have the team choose a setting where whispering, shouting, and normal speech can be integrated into one scene.

POINT OF CONCENTRATION: released throat.

EXAMPLE: Where—jail cell. Who—prisoners. What—planning a break. This scene had ample room for all three voice ranges and was a highly effective, dramatic presentation.

EVALUATION

Follow the usual lines of evaluation. Include the question: was the voice more resonant in normal speech after whisper-shout?

POINTS OF OBSERVATION

1. The need to be heard in the whispering sequence helps the student-actor to realize that the total body is involved in

speech. If he whispers properly, with full projection, his voice will be resonant and free from throat sounds. The teacher should listen carefully for tensed throats—this tension means the problem has not been solved.

2. To shout with released throat, the student-actor will have to keep his tones full, round, and extended. Instead of a clipped "Hello there," "Heelllooo theeerrrrre" is usually the result. If he just yells, then he is using throat tension and has not solved the problem.

3. When the players do the third scene, using normal speech, have the audience listen carefully to determine whether or not the group members are maintaining released throats.

4. The three scenes should take no more than a total of fifteen minutes. To insure this, give time warnings.

Radio And TV

The radio and television exercises are intended not to train the actor specifically for radio or television but to focus his energies within the limitations of each medium. The radio workshop is recommended at least once a month. However, it should not begin until after the students have handled enough improvisations to be able to use a Point of Concentration as the acting problem demands.

Here the actor works on the problem of showing his audience only through his voice. He must be able to select those things which will allow the audience to see the story "through their ears."

In radio exercises, the scenes take place behind the curtain, since we are concerned with the voices alone. The Point of Concentration is to show the Where and Who by voice and sound alone, without telling in so many words. Each improvisation should have one or two sound men who do nothing but open and close doors, push back chairs, ring bells, howl like the wind, etc. Sound effects are not to be planned any more than dialogue.

For formal theater, using the microphone technique to clean up a problem of voice in a character is often useful. This brings focus to the problem without giving it undue *critical attention.*

Among materials useful for radio exercises are a tape recorder and a curtain to separate actors from the audience's vision. It is wise to rig up a sound table with bells, buzzers, a small wind machine, a rain box, a door, a box of broken glass, a turntable, a few recordings, newspaper, chalk, blackboard, etc.

For preliminary work, a short discussion on radio itself is advisable, so that students will be able to clarify what they are trying to do. The problem of showing rather than telling in this medium is most challenging.

When you listen to the radio, what happens? The answer will arrive eventually: "The listener *sees* the story."

Then, when you do a radio improvisation, what are you trying to do? "Let the audience see the story in their minds."

How can we show we are in a classroom by the use of sound and voice alone, without telling our audiences where we are? "By using physical objects over the microphone."

Give some examples of physical objects which make sounds appropriate to a classroom? "Chalk could squeak on the blackboard . . . some could use the pencil sharpener . . . a lot of chairs could be pushed back from desks as the lunch bell rang."

On the problem of relationships, which also arises in the radio scenes: *How can we show a mother and son?* "The boy could come in and say, 'Hello . . . I'm back from the store. Can I go out and play now?' "

A discussion held in the same way as questioning during Where sessions will stimulate actors to find for themselves many sounds especially pertinent to a classroom, a kitchen, or a living room.

FIRST RADIO EXERCISE

Three or more players.

Who decided upon. Each actor makes list of the characteristics he is attempting to convey: age, weight, temperament, coloring, etc. The members of the student-audience are to make their own list of characteristics as the action progresses. When playing is over, lists are compared.

POINT OF CONCENTRATION: on showing Who. Through the same procedure but with a minimum of sound and dialogue, the Point of Concentration can be changed to: showing Where.

EXAMPLE: Where—a country schoolhouse. Who—the teacher and her class; teacher is about forty-five and rather dislikes teaching! one boy in the fourth grade is "slow." After the inevitable commercial, the program opens.

Teacher: Three times three equals?

Class: (in unison) Nine.

Teacher: Three times four equals?

Class: Twelve.

Teacher: Three time five equals?

Class: Fifteen.

Teacher: Did you open your mouth Johnny? Did you know the answer or didn't you? Speak up!

Johnny: No, ma'am.

Teacher: You will kindly come up and write down every answer the class gives.

Sound: Sound man pushes back chair and gets chalk ready for blackboard.

Teacher: Again . . . where were we? Oh, yes. Three times six equals?

Class: Eighteen.

Sound: Chalk on blackboard.

Teacher: That's an awfully sloppy-looking eight. Three times seven?

Class: Twenty-one.

Sound: Chalk on board.

Teacher: Johnny! What do you have in your pocket?

Sound: Sound man peeps like a little chick.

Class: Laughter.

Teacher: Johnny! I asked you what you have in your pockets!

Sound: Sound man peeps like a little chick.

Class: More laughter.

EVALUATION

After the improvisation, the student-audience compiles their impressions about each character to see how closely they coincide with the actor's lists.

How old was the teacher? What did she look like? How many students were in the class? How old were they. Was it a city or a country school? How did you know?

Did they show us Where and Who by sound and voice alone? Most often, some things are shown while others are told. How could they have made that point clear without telling us?

POINTS OF OBSERVATION

1. Try to avoid the omnipotent narrator. When students put their minds to solving Where and Who, there will be no need for him.
2. The acting problems in WORD GAME or THEME SCENE can also be used for radio improvisations; but the problems of Where and Who will more than likely keep a group busy for some time.

ANIMAL IMPROVISATIONS
See CHARACTER, p. 262.

Animal improvisations for building character can also help with speech. One boy with a high, thin voice was given the animal image of a hippo to help him with a character. By working on this visualization in his scenes, he was able to lower his voice tone considerably.

Children's Introduction To Radio

The seven-to-nine-year-olds will enjoy working at radio (using a tape recorder) and listening to playbacks of what has been recorded. This is the best way to work on speech with young children; for, since it is necessary for them to speak clearly in order to share with an audience, they learn to work on cleaning up their own speech. A "Man-on-the-Street" type of exercise is useful in introducing this age group to radio exercises, since it allows even the most timid child to speak and to hear his voice in playback.

MAN-ON-THE-STREET A

An assistant should be the "man-on-the-street" in all these exercises, since he is more skilled in drawing the children into conversation than another child would be.

Interviewer: "Hello . . . hello . . . and who are you, little girl?" The child then gives her name and address, etc.

MAN-ON-THE-STREET B

After the initial name-and-address interview, the assistant can suggest other characters, and the students must then respond.

Interviewer: "Well . . . here comes an old man. Hello, old man."

MAN-ON-THE-STREET C

Now have the interviewer suggest animal images which the children must take on when they speak.

Interviewer: "Well, here comes a cat! Hello, cat! How are you this morning?" "Meow, meow . . . I'm fine."

Many children will respond initially in this stereotyped expression of an animal. Suggest that they speak with the sound of the real animal in mind. Have them try to recall the speech rhythm of the animal as they have heard it—i.e., the dog would be staccato, the cow would be long and heavy, etc.

For variation, have the child suggest the animal by altering his speech patterns. The interviewer must then guess what animal he is interviewing.

Interviewer: "Well, here comes someone! And how are you today?" Child: "Eeeeooowww . . . IIIIIImmmmmm . . . fiiiinn nneeeooww."

When the interviewer cannot identify the animal, then the child is forced to clarify his speech. It is interesting to watch the swift development of young students in terms of speech and uses of tone of voice when this exercise is given.

TELEVISION EXERCISE

Four or more players (a director, a cameraman, and actors).

Director casts his actors and gives them a scene to enact. There should be a definite Where; scene should be simple (perhaps part of a larger scene), and should not be longer than three or four minutes.

A camera can be simulated with a large theater spotlight on wheels, a photographer's floodlight with long cord, or even a flashlight. The important thing is that light may be turned on and off. Microphone and earphone are not difficult to imitate with batteries and wires. They are not indispensable, although they add greatly to enjoyment of exercise.

Cameraman follows the scene with his light, moving in for close-ups, back for long shots, etc. Student-audience can tell what shots have been taken only by where the light falls. The light is the camera's eye—the picture being taken.

Players go through a dry-run rehearsal without camera. Director makes a few changes here and there. Cameraman moves in and out to warm up. Then the camera lights up, and they are on the air

EXAMPLE: Dining-room scene. Family is eating dinner. The little girl does not want to eat her spinach. The parents plead, cajole, and threaten. Finally she eats the spinach. End of scene.

EVALUATION

Did the actors take directions from the director? Have a full discussion of this. All will get a chance to be director and will soon understand the necessity in theater for following direction. The youngest actors become easy to handle during rehearsal of a play after they have been "Director."

Did the cameraman take the most interesting shots? First ask the cameraman himself, and then the student audience. Where might the cameraman have made his shots clearer and more interesting? How?

POINT OF OBSERVATION

Before beginning the exercises, a quick discussion on the basic camera shots (long shot, medium shot, closeup) is helpful.

Technical Effects

It is most important that every student learn to improvise using the technical aspects of the theater.

In early workshop sessions, the teacher-director would do well to initiate a short demonstration of the workings of the sound and lighting equipment, with particular emphasis on the resulting effects and moods. Students should take turns handling the equipment and producing the effects until they are familiar with the set-up.

When a basic understanding has been achieved, then assign technical crew members to each team, alerting them to improvise any sound or lighting effect the scene might demand. Or have each group select one or two of its members to handle lights and sound.

In improvisational theater the necessity that technical skill be used in improvisations should be obvious. Lights, sound, music and dialogue must all become an organic part of the unfolding scene. This spontaneous selection of effects and placing them into a scene at the time of improvisation gives the student-actors an added alertness and sensitivity to what is going on. As in the exercise SENDING SOMEONE ON STAGE, the actors on stage must respond and act upon the new element introduced into the scene.

INTEGRATION OF ON-STAGE
AND BACK-STAGE ACTION A

Two or more players on stage. Two or more players back stage.

Where, Who, and What agreed upon. Where should offer many opportunities for effects (a forest, desert, home, farm, etc.).

On-stage players must play scene and cue back-stage players for effects as they go along ("It's getting dark outside . . . do you think there'll be a storm? It's time for the rooster to crow . . .") or through physicalization. Reverse teams.

POINT OF CONCENTRATION: to integrate the on-stage action with appropriate technical effects.

POINTS OF OBSERVATION

1. This exercise can be done successfully with children as young as five years old. If the sound effects are simple to handle and a simple lighting set-up is available, any child can carry out the technical cues.
2. This exercise has an extraordinary maturing value for the very young actor, who suddenly finds himself handling the outcome of a scene, as he responds to the actors' need for him.
3. Many other acting problems can be adapted or developed with this purpose in mind.

INTEGRATION OF ON-STAGE
AND BACK-STAGE ACTION B

Same as A, except that in this exercise the back-stage crew originates the lighting and sound effects and the on-stage players must then improvise around these effects.

POINT OF CONCENTRATION: players must play their scene according to the effects provided by the back-stage crew.

CREATING MOODS ON STAGE

Three or more players on stage. Two or more players on back-stage crew.

Several Where's are written on slips of paper. Team selects a slip of paper and must then create the mood of this Where. Players agree on Who and What or may just enter stage letting Who and What evolve out of the effects.

Scene begins, with back-stage providing sound and lighting effects to create the mood and the on-stage players adding to the mood.

Once mood has been achieved, scene may be stopped or played through, as the director wishes.

POINT OF CONCENTRATION: to create the mood of the Where through technical effects and response of on-stage players.

EVALUATION

Did the lighting and sound effects coincide to set the mood? Did the players add to the mood or distract from it?

POINTS OF OBSERVATION

1. This exercise quickly shows which players are able to let the effects carry them without manipulating them.
2. Similar to ABSTRACT WHERE (p. 142) and can be used in conjunction with it. As with EXCURSIONS INTO THE INTUITIVE, a stage can be set up with lighting and props and story content added later.

VOCAL SOUND EFFECTS

Two or more players.

Where, Who, and What agreed upon. Players are hidden from audience's view. They use microphone.

Where is to be established through sound effects alone. The sound effects are not to be mechanically reproduced but are to done vocally by the players—i.e., birds, wind, sirens, bells, etc., are all to be produced by vocalization alone.

POINT OF CONCENTRATION: to produce sounds vocally that are usually given by recordings.

EVALUATION

Were the vocal sounds as effective as recorded sounds?

POINTS OF OBSERVATION

1. Players should work with sounds as they would with other players.
2. Almost invariably, one or more students will delight in this exercise and will develop skills in sound effects to such an extent that mechanical aids will be almost unnecessary.
3. For homework, ask the students to listen to the sounds around them and to try to reproduce them.

4. Some examples of scenes where sound is inherent are railroad stations, jungles, and harbors. Use of easily available materials to create sound effects can also be suggested. Straws can bubble water, cellophane crackles, pencils can be hit against empty glasses, etc.
5. Microphone essential to the success of this exercise.
6. As a warm-up, pass the microphone around and ask individual players to make any sound of their choosing. Their fellow players are to call out what was communicated (a rocket, an animal, horses running, starting a car, etc.).
7. Hidden teams agree on a Where to communicate to audience-players (a farm, a harbor, a jungle, etc.).

IX. Developing Material for Situations

The exercises in this chapter can broaden the student-actor's insight for finding fresh scene material. After a few experiments with WORD GAME (below), for instance, ideas should literally pour out as the student transcends his everyday orbit. Those involved in a community theater, interested in developing material around a certain event, should find WORD GAME B particularly useful.[1]

To be effective, these exercises should be supplemented with set pieces, lighting, music, sound, and costume. In short, the full technical theater should be utilized.

Although the following exercises are especially helpful in the handling of situational material—usable for performance—many exercises in this handbook can do this. If the Point of Concentration is understood by the student-actors and focus is kept on the problem (object) the Point of Concentration presents, in a sense, anyone and everyone can develop scenes.

WORD GAME A[2]

Two or more teams.

Each team selects a word and divides it into syllables. Floorplans are drawn, and a Where, Who, and What are agreed upon

---

[1]See Developing Scenes for Improvisational Theater, Chapter XVI.
[2]WORD GAME should be brought into workshops after the twelfth or thirteenth Where session.

for each syllable. Each team casts for the situations and selects back-stage workers.

The team then acts out the syllables of the word. At no time is the word itself (or the syllable being acted out) to be mentioned verbally. Every effort should be made to hide the syllable (and subsequent word) within the involved stage action.

POINT OF CONCENTRATION: to obscure the chosen word within the scenes.

EXAMPLE: "Let's use the word "industrial," which we can divide into in-dust-trial." *What can we do with the syllable "in?"* "We could be walking in a door." *If there are four of five people on a team, would it be interesting if all of them simply walked through a door? What are some possibilities for a real scene with a Where, Who, and What?*

This might lead to the discussion of a situation in which a student had an "in" with a teacher or a salesman with a receptionist. Reminding students to disregard the spelling of the syllable and think only of the sound sense might prompt someone to suggest a scene at an "inn." Any one of these suggestions could facilitate a complete scene.

Help the teams to realize the scene implications of each syllable. The "inn" might be in the country at night, with a cast of characters ranging from the wayfaring stranger to the sleepy bellboy. There might be a reconciliation between the stranger and a long-lost brother, or perhaps a robbery when the thieves see the moneybelt around the stranger's waist. Action that will help disguise the syllable and make it more difficult for the audience to guess the word should be encouraged.

What can we do with "dust"? "We could come from a mining camp and be dusting off our clothes." *Could that be developed into a full scene with Who, Where, and What? What else does "dust" imply? What do we associate with dust?*

They might think of gold dust and of a potential gold miners' situation; the dust-bowl period of U. S. history; a clue in a mystery story. The variations are unlimited.

"Trial" is obvious, but student-actors should be reminded to think of a situation so that attention is taken away from the word itself.

EVALUATION

Before the class evaluation of the theater aspects of the scene, allow the student-audience to guess the word enacted. It is advisable that the teacher-director know the word in advance, so as to provide hints to shorten the guessing period.

Did they solve the problem? Were the syllables they acted out hidden? Did they put in a major distraction to obscure the word? (For example, a team that acted out the full word "parcel" had a delivery boy bring in a mechanical servant, acted out by one of the players; the scene developed around the mechanical servant, and the word itself was obscured.)

Did selection of the costume piece bring the character into sharp focus? Could more have been done with lights and sound?

WORD GAME B

Two or more teams.

This exercise usually produces much satirical material. The team selects a word, as in WORD GAME A. Instead of giving them free rein in creating their scenes, the teacher-director provides specific themes on which the scenes must be based. The themes might be as follows:

1. religious
2. political
3. sociological
4. scientific
5. historical
6. fantasy
7. current events
8. blackout
9. automation
10. transformations
11. educational
12. *specific* community or school problems
13. clownishness

It is not at all necessary to limit the teams to one theme per syllable. Indeed, teams wishing to work on more than one theme per syllable often excite great selectivity trying to find material for five or six different situations.

Where, Who, and What is then set up, technical crew stands by, costume pieces are selected, and the games begin!

EXAMPLE: Suppose the team chooses the word "monkey." For their purposes, it is broken into two syllables: monk-key. The players must create a scene around the first syllable, monk, using one of the above-mentioned themes. For instance, a religious scene using monk is obvious; or perhaps a sociological scene, portraying a monk in relation to the lay citizen; or a historical scene, showing a monk at the time of the Spanish Inquisition. The possibilities are endless.

The second syllable, key, is handled in the same way. Political: the mayor hands over the key to the city to a visiting dignitary; scientific: a research chemist finds the key to preventing a dread disease; fantasy: a magic key takes the bearer to Shangri-La; transformation: anyone keeping the key becomes transformed.

And for the whole word, "monkey," infinite possibilities exist.

POINTS OF OBSERVATION

1. Make it clear to the teams that the sound sense of the word can be used instead of the actual spelling. (E.g., "mistake" becomes miss-take or mist-ache; or, using greater poetic license, "petrified" might become pet-try-fried.) Since all are after flights of fancy, as much freedom with words as possible should be allowed, so long as the words are not completely distorted.

2. Have the student-audience suggest other situations around the syllables and words enacted. Prompt them into suggesting ideas of transcending possibilities. Let the student-actor learn that he can make his theater reality whatever he so desires on the stage; if the group agrees, a scene can take place at the gates of heaven or in the bowels of the earth. Bring in unusual set pieces and costume pieces for them to choose from.

3. Two-syllable words are better than three-syllable words in a class situation because of the time limit. WORD GAME takes more time for preparation by the students than other acting problems, assignments of words, and themes may be given to the groups earlier so that they may work out the Where, Who, and What before coming to class. Care should be taken, however, that they do not plan out the How.

4. This exercise has been developed into a most successful evening of entertainment for an audience. It is particularly valuable in a summer camp situation, where the time element prohibits workshops and more formal presentations and where the arts and crafts classes can help in making props, set pieces, etc.

5. It has been found that WORD GAME has little value for children under nine years of age. The meaning of words before this time is generally too literal and connotative for them to use words in an abstract sense.

6. Like the run-through of a formal show, when two or three scenes are done at one time as they are here, the weaknesses and strength of the players are highlighted. This highlighting gives the teacher-director an excellent indication of where individuals need help and what kind of problems they should be given. If possible, it is most valuable to set aside extra time for WORD GAME *in addition* to regular workshop. If the student-actors show lack of involvement with objects, if they do not make contact and develop Where, Who, and What, if their stage pictures are cluttered and meaningless, it is time to retrace our steps and return to earlier exercises. And by now, the teacher will also know what exercises to give them.

7. The similarities between this and the old game of charades are evident, although here they have been adapted to meet our needs. The teacher-director should concentrate on heightening the students' selectivity and expanding their experience—not on producing charades experts.

8. It is probably clear at this point that the teacher or students have merely to peruse the dictionary now and again to find enough material to keep classes going for years. When students first play the game, the teacher should bring a list of words to class in case the students are at a loss. Let them bring the syllables to life. The simpler composite words are easier to use and make the WORD GAME more quickly understandable to students.

9. The student-actors should have worked on some technical problems before doing this exercise.

10. After WORD GAME has been played four or fiv times in work-

shop sessions, an awareness of the vastness and variety of choice of material possible for use in solving problems opens up for the student-actor.

11. If the situations develop into story and playwriting, suggest the team add an acting problem (of their own choice) to the syllable they are acting out.

ONCE UPON A TIME

Here the exercise outlined on p. 307 should be used.

USING OBJECTS TO EVOLVE SCENES

One player.

This exercise should help the student-actor to increase his awareness of the simplest of objects, a starting point for developing scenes. It constitutes an early step in excursions into the intuitive.

The player is seated on stage. Teacher-director whispers to him the name of an object. He is then to sit quietly until his concentration on the object sets him into motion.

Teacher-director may choose among such categories as: vegetation (growth), desk, fireplace, window, doors, light, a place to sit, box (container), weapon.

POINT OF CONCENTRATION: on the object, which then sets player in motion.

EVALUATION

To actor: did you sit quietly until something happened, or did you plan the use of the object before you went into motion?

To audience: was the object used in a pedestrian way? (Putting a log on the fire, or Satan rising from the fire?)

POINTS OF OBSERVATION

1. The player is to keep his eyes open while quietly viewing the stage and concentrating on his object. Closed eyes will withdraw him from his immediate environment; and this is to be avoided.

2. Coach the actors not to feel urgent or hurried about allowing their object to put them into motion. Suggest they concentrate on exhalation.
3. Watch the growth from the known to the unknown. Was vegetation just someone watering a garden, or did it become a man-eating vine?
4. If concentration is complete on getting the object to move them, and not on an activity relating to the object, students may do some charming fantasy or intensely dramatic scenes.
5. If actors remain tied down by uninteresting activity, stop the exercise and quickly go through the following exercises. When this has been done, then return to the single player's object-motion exercise.

DETAILING THE OBJECT (TRANSFORMATION)

Two players (advanced students only).

Where, Who, and What agreed upon. Players are to keep the object constantly in focus through handling it, etc., while playing the agreed-upon structure.

POINT OF CONCENTRATION: total focus on, and exploration of, the agreed object.

SIDE COACHING: *Stay with the object! Penetrate the object! See it in detail! Set it in motion!*

POINTS OF OBSERVATION

1. Be certain that players stay within the immediacy of the stage environment and the object and do not pull away from the problem by giving history, information, or any free associations. Direct seeing!
2. Preoccupation with the object creates either a change of relationship, of character, or of the object itself. It is difficult to say exactly why this works as it does, but as in the CONTRA-PUNTAL ARGUMENT and all the preoccupation exercises, an intuitive jump between players seems to take place through this total involvement with the single object. The object melts away, so to speak, and a transformation takes place, sometimes developing delightful fantasies, sometimes dramatic relationship changes. To achieve this, however, it is important

213

to penetrate the object in every way possible. The solving of this exercise requires intense absorption with the immediate object in the immediate present together with another player. Side coaching is essential.

3. If this exercise is done with students who are not too advanced it is, at best, a help in directing focus; only some activity will be generated around the object. This problem can be truly solved (and a transformation take place) only by the most advanced students. It shows quite clearly the potency of a Point of Concentration when it is understood and properly handled.

HERO EXERCISE

Two or more players.

Group decision on object. Where, Who, and What agreed upon.

POINT OF CONCENTRATION: on making the object the hero of the scene. The situation is around and about the object, and the scenes evolve from that. Many fairy tales use this form.

TRANSFORMING THE OBJECT[3]

Full group of players. (Similar to STORY-BUILDING, p. 179, and ADD AN OBJECT WHERE, p. 87).

First player creates an object and passes it to second player; second player takes it, handles it, and from it makes another object and passes it to third player; third player uses object second player gives him and alters its shape; and so on until it has gone through all the players.

A variant of the above is to play the game with two players. To help very young actors understand this problem, bring clay and have each student mold one object out of another. During TRANSFORMING THE OBJECT players *"play the object"* between them. In this way a miniature scene develops with each object before it is transformed.

---

[3]See SPACE SUBSTANCE, p. 81.

TELEVISION SCREEN

Teams of two or more players.

Set up a large shadow screen, 6′ x 4′ (can be made of stretched canvas); two spotlights; a well-supplied costume rack and prop table.

One team will be the actors; one team will be the family.

Actors go behind the screen. Family is seated in "living room," facing screen, where they have gathered for an evening of TV.

Each member of the family calls out his favorite show, goes to the TV screen, and "turns on the set." When he does so, the living room lights are dimmed, the lights behind the the "TV set" are brought up, and the actors must play the show called for.

The family may "change the channel" or call for a new show at any time. The actors never know when they are going to be "shut off."

POINT OF CONCENTRATION: agility in changing character, costumes, and content.

POINTS OF OBSERVATION

1. A variation of this exercise can be used by cutting a large opening in a cardboard box or building an actual oversized TV frame for the actors to play behind. In this variation, a great variety of props and costumes may be used.
2. Back-stage set-up should be extremely well-organized, so that the TV actors can obtain their costumes and props.
3. After a time, switch the teams around so that students have an opportunity to play both actors and family.
4. The scenes, for the most part, will center on take-offs on current TV shows.
5. If the teacher is working with adults, he may wish to exclude the "family" part of the exercise and just have one or two people on stage with the actors to call for shows, change channels, etc.

LEAVING SOMETHING ON STAGE

Two or more players (advanced students).

Where, Who, and What agreed upon. A scene is played in which an object, a sound, a light, or a thought are left on stage at the final curtain. There are no actors on stage when the scene ends, just the thing left there.

POINT OF CONCENTRATION: whatever is to be left on stage.

EXAMPLE A *(done by adults)*: POC was the plague. Where—a room in a home. Who—a man and his servant. What—avoiding contact with the populace.

The scene developed showing that the characters, fearful of dying because of a plague, never left their home. When they exited from the stage to retire for the night, a curtain fluttering on an open window in the empty room was the "something" left on stage—the concept of the plague.

EXAMPLE B *(done by adults)*: POC was an execution. Where—office of the prison warden. Who—girl, social worker, warden, minister, prisoner. What—a marriage.

The scene took place in the warden's office of a prison. A girl was permitted to marry a prisoner before his execution in order to legitimize their child. After all had exited from the room, the empty stage had a momentary blackout—the moment of electrocution.

EXAMPLE C *(done by teen-agers)*: POC was a searchlight. Where—inside the barbed wire fence of a concentration camp. Who—two prisoners. What—escaping.

Two characters were escaping from the camp, crawling and creeping along the ground trying to get through the barbed wire. A large searchlight kept sweeping the full theater and stage as the escapees flattended to the ground (this was a 1000-watt revolving spot in the rear of the studio-theater). When it appeared that the prisoners had finally escaped, a cry of "Halt!" a rattle of machine guns, and a scream were heard. The searchlight was left, revolving around the empty stage and through the theater.

EXAMPLE D *(done by children)*: POC was the sound of a baby crying. Where—bombed-out building. Who—women, children, old people. What—trying to escape falling bombs.

As this scene developed, the group of people had to leave the shelter because the bombs were coming close in. When all had left, and the bombing quieted down, a baby's cry was heard.

POINTS OF OBSERVATION

1. This exercise is extremely valuable for developing an understanding of building a scene and heightening theatrical response.
2. An equipped stage is necessary for this exercise, since lighting and sound usually play a great part in the scene's development. A studio theater with simple equipment and props makes it possible to set up these scenes within a short time; and as many as three or four such scenes have been done within one workshop period.
3. This exercise should not be given until the group have become technically adept and ingenious in setting up Where, Who, and What, with real props quickly and effectively.
4. The fluttering curtain in the Example A was achieved by using an electric fan and focusing it on a window frame with hanging curtains.

SCENE-ON-SCENE

Teams of four or more advanced students (closely related to STORY-TELLING, p. 312).

Each team divides into two sub-teams. Sub-team A sets up a scene in the present and, in the course of the scene, through conversation, brings to mind another scene (e.g., flashback, a moment in history, speculation on the future, etc.). Sub-team B must then act out the suggested scene.

There may be any number of these interjected scenes, as B completes the scene and throws it back to A and the present. A then suggests another situation, B plays it out, and so on. A may break in with the present and take the scene away from B at any time.

POINT OF CONCENTRATION: attentiveness as to when to come into focus.

EXAMPLE: Two old ladies (sub-team A) are chatting over their teacups. One reminisces over her girlhood and that wonderful night when she and George took their first sleighride together. Sub-team A now fades out, and Sub-team B comes into focus and plays out the scene. When they've completed the scene, they fade out, and sub-team A—the two old ladies—take it back into the present. And so on.

POINTS OF OBSERVATION

1. Lights, sound, music, and props should all be used for this exercise.
2. This is a complex problem, for the sub-teams are working from their own point of view. This constant attentiveness as to when to enter the scene requires the most intense involvement with everything that is happening on stage.
3. Both sub-teams should have a chance to initiate and follow. SIDE COACH: *Change! Change!*
4. This exercise should only be given to advanced students.

THEME-SCENE

Two or more teams.

This exercise is recommended for students who have worked several months on the advanced acting problems. It involves a more complex use of experiential data and is valuable as a step toward suggestions from the audience. Like WORD GAME, it should utilize full technical resources.

In this exercise, a "theme" is some activating phrase, such as "Big fish eat little fish" or "Stinginess leads to remorse." A "scene" can be any place at all: rooftops, cave, cloud, on top of the Eiffel Tower, etc.

Half the group writes theme ideas on individual slips of paper, while the other half writes scene ideas on individual slips of paper. The themes are scrambled together in one hat, and the scenes are scrambled together in another. Each team blindly chooses a theme and a scene and then works out a theme-scene

218

using Where, Who, and What. They proceed to play the theme-scene.

POINT OF CONCENTRATION: constant repetition of theme.

EXAMPLE A Love Is Where You Find It   Mountain Cabin
A married couple has gone to the mountains for the purpose of patching up their marriage. An escaped convict and his pal break into the cabin and hold the couple prisoners. The wife shows the gangsters how to get away, then returns to her husband. It was afterward suggested that the wife might (since the marriage is a failure) leave with the men, thus carrying out the theme more accurately.

EXAMPLE B The World Owes Me a Living   Rooftop
Two sweethearts on a New York tenement roof during a hot summer night. They are tense over the problem of her pregnancy, for he is not willing to take the responsibility of marriage and parenthood. He feels himself to be an artist, and nothing will make him take a drudging nine-to-five job. He is "special" and feels indeed that "the world owes me a living." The girl commits suicide by jumping off the roof.

POINTS OF OBSERVATION

1. This exercise can be extended and varied indefinitely. Any combination of theme and scene will work. The variations in characterization when one theme is used in several different scenes is amazing.
2. THEME-SCENE tends to become a structure for a story line and therefore to lapse into group playwriting. What we seek is total preoccupation of the players with the theme so that it moves them (as object) instead of them manipulating it.

SUPPLICATION
Teams of three or more advanced students.

Players are divided into three parts of a triangle: (1) Supplicant (who pleads for something); (2) Accuser (who makes a charge); (3) Judiciary (who makes the choice and determines whether supplicant is successful).

Either individuals or teams can play each corner of the

triangle. For instance, in a trial scene there would be a Defendant, a Prosecutor, and a Judge (the audience would be the Jury, an extension of the Judge).

POINT OF CONCENTRATION: each part of the triangle has a different POC (pleading, accusing, determining success of supplication).

EXAMPLES: a Salem witch trial; an ordinary misdemeanor trial; a murder trial; an Indian pow-wow arguing some important point; deliberations with prisoners during a prison break.

POINT OF OBSERVATION

The Supplicant should be encouraged to work with the student audience (playing the jury, a mob, etc.).

ORCHESTRATION

Four or more players.

Each player decides what musical instruments he will be. Players agree on Where, Who, and What in which they can be their instruments. Players are not to become their instruments literally, as in fantasy, but are to "play" as if they have taken on the qualities of their instruments. This may be done through voice quality, body movement, etc.

At various times throughout the scene, the teacher-director should coach: "Orchestrate!" All the players must then "play" together.

POINT OF CONCENTRATION: to take on the qualities of a musical instrument and to play as part of the "orchestra."

EXAMPLE: a cocktail party, where different "instruments" can play in harmony with one another.

POINT OF OBSERVATION

As an interesting variation, ask group to select a "conductor." In the preceding example, for instance, it could be the host. He must then, through the scene's progression get his "instruments" (guests) to play together, as duets, solos, or full orchestra. This gives the actor playing the host a director's view while working inside the scene. This is a most advanced use of a similar technique used with young children in activizing them within a scene.

RANDOM WALK

Any number of players. Requires a pianist capable of improvising.

Actors walk at random around stage, exiting and entering. The mood, rhythm, etc., are usually set by the playing of music. At intervals during the walk, activities of one sort or another are called out to players who move from the walk into the activity. This is a most exhilarating exercise, it creates a tremendous freedom, gaiety, and unusual spontaneity in the activities. The end of the walk comes in a slowing down of the music and walk to a standstill.

RANDOM WALK has great value in connection with exercises in seeing. While players are walking to the piano rhythm, simply call out various things for them to look at—a tennis match, a bull fight, etc. This is to be done without interrupting the rhythm generated by the walk.

HIDDEN PROBLEM

Teams of two or more advanced players.

They set up Where, Who, and What as usual. They decide on a category or emotion but are never to bring it out in the open. Categories could be: teaching, fantasy, love, hate.

EXAMPLE A *(teaching):* Where—kitchen. Who—mother-in-law and daughter-in-law. What—a visit by the former to the latter. Hidden problem—to teach.

POINT OF CONCENTRATION: keeping the problem hidden.

SIDE COACHING: *Keep activity going between you!*

POINTS OF OBSERVATION

1. In the foregoing example the mother-in-law hid her teaching by helping, insinuations, suggestions, etc. It developed into an intensely interesting scene in which "to teach" never came up. See Conflict, p. 248.
2. The Where, Who, and What are to be unrelated to the hidden problem. Teaching, for instance, is not to be placed in a schoolroom.
3. Variant: players act to alter opposite players' attitude.

EXAMPLE B: *(fantasy):* The following example was a scene improvisation titled "The Orange Tree." Where—living-room, dining-room combination. Who—husband and wife. What—wife's birthday (husband brings her a miniature orange tree). Hidden problem—fantasy.

This scene developed into a charming, whimsical piece on the growth of this little tree in this simple home to an orange grove within the apartment building, and the couple retiring on the proceeds from orange-juice

EXAMPLE C *(love):* Two players. Where, Who, and What agreed upon. A strong emotion is felt between these people but never expressed because for some reason it is impossible or inappropriate or unknown. The POC is to keep up a mutual activity without ever mentioning the emotion. See NO MOTION, p. 189.
Where—old people's home. Who—man and woman in their eighties. What—gardening.
An interesting shift of the above could be to make a wide age difference between them. Young doctor and old woman or very old man and young nurse—any situation where the difference of age, race, class, etc. make consummation or declaration of love impossible. Again it could be love as in friendship, for example: Where—fishing wharf. Who—Civil War veteran and young boy. What—fishing.

EXAMPLE D *(hate):* Where—bedroom. Who—husband and wife. What—preparing for their fiftieth anniversary celebration.

SUGGESTIONS BY THE AUDIENCE[4]

Taking suggestions by the audience can be a delightful part of an improvisational theater program and quickly makes the audience part of the game.

Organization for taking SUGGESTIONS BY THE AUDIENCE has many variations. Some improvisational theaters base their whole structure on this technique. This can be dangerous, however, for it may easily become a gimmick that can kill the art form. The following are a few ideas for structuring this form:

---

[4]Suggestions by the Audience, which has become the hallmark of improvisational theater throughout the world, was first created by the author in 1939, in

1. On-the-spot scenes developed without preparation off stage.
2. Use of individual members of the audience as actors,
3. Off-stage preparation.
4. Use of one outside person who can take the position of a narrator or story-teller or just an extra player when the scene needs or requires him. See SENDING SOMEONE ON STAGE, p. 144.

Players should structure for an action or problem and not a story or joke, otherwise many of the audience's suggestions fizzle as players struggle to be "funny." Sometimes the players will let the audience in on the problem, sometimes it is just used by the players as their POC while working out the suggestions. What category the audience suggests is up to the players. Where, Who, What, Objects, Events, Emotions, and Styles of Playing may be varied and combined. If Where is suggested, for instance, it can become OBSTACLE WHERE or HELP EACH OTHER WHERE. If it is objects, TRANSFORMATION OF OBJECTS, or LETTING OBJECTS MOVE YOU, or GIVING LIFE TO OBJECTS can become the acting problem used to put the audience suggestion into motion. The object suggestions can be used within Where, Who, What or handled simply as objects with either single or more players. Many combinations are possible.

Whether the audience knows or not, an acting problem is valuable to use when players structure scenes. If the audience is asked for a problem, then players supply the Where, Who, and What; if the audience is asked for Where, Who, and What, then players must supply the problem. Whether doing an on-the-spot improvisation or preparing one off stage (during intermission or while other plays are performing), ability to solve problems and quickly picking an exercise that will free all for playing will determine the quality of scenes. For even, as in workshops, if the scenes do not always quite come off as "story," the very act of playing is exciting to watch.

Agility and speed in getting a character, setting up Where, and selecting and acting problem are necessary to the success of this stage activity, and all such exercises in the book should be

Chicago, with children performing for children. *All* were involved in the excitement of playing.

used continuously in the workshops. WHERE WITH THREE OBJECTS and all the exercises of character agility are especially useful. Many of the exercises in the book can be used exactly as they are done in workshops, with exhilarating results.

The following is an agility exercise in quickly thinking up problems that might generate stage action. Paper and pencil. Student actors write down as many answers to the following they can within an agreed time limit. The teacher director may add any other categories he wishes.

1. Getting rid of something.
2. Getting rid of someone.
3. Getting out of something.
4. Wanting the same thing someone else has.
5. A moment of indecision.

Audience's suggestion	*Players' structure*
Where: Underwater	Where: Use the THREE OBJECT WHERE exercise
Who: Divers	Who: Select a character by quickly selecting a rhythm image as played in CHARACTER AGILITY game.
What: Seeking treasure	What: This is the What acting problem to use (i.e., "jump emotion," "unknown problem," "teaching," etc.)

In this way the actors place their own organization within the structure given by the audience and go ahead solving the audience suggestion exactly as they would any workshop problem. When theater games become "flesh on bones," no acting problems as such are necessary, for stage actions will be spontaneously selected during the playing.

X. Rounding-Out Exercises

Speech

SINGING DIALOGUE[1]
Two or more players. Where, Who, and What agreed upon.

POINT OF CONCENTRATION: players are to *sing* the dialogue instead of speaking it.

EVALUATION

Did they explore all the areas into which sound might go?

POINTS OF OBSERVATION
1. Good singing voices are not necessary for this exercise. Just as we had extended movement of the body, this is an exercise in the *extension of sound*.
2. If a pianist is available, have him follow the group and improvise melodies as they go along.

TELEPHONE
Single player.

Phone rings. Player answers. Conversation should be guarded (from the audience) and should be hidden. Player must not tell

---

[1]See also madrigal and cantata for improvised singing, p. 180.

audience who is at other end of line. Player can call out if he wishes.

EXAMPLE: A girl might be calling a boy, but she is afraid to come right out and ask him for a date.

EVALUATION

Who was on the other end of the line? What did the answerer think of the other person? Did he tell us? Did he use his body?

GIBBERISH #8—GIVING A LECTURE

Single player.

Player is to decide upon a lecture he will give. It will be a long lecture on any subject he may wish—classical literature, Social Security, geology, etc.

POINT OF CONCENTRATION: on communicating.

POINTS OF OBSERVATION

1. This is for advanced students only. The communication made on these serious and lengthy subjects is almost complete if the problem is solved.
2. The POC must be held to very strongly. On the *communication*. If this is done, with no more overt action than any speaker might make during a lecture, players will communicate a lecture.

GIBBERISH #9: FOREIGN-LANGUAGE RHYTHMS

This exercise requires knowledge of language rhythms. Up until now, we have tried to keep gibberish free from any particular language rhythms. Now, have students deliberately work for such rhythms: gibberish that sounds like Swedish, Russian, Japanese, etc.

The exercise can be integrated with GIBBERISH #6, but care should be taken to keep away from these rhythms in GIBBERISH exercises #1 through #5.

Physicalization

DEAF AUDIENCE[2]

Two or more players.

Who, Where, and What agreed upon. Members of the audience are to plug up their ears while watching the scene. Players are to go through scene as they normally would using both dialogue and action.

POINT OF CONCENTRATION: communicate a scene to a deaf audience.

EVALUATION

Did the scene have animation? Did you know what was going on, even though you could not hear them? Where could they have physicalized the scene?

POINTS OF OBSERVATION
1. This brings to the student-actors (by being audience) a realization of the necessity for showing, not telling.
2. The lifelessness of a scene when actors talk instead of playing becomes evident to the most resistant.
3. This is a particularly good exercise to use to freshen up improvisational actors who are performing and rely on jokes and ad-libbing to carry their scenes.
4. Variant: have audience close eyes instead of plugging ears.

DUBBING

Four players.

DUBBING is effective in creating close relationship with fellow actors. A live microphone adds greatly to the impact of the exercise but is not vital to its success.

Sub-divide the group into two sub-teams. Sub-teams decide together on Where, Who, and What.

Sub-team A goes up onto stage. Sub-team B takes up position where they can see the stage and can be seen by sub-team A. If possible, sub-team B should have mike.

---

[2]This is closely related to, and can be used in conjunction with, GIB-BERISH exercises.

Sub-team B is to perform as if they were providing the English soundtrack for a foreign film—as if they were dubbing in the dialogue in English. Sub-team A is to perform as though they were the actors in the foreign film, providing all the visual action. They are to use action alone and are not to speak at any time, but they may silently mouth dialogue to one another.

POINT OF CONCENTRATION: to allow the dialogue and action to become as one. Initiate/follow; follow/initiate. Follow the follower.

EXAMPLE: The scene is usually initiated by the actors, with the dubbers picking it up after action has already begun. A couple might come on stage as if entering their house, take a few silent moments to put away hats, coats, etc.—perhaps the dubbers might provide humming or whistling or something of the sort— and then suddenly launch into an argument, hashing something over which they held back for the privacy of their own home. At this point, the dubbers would come in, providing the voices and dialogue to match the action. At first, the actors and the dubbers may work separately—the actors altering their stage action each time the dubbers speak, and the dubbers altering their speech each time an action is made. But after a time, the two teams will work together; and the resulting combination of action and dialogue will create a highly integrated and lively scene. In a variation of this exercise, the director switches the initiative for dialogue back and forth by side coaching: "Actors!" "Dubbers!" etc. Still another variation is to have sub-team B follow sub-team A around (shadow) the stage. The actors initiate dialogue, but the dubbers speak as nearly as possible simultaneously.[8]

EVALUATION

To actors: Did you find that you altered your stage action as a result of the dialogue?

To dubbers: Did you follow the action as it came from the stage, or did you interject other action through your dialogue?

---

[8]This is similar to the Greek theater technique where the prompter keeps the dialogue running along with the actors. In this case, however, the dialogue by the original actor is ad-lib, which makes the dubbers' role most challenging. Like mirroring and shadowing, dubbing exercises develop strong connection with fellow players.

To audience: were the dialogue and the action integrated?

POINTS OF OBSERVATION

1. This exercise should be used only with advanced students. Has performance value.
2. Teacher-director, or group leader, or group can add variations.
3. Try going *against* the rhythm within the scene.

METRONOME EXERCISE

Two players.

Where, Who, and What are agreed upon. Players repeat scene four times. Their pacing and timing in each scene are determined by the speed of a metronome. The first three scenes are done *with* the metronome, and thus the metronome might be set at normal speed for the first, fast for the second, and slow for the third. (If no metronome is available, have someone beat on a drum or something similar.) The fourth scene is the actors' choice—they may choose any of the previous speeds they wish—but they are to do the scene *without* the metronome, recalling the beat from the first time they did the scene. The Point of Concentration is in picking up the beat of the metronome.

EVALUATION

To actors: Did the metronome give you a greater awareness of stage relationships? Did the beat of the metronome affect you physically and individually?

To audience: Did the different timings alter the content and moods, even though the scene was basically the same? What different character qualities came up with each of the different beats?

POINTS OF OBSERVATION

1. In the fourth presentation, the actors' choice, instruct the actors to choose other than the normal speed.
2. Let the actors play around with different speeds; don't limit them to the extremes of fast, normal, and slow. Experiment with more subtle beats.
3. For variation, try changing the beats within the scene.
   As with all the exercises, it is up to the teacher-director to de-

termine at what point his students will gain the most from this problem.

This exercise should bring a further experience in attentiveness to outside phenomena (rhythm) shaping the scene's progression.

GIVE AND TAKE

Two or more players (two preferred).

Where, Who, What, time, weather, etc., agreed upon. Scene is played. Side coaching is used throughout scene. As the teacher-director calls out to the players, they are to respond accordingly.

SIDE COACHING: *Give! Take! Give and take!*

POINT OF CONCENTRATION: to be attentive to the side coaching and give the total focus to the other player, or take focus from him, or give and take where required.

EVALUATION

To actors: Did you feel a rise in energy when directed? Did the problem (material in the scene) between you become more intense?

To audience: Were the human relations sharper? Did tension in terms of the scene appear? Were character traits developed? Did the scene maintain a complete improvisational development? (Scene-building must come through immediate involvement and not through outside plot or story.)

To total group: did you experience true improvisation?

POINTS OF OBSERVATION

1. Some players keep abruptly changing character tone throughout this exercise and become most permissive on give and very aggressive on take. This is not necessary for solving the basic structure, since all we are after is giving the focus or intensity to each other (as in the following CAMERA EXERCISE) and taking the focus from each other.[4] Therefore it should be noted whether or not the expression of emotion shown grew

---

[4]TWO SCENES, p. 160, employs a similar change of focus.

out of the problem or merely was stuck on the scene at the moment of give and take. However, any emotional changes that come about genuinely through the give and take should be discussed, since physical intensity will produce emotional changes in a character. In fact, this exercise often produces strong character traits as a result of intensity with focus on each other.

2. If actors still appear isolated or are still using outside devices to move scenes—if they show little stage energy—then the teacher has given this problem too early.

Seeing

CAMERA

This is a good lead-up step to "give and take" and can be given early in "where."
Two players.

Players agree on simple activity, such as eating, sitting on a park bench, etc.

Throughout scene, side coach is to call out the name of one or the other player. When player's name is called, he is to put head-to-foot focus on the fellow player. Activity is not to stop, but is to continue throughout these "camera changes."

POINT OF CONCENTRATION: to put full focus and energy on the other player.

EVALUATION

Did the players give their total bodily attention? Did they see their fellow player with their feet? Did stage activity continue?

POINT OF OBSERVATION

In explaining the problem, use the image of "becoming-a-camera" or that they are one large eye (from head to foot) to help the players in concentrating and focusing their energies on one another. Well-timed side coaching essential.

SEEING THE WORD[5]

Single player.

Actor goes on stage and describes an experience he's had, such as taking a trip, watching a football game, or visiting someone. Tell him he is to continue his talk but to shift his Point of Concentration according to the side coaching he will get.

No matter what the teacher calls out, player is to continue narrating the scene. He is *not* to shift his narration to meet the coaching.

SIDE COACHING: *Concentrate on the color in the scene! Concentrate on the sounds in the scene! Concentrate on the way you feel about the way the game is going! Concentrate on the student in the second seat! See yourself!*
If the talk is on playing ball, the side coaching might be: *What color shirt is the pitcher wearing? Is the wind blowing? Is the sky grey or sunny?*

POINTS OF OBSERVATION

1. As greater perception is awakened in the student by side coaching, notice at what moment he begins to leave the *word* and relate to the *scene* he is talking about. His speaking voice will become natural, his body will relax and words will flow out of him. When a student is no longer depending on words but is concentrating on the environment he's describing, then all artificiality and stilted speech disappear. This exercise should not be played often, for it deliberately uses recall and therefore must be carefully handled.
2. For the formal theater, this exercise is very useful for the actor with long speeches. Breaking down the speech into a series of Where, Who, and What will give the lines the physical objects necessary to make dialogue organic. (See VERBALIZING THE WHERE, p. 128.)

---

[5]This exercise is helpful in training the student-actors to use words with more dimension. It stimulates scenes in full sense perceptions and is also a great asset in correcting artificial reading habits for the formal theater. See the remarks on dialogue and words in Chapter II.

Developing Scenes From Audience Suggestions

ON THE SPOT A

Teams of four or more.

This exercise trains the actors in developing immediate response to audience suggestions. It is one of the preliminary steps toward actual improvisation of audience suggestions at public performances.

Student-actors write out on individual slips of paper a Where, Who, Time, Weather, etc. Papers are then put into individual piles according to categories, and each team picks a slip from each pile.

Each team develops a scene by combining the information set down on these slips of paper.

EVALUATION

Was the scene set up quietly? Could the scene have been organized faster?

Ask the actors: *What could have been done to expedite the organization?* Ask the audience the same question.

POINT OF OBSERVATION

The method of writing on slips of paper and having students pick at random can be used with many other exercises. Players enjoy this way of selecting problems. See SUGGESTIONS BY THE AUDIENCE, p. 222.

ON THE SPOT B

Teams of four or more.

This exercise will aid the student-actors in developing higher organizational skill and more speed in preparing their scenes. Audience vocally gives a Where, Who, What, Weather, Time, etc. to the team on stage. The team prepares the scene in front of the audience.

EVALUATION

Could they have cast more effectively? Did they work as a cooperating unit in planning? Did they give and take effectively (build upon each other's material)?

Did team improvise a scene or write a script? Organization of the material, preparing the set, and time used in preparing scenes should be discussed.

POINTS OF OBSERVATION

1. The teacher-director should watch for sloppiness on the part of the players. Scenes must be set up quickly and quietly. Do not allow cleverness and gags to replace discipline and integrity.
2. Mirror exercises continue to be exciting to the students and a valuable tool in getting student-actors to work very closely with one another. They are also quite charming for performances.

MIRROR EXERCISE #4

Four or more players.

They are to use a three-way mirror.

EXAMPLE: man trying on clothes.

MIRROR EXERCISE #5

Five or more players.

Where, Who, and What agreed upon. Three players are mirrors, and two play scene, or one is player and four are mirrors, or whatever combination is desired.

MIRROR EXERCISE #6

Many players.

Where, Who, and What agreed upon, using whatever combination they wish. The "mirrors" distort as in an amusement park.

MIRROR EXERCISE #7

Many players.

Players play mirror or looking into mirror without specifying when the change back and forth will happen. Follow the follower.

MIRROR EXERCISE #8

Teams of any number.

Ask players to do a problem around reflection of any kind.

POINT OF OBSERVATION

Exercise #8 will produce a number of new problems which can be made into further exercises.

AUDIENCE DIRECTS (SIDE COACHES)

Full group (after students are familiar with acting problems).

Teams set up in usual way. During playing, the teacher calls out various problems for them to solve. What is called out will depend upon what is wanted from the scene.

EXAMPLE: Where—kitchen. Who—mother and son. What—dinner time. Problem—boy wants to leave home.

When playing starts, "Contact!" may be called out, and players then must put their Point of Concentration on contact. They continue this until another problem, such as "Gibberish!" or "Extended movement!" is called. If "Blind!" is called out, of course, the players will have to close their eyes.

When the scene is completed, the teacher asks for it to be redone but this time does not call out. Instead, the teacher chooses someone in the student-audience (or many) to call out the Point of Concentration. Training for scene improvisation develops directing skills in everyone.

EXPLORE AND HEIGHTEN (TRANSFORMATION)

Teams of two or more.

This exercise calls for transformation of the beat and should not be done until CONTRAPUNTAL ARGUMENT C (transformation of the point of view) and TRANSFORMATION OF RELATIONSHIP have been understood and solved. The purpose of the exercise is to help players recognize and act upon the varied formations arising out of their playing. From the formations (plays, as in a game) come beats, and from a heightening of the beats emerges a scene. Often players fall into invention, plot, and ad-libbing because they are at a loss and do not see the beats rising out of the stage life. This exercise alerts everyone to even the minutest possibilities that appear during playing. Sometimes a simple gesture is explorable, sometimes an idea, an object, a sound.

As in AUDIENCE DIRECTS and GIVE AND TAKE, team starts off with a Where, Who, and What. After players are in motion, members of the audience (including the teacher-director) side-coach when they see an opportunity to explore and possibly "transform." Players build on the coaching.

SIDE COACHING: *Explore that idea! Explore and heighten that chair! That involvement! That cough! Transform that relationship! That beat! Explore the silence!*

EVALUATION

Were actors given enough time to explore before new coaching was called out? Were possible beats explored, or just words?

POINTS OF OBSERVATION

1. In all transformation exercises, invention, story-telling, and ad-libbing are clearly noticed by student-actors and student-audience alike, for true transformation brings fusion and unmistakably new formations.
2. Because in transforming the beat a limitation is set up by the Where, Who, and What, all the changes must remain under one roof, so to speak, and do not appear at random.
3. As in the other transformation exercises, the moment of playing must be apprehended and exhausted for a change to occur.

XI. Emotion

From the beginning student to the performing artist, great argument ensues as to how to get emotion or feeling for a particular scene.[1] The problem of clarifying what is meant by emotion is far from simple, but if emotion is to be handled as a direct acting problem in the training, a position must be formulated. One thing is certain. We must not use personal and/or subjective (what we use in daily living) emotion for the stage. It is a private matter (like feeling and believing) and not for public viewing. At best "real" emotion put on stage can be classified as psycho-drama no matter how skillfully it is written or played, and it does not constitute a theatrical communication.

The emotion we need for the theater can only come out of a fresh experience; for in such experiencing rests the stirring of our total selves—organic motion—which when combined with the theater reality spontaneously brings forth energy and motion (stage) for actors and audience alike. This prevents the use of old emotion from past experiences being used in a fresh moment of experience. It could well be the same formula that created the original personal emotions to begin with, and if this is so, all the emotion we use in daily living should evolve out of organic motion—out of the Where, Who, What, the involvements and relationships of our personal lives.

---

[1]While one book on acting may say that "joy is expressed by raising the hands over the head in a figure eight," student-actors will learn that joy can also be shown by wriggling the toes ecstatically.

In this way creating our own structure (reality in the theater) and playing it instead of living out old emotions, a whole process is set going which manufactures its own energy and motion (emotion) then and there. This prevents psycho-drama from appearing on either side of the stage, for psycho-drama is a vehicle specially designed for therapeutic reasons to abstract old emotions from the participating members and put them into a dramatic situation to examine them and so release the individual from his personal problems. This dramatic structure then, is the only resemblance to the play. In theater training, emotion can easily be provoked by many devices, and great care must be taken not to misuse individual emotion or allow the players to do so.

When psycho-drama is confused with a play or scene, is in fact considered to be the scene, it leads the actor to exploit himself (his emotions) instead of experiencing total organic motion. What can psycho-drama do but abstract the tears that should come out of our personal grief alone, thus making artistic detachment impossible? Emotion newly generated on stage, however, remains detached because it is usable only within the structure of agreed reality.

When exercises in the workshops are used for emotional release they must be stopped; for the players are working out of and on their personal feelings alone. However, as Point of Concentration is understood and used, subjective emotion becomes a thing of the past, where it truly belongs.

By taking the whole problem of emotion, then, and physicalizing it, we move it out of its abstracted use and place it within the total organism making organic motion possible. For it is the physical manifestation of emotion, whether it is a quiet widening of the eyes or a violent throwing of a cup, that we can see and communicate.[2]

Therefore we must not bring students to the exercises of emotion too early if we wish to avoid exhibitionism, psycho-drama, and general bad taste. The student-actor must not withdraw into his subjective world and "emote," nor should he intellectualize about "feeling," which can only limit his expression of it. An

---

[2] There are many ways to heighten emotion on stage for the audience's enjoyment through music, lighting, props, etc. Here we are dealing with the student-actor alone.

audience should not be interested in the personal grief, joy, and frustration of the performing actor. It is the skill of the actor playing the grief, joy, and frustration of the character portrayed that holds us captive.

Physicalization

SILENT SCREAM
Full group.

To help the student-actors feel emotion physically (inner action), ask the seated group to scream without making a sound. Coach them: *Scream with you toes! Your eyes! Your back! Your stomach! Your legs! Your whole body!*

When they are responding physically and muscularly as they would for a vocal scream—and this will be very evident—call: *Scream out loud!* The sound should be deafening.

This exercise not only gives students a direct experience to remember but is very useful for rehearsing mob scenes. Watch for the self-protective student-actor who will "act" out this exercise instead of doing it.

INABILITY TO MOVE A
Single player.

Player goes on stage and presents a situation in which he is physically immobilized and is being threatened by an outside danger.

POINT OF CONCENTRATION: inability to move.

EXAMPLE: Paralyzed man in a wheelchair senses someone behind him (Another player could actually be moving behind him.)

INABILITY TO MOVE B
Two or more players.

A group of people are in a situation whereby it is impossible for them to move because of some outside danger.

POINT OF CONCENTRATION: players' immobility because of outside danger.

EXAMPLE: Soldiers stranded in a minefield. Robbers hiding in a closet.

POINTS OF OBSERVATION

1. Only now will the introduction and discussion of activity and inner action be meaningful for students. Action does not necessarily mean activity, nor does activity always mean action. For our purposes, the word "activity" is used to denote outward stage movement, and the words "inner action" to explain internal movement. The term "inner action" means physicalization of feeling and replaces the term "emotion" whenever necessary.

2. To help students acquire this new awareness, bring up a discussion of the two terms. They must understand which comes first—activity/dialogue or inner action. Does the actor, like the White Queen in *Alice in Wonderland*, cry out before the pin has stuck the finger? All have probably seen the roughness and lack of reality in the scene where the actor reads, "It's cold in here" and then proceeds to shiver; for although the two might in some cases occur simultaneously, inner action generally precedes activity/dialogue:

1) Inner Action	2) Activity	3) Dialogue
Hunger	Go to refrig-	"What's there to
Physical response:	erator	eat?"
Salivary glands		
work, etc.		

3. An infant acts with his whole body (internally and externally), he laughs or cries from head to toe. However, as we grow older, we muscularly *hold* many manifestations of feeling. As a result of cultural pattern, we are forced to hold our tears and stifle our laughter. An emotion may work in our stomach, tingle along our spines, or give us cold chills, but outwardly, we have become conditioned to show this emotion physically only in isolated areas. We grit our teeth, clench our fist, and keep a stiff upper lip. It is essential to release these holds for full natural movement.

4. From now on use side coaching to remind the student-actors: *More inner action, please! Physicalize that feeling! Feel it in your toes!* This Point of Concentration will enable the student-actors to really *show* how they feel instead of merely talking or purusing meaningless activity.

CHANGING EMOTION

Single player.

When student-actors thoroughly understand inner action (physicalizing), show them how it can shift and change, even though the activity remains the same. In this exercise, the player completes an activity. Then, for some reason, the activity must be undone after it is completed, using the same objects the second time, but in reverse and with a different inner action.

POINT OF CONCENTRATION: physicalizing emotion or feeling through the objects.

EXAMPLE: Activity—a girl is making up and dressing for a dance. First inner action—*pleasure,* caused by her feelings about the event. Second inner action—*disappointment,* caused by learning that the dance has been canceled.

As one part of the activity, while influenced by the first inner action the girl might have taken the dress from the closet and held it against herself as she danced dreamily around the room. After learning that the dance had been canceled, she might have held the dress against herself and then rolled it up and thrown it back into the closet—thereby reversing motions in the same activity and responding to the second inner action.

SIDE COACHING: *More inner action, please! Physicalize that thought!*

EVALUATION

Was the activity identical before and after the turning point? Was the inner action communicated to the audience through body changes? What does pleasure do to one physically? What does disappointment create kinesthetically? (See remarks on showing inner action through the use of objects, p. 245.)

POINTS OF OBSERVATION

1. The same activity must be carried out both times. As in the

example, if the girl applied her make-up and then took the dress from the closet, she would put the dress back and remove the make-up after the turning point.

2. When the first inner action is well set, the teacher-director can ring the phone or send another student on stage to provide the necessary information to change the inner action, if necessary.

3. It would be well to note that the students can communicate their feelings very effectively by their handling of objects (as shown by the girl's handling of her dress before and after the turning point).[3]

4. If changing inner action is shown only through facial mannerisms, students are "acting" (performing) and have not understood the meaning of physicalization. Go back to early exercises of involvement with objects.

CHANGING INTENSITY OF INNER ACTION

Two or more advanced students.

Where, Who, and What agreed upon. Emotion must start at one point and then become progressively stronger. For instance, the sequence might run: from affection to love to adoration; from suspicion to fear to terror; from irritation to anger to rage.

The inner action can also run in a circle, concluding back at the original emotion (e.g., affection to love to adoration to love to affection). However, this must be accomplished only through side coaching by the teacher.

POINT OF CONCENTRATION: changing the emotion from one level to the next.

EXAMPLE: Where—a camp scene. Who—a group of teen-age girls. What—they think their counselor has deserted them for another group. *Changing inner action*—loss to sadness to grief.

In this scene, the inner action was carried through a full cycle by side coaching. When they arrived at grief, the coaching began; and they responded emotionally in the following order:

---

[3]See PHYSICALIZING OBJECTS, p. 78.

1. self-pity	7. affection
2. anger	8. love
3. hostility	9. self-responsibility
4. guilt	10. understanding
5. grief	11. self-respect
6. sadness	12. admiration for each other

EVALUATION

Were they acting (emoting) or showing inner action (physicalizing)?

POINTS OF OBSERVATION

1. In this exercise, the teacher-director should work very closely with the players, taking his cue from them as they pick up their cues from him. Follow the follower.
2. If the group is ready, these scenes can produce very exciting energy. However, if the scenes end up in mere chit-chat, the exercise has been presented too soon and the students need more foundation work.

JUMP EMOTION

Two or more players.

Where, Who, and What agreed upon. Each player chooses some radical change of inner action, which he plans beforehand, and fits into the scene (e.g., fear to heroism, love to pity, etc.).

Floorplans should be used here, particularly if the actors are getting sloppy about stage set-ups.

POINT OF CONCENTRATION: changing from one emotion (inner action) to the other.

EXAMPLE: Where—foxhole. Who—two soldiers. What—a dangerous mission. Jump changes of inner action—#1 anger to underderstanding; #2, fear to heroism.

Soldier #1 was angered at the cowardice shown by soldier #2, a shy sensitive boy whose seeming cowardice was a revulsion against killing another person. During the scene, a bullet struck soldier #1, wounding him; and soldier #2 bravely undertook the mission, although it was not his duty to do so. As the players kept their concentration on trying to make their shifts of emotion during the action, the scene developed to unusual dramatic height.

EVALUATION

Same as in previous inner-action exercises.

POINT OF OBSERVATION

To make a game of this exercise, designate examples of changing emotions on some slips of paper, put Where suggestions on others, and then let the players draw from each pile, as in the THEME-SCENE exercise (p. 218).

SHOWING EMOTION THROUGH OBJECTS #1

Two or more players.

Special Materials Needed

balloon	bell
sandbag	feathers
ball	egg beater
chains	rubber band
triangle	jumping rope
bean bag	party toys
horn	trapeze (or swinging rope)
	ladder

This is only a sample list; items may be substituted or added as desired.

Where, Who, and What agreed upon. All objects are on a table which is easily accessible to all players on stage without disturbing their set or stage movement.

POINT OF CONCENTRATION: to use an object, selected spontaneously at the moment the actor needs it, to show a feeling or relationship.

EXAMPLE A: Where—bedroom. Who—three sisters, two older and one younger. What— two older sisters are dressing to go out; younger sister wishes she could go along with them.

While dressing, the two older sisters discussed their anticipation of the evening's fun. They threw balloons, blew feathers, and jumped rope. The younger sister, sadly bewailing the fact that she could not go with them, walked around the bedroom weighted down with a sandbag, which she sometimes put on her shoulders and sometimes dragged along on the floor.

EXAMPLE B (for formal theater): A love scene between a bashful couple could make use of a ball rolled back and forth between their feet.

EXAMPLE C: A scene where someone was trying to "pass the buck" could be physicalized by tossing a bean bag back and forth among the two or three players involved.

EVALUATION

Did the objects follow the action?

POINT OF OBSERVATION

This exercise is especially helpful for the director of formal theater. It can give unusual nuances to actors, even those with small amounts of training.

SHOWING INNER ACTION THROUGH OBJECTS #2

Players repeat same scene as in SHOWING INNER ACTION THROUGH THE USE OF OBJECTS #1, attempting to retain the feeling of the objects without using them.

EVALUATION

Did they retain the quality of the scene when they worked without the objects?

POINT OF OBSERVATION

The second time the scene is done, keep reminding the players (through side coaching) of the objects that were used for the first scene.

EMOTION GAME

Entire group.

One player starts game, which can be enlarged to include other players (as in Where and Orientation games). He communicates Where he is and Who he is. What happens to him should be around a disaster, accident, hysteria, grief, etc. Other players enter the scene as definite characters, set up relationships with Where and Who, and play the scene.

EXAMPLE A: Where—street corner. Who—elderly man. What—car hits man as he crosses street.

The old man tentatively steps into the street. He is hit by a car and falls screaming to the ground. Other players enter as driver of car, cops, friends, passersby, ambulance driver, doctor, etc.

EXAMPLE B: Where—hospital room. Who—woman. What—seated at bedside of dying relative.

Player moves around room showing hospital environment. She shows us her relationship with the patient in the bed and her grief at his state of health. Other players enter scene as relatives, doctor, nurses, priest, another patient, etc.

POINTS OF OBSERVATION

1. If the teacher-director observes that the players are not entering into the game with enthusiasm, energy, and excitement, then it has not been presented properly, and steps should be retraced.
2. This game may be scattered throughout training or presented at the time emotion is introduced to the group. It is very useful when working on crowd scenes.

REJECTION

Two or more players.

Where, Who, and What agreed upon. Players must reject other players, adopting one of the following patterns:
1. One group rejects another group.
2. A group rejects an individual.
3. An individual rejects a group.
4. An individual rejects an individual.

POINT OF CONCENTRATION: on effective rejection.

EXAMPLES: New person in neighborhood is rejected. Someone is rejected because of race, color, or creed. Substitute teacher is rejected by the class.

EVALUATION

Did they solve the problem? What was the weather? Did they show us the time?

POINT OF OBSERVATION

By now, all the scenes should have a definite theatrical life. Evaluation is a way to remind players they might be getting careless in setting up the details of a scene.

EMOTION THROUGH CAMERA TECHNIQUES

Two or more players.

Where, Who, and What agreed upon. Players begin scene. From time to time during the action, the teacher-director calls out to "frame" different actors. Each time, the other actors on stage become "cameras" and focus on the one framed. The actor thus framed continues to play the scene normally; but he now has the intense attention of all the players around him. The scene continues to play with all actors remaining in their characters, whether cameras or subject. The framing is simply a way of heightening the scene.

POINT OF CONCENTRATION: intense body energy is to be focused on the actor being framed.

EXAMPLE: Where—throne room of a palace. Who—king, courtiers, a courier. What—waiting for news. The courier, badly beaten, comes into the palace with bad news. The court must decide what to do.

EVALUATION

Was the full body energy used to focus on the framed actor? Did they show us where they were? How old was the king (or whoever was in the scene)?

POINTS OF OBSERVATION

1. The interchange of the word "light" with "frame" will aid in evoking the intensity needed. Side coaching should shift the camera as necessary.
2. Exercises like this one when used during rehearsals of a formal play, where actual lights can be brought in simultane-

ously with the players' framing, can put much heightened stage energy into the players' performance.
3. This exercise is particularly good for student-directors, since they can easily take over the side coaching.
4. This exercise is similar to TWO SCENES (p. 160).

Conflict

Conflict should not be given to students-actors until they thoroughly understand holding the focus (object) to create relationships. If conflict conditions are given too early, involvement will take place between the players themselves, thus creating subjective emotional scenes or verbal battles between them. This is an important point and one difficult to understand. In fact, this writer used conflict extensively in the early years of her work as part of the Where exercise. It seemed useful, for it invariably created some stage energy (when it wasn't on a "you-did-and-I-didn't" level). This was because by creating involvement with each other directly, it stirred up personal feelings and tension in the players and in many instances was close to psycho-drama. This gave the players the feeling of "acting". As we are working in an art form, the personal emotions of players must be distilled and objectified through the form in which they are working—an art form insists upon this objectivity. In spite of this obvious fact, however, conflict seemed to bring "life" into the Where exercise and was a definite step towards contact, and so was retained as one of the problems given during the early stage of Where.

In time, it became apparent that unless the players used the *physical objects* in Where, for instance, to show conflict, many aspects of subjectivity (such as emotionalism or verbal battles) were bound to result. Further, very little if any scene progression took place. It was important to note that despite the unpleasant aspects, tension and release freeing energy (physical action) were always generated between players. Only after the author came to Chicago to direct workshops and discussed this many times with Paul Sills (original director of Second City) was the question of conflict finally resolved. The same tension and release generated through conflict can be accomplished with the student-actor when he is kept on the problem as presented by the Point of Concentration (focus) and not allowed to wander off into story-telling or playwriting.

It became evident that the players' involvement with each other (as produced by conflict) instead of involvement with the focus (as produced by the Point of Concentration) was for the most part a mutual pushing around (which is confused in our minds as dramatic action) to get to one's goal and in no sense a process out of which scene improvisation could develop. On the other hand, relation between players created by involvement with the object made objective tension and release (physical action) possible and at the same time produced scene improvisations. This would seem so because conflict remained in the area of the emotional and could therefore never make the spring into the intuitive, which consistently happens when we allow the Point of Concentration to work for us.

If players are absorbed with story (content) only, conflict is necessary. Without it, the scene gets bogged down, and little or no action can possibly take place. At best, however, it is titillation and imposed action and for the most part produces psycho-drama. However, when process is understood, and, further, that story is the residue of process, dramatic action is the result, for energy and stage-action are generated by the simple process of playing. By constantly stopping student-actors from playwriting and continuously clarifying the whole point of process *versus* content, the teacher found that conflict was no longer needed to generate stage-action, and so this exercise with its emotionalism and verbal battles fell into disuse.

Now conflict takes its place along with the later exercises. It is useful; it can be fun to do. A teacher-director may be tempted to use it earlier than advisable, when there are difficulties in understanding process and playing, to "stir up" some action. If he does this, however, he must know that it is a device—and because of the personal emotions it stirs up, it constitutes a "bribe." Its use in this way may be permitted us when it becomes most important to hold a student's interest until process and therefore playing are understood.

To summarize. When players work with story alone, they need a conflict to generate energy and stage-action. When they understand playing (process), however, tension and release freeing energy are clearly seen as an integral part of playing—in fact this *is* playing.

CONFLICT EXERCISE
Pairs.

PRELIMINARY

To give the communication of conflict being tension between two people, have student-actors go on stage in twos and have a tug-of-war with a real rope. Discussion on the tug-of-war should be around the physical tension in each one of them as they strive to pull their opponent over the center line. Further discussion should be on the outcome of the tug-of-war, when one pulled the other over, both fell over, or a stalemate was reached.

EXERCISE

Two or more players.

Where, Who, and What agreed upon. Add a conflict.

POINT OF CONCENTRATION: the conflict (rope) between them.

SIDE COACHING: *Pull the rope! Stay with the Point of Concentration!*

EVALUATION

Did they stay with the Point of Concentration? Did each individual actor hang on to his end of the rope?

POINT OF OBSERVATION

In preparing the scene, listen to groups carefully to see that the conflict will be such that it will permit physical action and not just an argument. Conflict and/or rope are used interchangeably to help physicalize the conflict for the players.

HIDDEN CONFLICT
Two or more players.

Where, Who, and What agreed upon. Each player takes a

conflict and states it to himself in the first person without letting the other know what it is.

POINT OF CONCENTRATION: never to verbalize the problem (conflict).

EXAMPLE: Where—kitchen. Who—husband and wife. What—breakfast.
Hidden conflict: Husband—I am not going to work. Wife—I want him to leave. I'm expecting a visitor.

POINTS OF OBSERVATION
1. Let audience know each player's hidden conflict.
2. When the hidden conflict is stated, the scene is over.
3. Variation of this is to write a series of hidden conflicts on slips of paper and let actors pick after they have decided on Where, Who, and What.
4. HIDDEN CONFLICT forces use of objects and was one of the early exercises that started the semantic shift from "conflict" to "problem," thus opening up new doors of inquiry.

WHAT TO DO WITH THE OBJECT
Two players.

Players agree on object between them. Object is to be set in motion in some agreed way such as: selling it, destroying it, building it, hiding it.

POINT OF CONCENTRATION: on *what* to do with the object.

POINT OF OBSERVATION
This is similar to the Involvement exercises in the orientation session. It takes the players further, however, for it can be used to set up emotions directly involving players through the object. While the Point of Concentration in the earlier exercises was on the object between the players, the present Point of Concentration is on what is happening to the object. It therefore sets up a different relationship between the players. If a story is imposed on the object and players "act," limit them to a simple activity. Return to this exercise at a later date when the group has learned how to let the POC work for them.

CONFLICT GAME

Full group.

Played as in Orientation and Where games. Two players go on stage. They agree upon a conflict that can allow for many others to take part. Other members of workshop decide Who and enter scene to take sides.

EXAMPLES: Where—a street corner. Who—a policeman and a soap-box orator. What—an arrest. Conflict—policeman arresting orator because of the content of his speech. Players entering scene can be workman, bums, housewives, more policemen, etc. Where—playground. Who—two boys. What—playing. Conflict— one boy is a bully. Those entering scene can become other children, teachers, mothers, etc.

XII. Character

Character is presented as the last large problem in the handbook. It should not be given as a direct exercise until the student-actors have solved the earlier workshop problems and have learned to work with the POC. Although it may be tempting to present and discuss character exercises in earlier workshops, it is best to wait until students appear to be fully in contact with each other and fully involved with the acting problem (see Chapter XI).

Character is intrinsic in everything we do on stage. From the very first acting class, this thread has crossed and re-crossed the fabric of our work. Character can grow only out of personal integration with the total stage life. If the actor is truly to play his role, character must not be given as an intellectual exercise independent of this involvement.

Premature attention to character on a verbal level may throw the student-actor into role-playing, keeping him from involvement with the POC and moving relations with his fellow players. Instead of reaching out into the stage environment, he will withdraw further behind his self-protecting walls. It will be himself acting out his private needs and feelings; it will be himself mirroring himself; it will be himself giving an interpretation of a character, an intellectual exercise.

In the unskilled student this will be quickly uncovered, but it is far more difficult to catch in the more clever and skilled actor. Character must be used as further theatrical communication, *not as withdrawal*. To insure this, do not work on character until students are playing. Always keep them from "acting" (performing) in their early work, by stopping an exercise if necessary. Avoid discussing character except in the most casual way, on a simple Who basis (relationship). Remember, since most students know that character is the essence of theater, this absence of direct character discussion may be very confusing to them until they begin to see character emerge out of the stage life and realize that "acting" is a wall between players.

When they learn to be involved with the Point of Concentration, relate to each other, and solve the group problem, they will "trust the scheme" and be ready for direct exercises in developing physical qualities for a character. An actor must see and relate to a fellow actor, not a "character." We play football with other human beings, not with the uniforms they are wearing. This simply means that both players know the other is playing and go along with the game.

Developing A Character

When student-actors plan W.W.W. around an acting problem, what is it that determines who among them shall play the grandmother and who the maiden aunt? This is all implicit in what is known as characterization.

In Orientation, the students—by simply observing whether others are comfortable or uncomfortable—are able to catch mannerisms. ORIENTATION GAME, HOW OLD AM I? and WHAT DO I DO FOR A LIVING? all introduce character without calling attention to it. In Where we ask: "How do you know what people are to each other?"; and the youngest student answers, "By the way they act together." And every early Who exercise handles the problem of character.

In Evaluation we raise such questions as: "How old was he?" "Did he show us he was a man who farmed for a living?" "Did the miser look as if he loved gold more than people?" If we question carefully, even the youngest child will be able to express the differences between people—whether the distinguishing quality is in mannerism, tone of voice, or tempo of movement.

After many years, our usual facial expressions, posture, and movements become muscular reflections of our inner state. Emotion can be expressed only through character. In *The Thinking Body,* Mabel Elsworth Todd states:

"Emotion constantly finds expression in bodily position; if not in the furrowed brow or set mouth, then in limited breathing, in the tight held neck muscles, or in the slumped body of listlessness and discouragement."

It could be said that, in time, a man might well become a portrait of himself—for a man becomes the physical expression of an attitude (a life attitude). How many of us can pick out a doctor, a public relations man, a schoolteacher, or an actor in a crowd and be 85 per cent correct?

Simple involvement with objects can come to life only through character. In developing material for scenes (Chapter IX), character development is handled more directly as the "play" is set up and the need for definite characters arises. GIBBERISH, CONTACT, BLIND, and other exercises insist upon strong stage relations which create definite character attitudes and actions.

What is acting with the whole body (Chapter V) but a way of showing the actor how his body can be an expressive instrument? And for what purpose? To communicate with an audience more comprehensively. To communicate what? A character within a play.

Experiment with a group. Tell them that they will be given a quick command. When the teacher-director claps his hands, they are to carry out the command instantly without thought.

"*Portray an old man!*" is called. Invariably, almost 90 per cent of the students will lean forward, hand on hip, as if resting on a cane. Discuss their generalization (cliché) with them. Do all old men necessarily lean forward? There are millions of old men— some are straight and tall. What makes a person old?

The generalization (cliché) is not necessarily untrue, merely abstracted and thus limited. To the student-actor, the old man may well be a person who leans on a cane, has white hair, and moves slowly, and this economy of selection is important to keep.

Old age is, after all, recognizable. The students, in selecting the characteristics which would instantly communicate an old man, chose the simplest of them all, infirmity. And that was what they gave in answer to the command. It is from this kind of simple recognition that the actor develops his characterization.

What will finally emerge as they gain perception is that an old man can show his age and his feelings in his feet, his elbows, and his voice, as well as in his white hair and cane.

Developing a character is the ability to intuit an essence from the welter of the complex whole person. This ability to show the essence rather than a description of the detailed whole springs spontaneously from within. See HOW OLD AM I REPEAT, p. 69.

The actor's skill depends upon his response and ability to communicate it. *All* can respond: the immature will do the obvious (leaning on a cane); the artist who trusts his intuition accepts what emerges with certainty (arthritic hand, cataract-blinded eye, thickened tongue, etc.)[1] But no matter what is used, simple or profound, and whatever the age or experience of the player, when he responds to his stage life, at the same time character appears; for characterization grows out of the total stage life as well as intuitive recognition of a fellow man.

The actor is surrounded by a circle of characteristics—voice, mannerisms, physical movement—all of which are given life by his energy. The student-actor will develop *himself* as an alert, perceiving, free person, capable of reaching beyond his day-to-day life. He will be able to "play" a role. He will be alive, human, interdependent, working with his fellow players. He will be *himself*—the actor—playing the game of the character he has chosen to communicate.

How much better to think of him this way, as a human being working within an art form, than a schizophrenic who has changed his own personality for the sake of a role in a play!

---

[1]The player need not "become" the old man. Rather, he presents the old man to us for purposes of communication.

Physicalizing

A student can dissect, analyze, intellectualize, and develop a valuable case history of a character; but if he is not able to communicate this physically, it is useless within the theater form. Reaching the intuitive, on which the insight into a role rests, does not come from a logical, intellectual knowledge of our character.

The following group of exercises deal with the problem of character on a physical structural basis, from which a character may emerge. The question arises as to whether an actor should assume outward physical qualities to get a feeling of a character or work on feeling to get the physical qualities. Sometimes a physical attitude or expression will give us an intuitive jump. In these exercises we play the game every way. (See also Chapters X and XI.)

Who Games[2]

Absorb the following exercises carefully so as to be able to present them to student-actors at the time when they will most effectively act as a series of simple steps toward character development. They can be used as warm-ups or developed into full exercises.

WHO GAME B

Two or more players. Who, Where, and What agreed upon. (Players should choose a simple relationship and activity, such as husband and wife watching TV.)

Have each player write on individual slips of paper a list of facial features and then descriptions of those features. The descriptions should be emotional rather than structural. Players should make out slips for each facial feature. For instance:

> lower lip–sad
> upper lip–petulant
> tip of nose–sharp

---

[2]Some of the Who games are presented in Chapter IV.

nostrils–annoyed
eyes–beady
eyebrows–serene
forehead–overhanging
chin–belligerent
shape of face–saucy

When the slips have been completed, separate them by features and put the slips into piles. Let each player pick one slip from each pile. The players are to take on as many of the descriptions as they wish and retain them while playing their scene.

POINT OF CONCENTRATION: To keep as many of the facial qualities as possible while going through the scene.

EVALUATION

To actors: Did holding these physical aspects make you feel mechanical? Did you gain any new insights?

To audience: did any of the actors show a new character quality? Did the facial qualities seem integrated with the scene?

POINT OF OBSERVATION

Mirrors for the players when they first try to take on their physical characteristics can be helpful.

WHO GAME C

Instead of choosing facial descriptions, the players are now to list emotions for body attitude. For instance:

shoulders–sad
stomach–angry
chest–joyous
legs–suspicious

POINT OF CONCENTRATION: showing feeling through body attitudes while going through scene.

POINTS OF OBSERVATION

1. WHO GAMES B and C may also be used for developing physical rather than emotional attitudes. To do so, just substitute descriptions (e.g., stiff upper lip, a harp nose, bowed legs, etc.)

2. Both WHO GAMES are very useful for the director of the formal theater.

WHO GAME C, ADDING CONFLICT

Same as WHO GAME A, p. 109, with addition of pre-planning the state of the unknowing player (conflict or tension).

EXAMPLE: A on stage. B pre-plans that A is a mean, taciturn parent while she herself is a teen-ager. Where—living room. Who—mean taciturn parent (seated); teen-ager (enters). What— teen-ager comes home late from a date.

POINTS OF OBSERVATION

1. This exercise can usually be continued beyond the solving of the problem, for tension between the two players comes up automatically.
2. Again, letting the audience in on the reverse point of view is intensely interesting.

Physicalizing Attitudes

HOLD IT! A

Four or more players (even division of males and females desirable).

Have players sit on stage. Ask each of them individually to give a short expressive statement such as: "Nobody loves me." "I never have any fun." "I wish I had nice things." "Tomorrow will be better."

When the player has achieved a definite physical expression (full body) as a result of his phrase, tell him to "Hold It!" When all the players have their "held expressions," put them through a series of three- to four-minute scenes. For example:

children in nursery school
a grammar-school graduation platform or classroom
a street corner
an office party
marriage proposal (if there are two or more couples, place them in "parked cars" and combine give-and-take with this exercise)

middle-age (party at someone's home)
old age (meeting for card game or such)
POINT OF CONCENTRATION: to keep the original facial and body
expression throughout the scenes.

EVALUATION

Did the expression become an attitude towards others within
the scenes? Were the basic expressions (attitudes) maintained,
even if somewhat altered in each scene? (Naturally, the love
scene would have some alteration, as would the nursery scene
versus the old-age scene).

POINTS OF OBSERVATION

1. If a phrase does not evoke an attitude, suggest that the player
   take on an exact physical expression (e.g., belligerent chin,
   petulant mouth, overhanging forehead, wide-open eyes, etc.).
2. Do not use this exercise with young students. Players should
   be at least in their teens.
3. HOLD IT! can be given around the eighth or ninth Where workshop session and repeated at later dates.
4. One student, on completion of HOLD IT! said: "I feel as if I've
   gone through a lifetime!"

HOLD IT! B

Vary HOLD IT! A by having the players take on body expressions (hunched shoulders, firm aggressive step, pigeon-toed, ex-
panded chest, flabby stomach muscles, etc.). Carry them through
six or seven scenes.

EVALUATION

Did their body attitudes (expressions) alter their ways of
speaking?

HOLD IT! C

Two or more players.

Where, Who, and What are agreed upon after the students

have each achieved a physical expression and been told to "Hold it!"

POINT OF CONCENTRATION: retaining one or two physical aspects throughout (pulled-in chin, extra weight, etc.)

EVALUATION

Did the chosen physical characteristics influence the players' choice of Where, Who, and What?

Physical Visualization

The use of images in getting a character quality is an old and tried technique and can sometimes bring a totally new dimension to an actor's role. Images can be based on pictures or any object, animate or inanimate, that the actor chooses. However, getting character in this way is at best a device.

In the formal play, such images should be used only when the character development has not evolved from the total stage relationship. Actors who have had some experience with this way of working are eager to begin work on the character immediately and sometimes set about taking some image privately without letting the director know. This becomes a serious handicap, for the director and actor may be at odds with one another. The director may be working to get rid of the very mannerisms the actor is hanging on to because of the image he has created for himself.

It is, however, useful in emergencies. Once, for example, a girl was asked to step into a small part on a few hours' notice, because of the sudden illness of the regular actor. She was playing in another one-act play on the same bill. In rehearsal, it was soon evident that she could not easily shake the characteristics of the other role. Her regular part was that of a shy, frightened girl; but the new one was a portrayal of a perky, talkative woman. By suggesting that she take an animal image, specifically a turkey, the director enabled her to project the necessary qualities for the role almost immediately.

In improvisational theater, when suggestions by the audience arc part of a program, images can give the actor an instant character quality which adds to his versatility.

ANIMAL IMAGES[3]

Four or more players.

If at all possible, take the workshop group to a zoo or barnyard to observe the movement, rhythm, and actual physical characteristics of animals—the bone and facial structures are as important as the more obvious movement. In this way, student-actors will have an actual impression to recapture, not simply a picture in a book. Generalization is to be avoided if the exercise is to have any value.

Separately, each player decides what animal he will portray. The players do not need to discuss their choices with one another. Each player is to take on the exact physical qualities of his animal and is then to move around the stage as the animal. Side coaching must go on throughout the exercise to free the actors to work on the problem.

When the students have released their total selves into the animal qualities and have captured some new body rhythms, then coach them to make the sounds of their animals. Continue coaching until all resistances are gone and the sound and body movements are integrated.

Now, coach the players to become human again, to stand upright and move about the stage, absorbing the animal characteristics and sound into their human actions and speech. They are to keep the rhythm of the animals in their bodies and the sound of the animals in the words they are mouthing. As before, they are to move about the stage at random.

When they are all moving around upright and have absorbed the animal characteristics and sound, the teacher-director quickly sets up a Where, Who, and What for them.

POINT OF CONCENTRATION: to make the body rhythm, facial expression, and vocal sounds of their animals their own.

SIDE COACHING: *Re-shape your forehead! The nose! The jaw! Concentrate on the spine! Concentrate on the tail! The back legs!*

---

[3]The basic exercise is attributed to Maria Ouspenskaya.

When they are moving freely around the stage, coach: *Give the sound of your animal!*

When the sound and body movements are integrated, coach: *Become human! Stand upright! Keep your animal qualities! Keep your animal rhythms! Sound like your animal! Use a human voice with the animal sound!*

EXAMPLE: Four players took for their individual visualizations a parrot, a cat, a hippopotamus, and an owl.[4] In solving the problem, the parrot became a shrewish talkative person. The cat was lithe and shy, the hippo heavy-voiced, lumbering and sullen, and the owl was a wide-eyed naive young girl.

The combination suggested an office, perhaps a school office. A table, chair, and bench were quickly set up. Windows and doors, drinking fountains, etc. were pointed out to define Where (this was done very swiftly, reminding the actors to keep their Point of Concentration). Where—school office. Who—assistant principal, parents, children. What—settling childrens' problems.

The parrot was the assistant principal, who decided which person could gain admittance to the inner office. Her staccato, repetitive phrasing lent itself well to this. The others were parents and children waiting to see the principal.

Parrot: (Asst. Principal)	All right, all right . . . who's next? Who's next, I said? Who's next? I haven't all day, you know.
Hippo: (Father)	(Moving slowly, rubbing his hands on his legs.) It's me, I guess. . . .
Parrot:	Hurry up! Hurry up! Hurry up! I haven't all day you know. Just look at all the people we have to see today. Dear, dear, dear!
Hippo:	(Head forward, shoulders hunched, slow heavy voice.) It's about my daughter.
Parrot:	(Voice rising.) Did you hear that? Did you hear that? (Cackles.) Of course! Of course! That's what you are here for. Your daughter is

---

[4]This scene was done by twelve-to-fourteen-year-olds.

	right there. I know her well. (Looks at owl who is on the verge of tears.) And this young man!
Cat: (Boy)	(Turns his head and body away from her sharp scrutiny and slides down to the edge of the bench.)
Parrot:	Well, well, what are we going to do about these children?
Hippo:	I dunno . . . she said she didn't mean to do nothin'. (To Owl.) Didn't you?
Owl: (Daughter)	(Wide-eyed, lips pursed, tearful) Ooooooh . . . Oooooooooo . . . Ooooooooooh!
Parrot:	(To Cat.) Now you! You there! You! Where are your parents. They were to be here! You know that!
Cat:	They c-c-couldn't beeeoooooowwww here!

POINTS OF OBSERVATION

1. If the actors lose their animal rhythms of body and voice when they stand upright, have them go back on all fours again to the original animal image. This should restore the qualities they are using.
2. When the actors speak as humans, they must sound like humans with the added animal quality; not like an animal talking.
3. To avoid breaking the flow generated by this exercise, set up a situation for the student-actors as they are moving about the stage. By close observation of body attitudes, rhythm, and voice quality that appear when they are "human," a situation will spontaneously suggest itself. Quickly, giving the acting group a Where and What, come on stage and set it up for them. Cast each player and have them move directly into the situation.

STATUES

Two or more players, one back-stage worker (optional). (This is based on the common children's game.)

An outside person swings the players around and then lets them go so that each one falls into some random position. Players must then hold these positions until each position suggests to its player one of the following: a Where; a character (Who); an emotion; an activity; a relationship. The players then make contact with one another and develop a structure using one or all of the above categories.

POINT OF CONCENTRATION: body position and responding to fellow players according to category selected.

EVALUATION

Did the actors fall into position naturally when swung around, or did they set a position for themselves (thereby controlling or playwriting)? Did the action evolve spontaneously between them?

To actors: did you individually decide Where, Who, etc., or did it spring from the group contact? Did back-stage effects implement stage action or impose upon it?

POINTS OF OBSERVATION

1. Watch for the playwriters. They will try to maneuver the others into what they decide is the way the scene should go.
2. Each category can be given singly in place of offering a choice. For instance, if Who (character) is the category, then the Where, What, Involvement, etc. must take place spontaneously out of Who.
3. Because many immature actors feel uncomfortable in long silences (see SILENT TENSION, p. 188), side coaching on the Point of Concentration during the pre-scene quiet period will help relieve students of the urgency to premature activity.
4. A variation of this exercise is to instruct the players to end the exercise by returning to their original positions.

Physical Attributes

PHYSICAL EXAGGERATION[5]
Two or more players.

Where, Who, and What agreed upon. Each player is to take

---

[5]See also Chapter V.

on some exaggerated physical quality, which he is to retain throughout the scene.

EXAMPLES: 10 feet tall, 2 feet tall, weighing 500 pounds, wearing size 20 shoes, a large chest, foot-long index fingers, legs and feet are pogo sticks, legs and feet are springs, legs and feet are round balls. This exercise can be done with full group. Players walk around stage and take on exaggerated qualities as coached.

COSTUME PIECE

Two or more players

Each player selects a costume piece (cane, derby hat, scarf, umbrella, etc.). He is to assume character qualities (attitudes) suggested by his costume piece. Who, Where, and What agreed upon.

POINT OF CONCENTRATION: actors are to retain the character qualities (attitudes) suggested by their costume bits.

EVALUATION

Did he impose character on his costume piece, or did he let the costume piece determine his character for him?

POINT OF OBSERVATION

For further information on using costume pieces for characterization, see Chapter IX.

PHYSICAL IRRITATION A

Three or more players.

Where: a public speaker's platform. Each player is to make a speech. During the speech, he has some sort of physical irritation which is bothering him but which he cannot remedy because of all the people watching him. The irritation might, for example, be a tight collar.

POINT OF CONCENTRATION: (1) the discomfort; (2) masking all attempts to relieve the irritation while continuing with the speech.

EXAMPLE: A scene was set up in which two students were waiting politely on a lecture platform for a third to finish his speech so they could make theirs. When curtain was called, the first student launched into his "speech." His physical irritation was a piece of corn caught in his teeth, which he kept trying to loosen unobtrusively as he continued his speech.

One girl took the problem of surreptitiously fixing a snapped garter while she had to speak (holding a stocking up).

The other student had an itching sunburn between her shoulder blades.

EVALUATION

Did they make taking care of their physical irritation part of what they were doing, or did they isolate it?

POINTS OF OBSERVATION

1. Although this exercise often produces very humorous scenes, the teacher should stress that it is not being given for its "gag" value.
2. The student who solves the problem will be the one who most subtly tends to his irritation. However, the teacher-director should not tell the students that he is looking for subtlety. Leave this for self-discovery.
3. This exercise is a great measure in determining the students' development.
4. If players are too overt in "hiding" their physical irritation, redo exercise as in HOW OLD AM I? REPEAT where point of concentration is held on the physical irritation alone and moves the player instead of him trying to manipulate it.
5. This exercise often brings interesting new character qualities to the players, and is useful in conjunction with the formal play.
6. Don't confuse a social comment with creating a character.

PHYSICAL IRRITATION B

Two players.

Players portray an encounter where one person is under close scrutiny by the other and must cover up an embarrassing blemish.

EXAMPLES: A is being interviewed for a job by, or having a business meeting with, B. A has a spot on his tie, or he has beer on his breath, etc.

B is a school girl meeting with her counselor. B has a run in her stocking.

POINT OF CONCENTRATION: concealing the problem during the interview.

NERVOUS HABITS OR TICS

Two or more players.

Where, Who, and What are agreed upon. Each player is to adopt a nervous habit or a tic. They should choose these from actual experience—recalling someone they have met who was actually afflicted with such a habit.

Action should be handled just as in PHYSICAL IRRITATION. Teacher-director should stress at the outset that the player is not to poke fun at this affliction but is to understand it and work with it.

POINT OF CONCENTRATION: adopting a nervous habit or tic.

EVALUATION

All players agree that people with nervous habits do not want them, nor do they necessarily have them at all times.

Do you think that a nervous habit is caused by something, or that it belongs to a person from birth? While we may not know the clinical reasons why a person has a nervous habit, let us never forget that it is the physical manifestation of some inner action.

In the case of stuttering, for example: *What do you think might be causing that? How many of you have ever stuttered?* It is surprising to see the show of hands. Most people have stuttered at one time or another.

Can anyone remember what caused them to stutter? What made it difficult for the words to come out? In almost every instance the reply is: "I was afraid." "I didn't know the answer." "Someone scared me." "I was asked to say something too fast." It seems, on this level, most stuttering is related to fear or sudden shock.

If we agree, then, that stuttering is the result of fear or shock, what does this do to us physically? Have students remember a moment of personal fear or shock. Note they almost invariably make a sharp breathing sound and then hold their breath when they have remembered something.

Have students go on stage as refugees from a war zone. Explain that when they hear a loud sharp noise, they are to treat it as bombs falling. *What happened in almost every case of reaction to the bombs?* "We stopped dead," they recalled. "We fell to the ground and stiffened out."

It is obvious to them that fear and shock brought a physical tension—not only to speech but to their bodies as well. They held their breath from head to toe. It well could be that physical manifestation of this sort in people are moments of past fear retained in a present environment.

POINTS OF OBSERVATION

1. Whatever the exact cause of an affliction, the student should be aware of some personal as well as physical problems of the sufferer. The exercise is not to be treated as a bit of comic business.
2. This exercise is useful because it clearly shows a student-actor that emotion and the physical expression (character) of that emotion are one.

Developing Character Agility

The following exercises are obviously valuable for the actor in the improvisational theater. They are equally valuable for the actor in the formal theater, in that they expedite the search for character attitudes.

CHARACTER AGILITY A
Full group.

Teacher-director supplies pencils and paper to the players and gives them the following categories, which they write down. Additional categories can be used. Time limit for each.

1. Animal
2. Image
3. Rhythm
4. Props

5. Costume Pieces
6. Color

Teacher-director now reads off a list of characters one at a time. Players must write down whatever comes to them regarding each character for each of the categories. Possible characters might be:

Professor	School Teacher
Old Man	Astronaut
Psychoanalyst	Father
Little Boy	Aunt
Banker	Grandmother

POINT OF CONCENTRATION: on writing down the first impressions that come to mind, under the given categories, for each character.

EXAMPLE

Character: Professor
1. Animal: owl
2. Image: rock
3. Rhythm: staccato
4. Prop: pointer
5. Costume Pieces: muffler, overshoes
6. Color: purple

CHARACTER AGILITY B

Instead of giving a variation of categories, name only one specific category. The players must then write as much about the character in this one specific category as they can within a one-minute time limit.

Or, the teacher-director might supply varied and seemingly unrelated categories, which the players must then fill in, also within a limited amount of time.

EXAMPLES: Single category—image.

Varied categories—physical details; foods, tastes; background, friends.[6]

---

[6]The varied categories can be used as "biography" for a character in a formal play.

CHARACTER AGILITY C

Two players.

Student audience suggests characters (e.g., a spinster school teacher and a grocery clerk) for each. Players are given limited time to concentrate on their characters. (Have them sit quietly as in EXCURSIONS INTO THE INTUITIVE, p. 191.) When ready (in their own time) players move into a Where which emerges in the space.

POINT OF CONCENTRATION: to allow the "random thoughts" to take over without intellectual selection.

EVALUATION

To players: did you allow random ideas to appear, or did you categorize your thoughts? Did your character come to life? Did you *play* the character?

To audience: was there a difference in the characters between random and categorized associations? Did this problem excite the actors into new aspects? Were there many body changes?

CHARACTER AGILITY D

Teacher-director supplies pencils and paper, gives the image, mood, rhythm, etc., and has student-actors quickly write the character suggested.

CHARACTER AGILITY E[7]

Full group. Used as a warm-up game.

Players sit in a circle with one in the center. The center player calls out various character categories while pointing to each player in turn as he does so. The center player then stops and points to one of the players, giving him a particular category and counts to ten as he does so.

The player must respond before the center player stops counting. If image or mood or rhythm, color, etc., is used by the center player, a specific character must be named. If character is called by the center player, then an image must be given by the count of ten.

---

[7]This is played like the game called Beast, Bird or Fish in Neva L. Boyd, *Handbook of Games* (Chicago: H. T. Fitzsimons Co., 1945), p. 101.

POINTS OF OBSERVATION

1. See that these exercises do not become an intellectual game, a series of clichés for student-actors. Play it frequently, and students will soon be getting substance for their characters from a far deeper source than is usual.
2. The agility in spontaneous selection which this exercise develops in the actor is very important to handling characters as presented by suggestions from the audience.

TRANSFORMATION OF RELATIONSHIP
Two players.

Players begin with a relationship (Who) and keep transforming it into new relationships. As in TRANSFORMATION OF THE OBJECT (p. 214), change must not be made through invention or association. Players must "let it happen," not meddle. Either player may initiate change, and "relationship" may include animals, machines, etc. as well as people.

When players are working on the problem and solving it, the spontaneous changes that appear are seemingly endless. Some transformations bring dialogue along with them, some are silent, Where has great clarity, props instantly exist, and physicalization is strong.

If players stand around and tell stories, however, change comes only through word association, and they are not solving the problem and must be stopped. When the problem is understood, however, extraordinary breakthroughs occur as players sense that an endless succession of characters, relationships, and ideas exist within them for their use.

After success with this theater game, bring students back to CONTRAPUNTAL ARGUMENT C (transformation of point of view), and they will move more readily into transforming a thought.

Transforming, whether it be of character, object, or idea, seems to be essentially what must take place within every scene improvisation. It is the excitement and energy of every scene—its life process.

EVALUATION

To actors: did you invent or let it happen? They will know because they will be fully feeling, at last, the difference between inventing and creating.

POINTS OF OBSERVATION

1. Repeat SPACE SUBSTANCE (p. 81) just prior to introducing this exercise.
2. In every case the changing characters and relationships reveal a scene in microcosm before it shifts.
3. Three or more players can be used if the group is advanced.
4. In most cases the teacher-director will have to call the exercise to a halt, for transformations can go on indefinitely.
5. When this theater game was used for public performances in Chicago, the audience suggested the first and last characters.
6. Any performing group that uses this game should be cautioned: "let it happen"; do not imitate old changes or "invent" new ones, or the game will "dry up." To strain and plot for transformations will kill the goose for a mere handful of golden eggs.

CREATING A STAGE PICTURE

Any number of players.

Players agree on Where, Who, and What. Age is decided upon. When curtain opens, they should be posed as in a picture.

All sit on stage in the Where they have decided upon. As in HOW OLD AM I? REPEAT they sit quietly with blank mind. When inspiration comes to one of them, he moves into the scene.

Categories other than age can be decided upon. This is a sort of combination of EXCURSIONS INTO THE INTUITIVE and NO MOTION put together in a frame. Players are to come back to original "picture."

Children and the Theater

XIII. Understanding the Child

Children nine years old and up can follow the steps set up in the first part of this handbook with exhilarating results. In fact, the non-verbal system of problems and rehearsal was developed *with* and *for* children. While many of the earlier exercises can be altered for the younger student-actor, just as some of the following exercises can be used for the older student, this chapter is geared to the particular needs of the six-to-eight-year-olds. Many of the special exercises in listening, seeing, and give and take have also been used successfully with the six-to-eight-year-olds when given to a well-established group. It is suggested, of course, that the Points to Remember from Chapter II be read carefully before presenting this material, as well as the section on directing the child actor in Chapter XVII.

For ten or more years, summer workshops were held at the Young Actors Company in Hollywood for children from nine to fourteen years of age. The program consisted of a total of thirty hours per week, plus extra time for those children who wished for more activity in the technical aspects of the theater. With the exception of active games and folk dancing, every hour was spent on theater activity. There was never a moment's lag in interest. One summer the six-to-eight-year-olds participated in the program. They absorbed a good eight hours of work and wanted more. In fact, the combination of the theater games, body work, and rehearsal of plays made their eight hours almost too few.

The Teacher's Attitude

A child can make an honest and exciting contribution to the theater if he is allowed the personal freedom to experience. He will understand and accept his responsibility to the theater communication; he will involve himself, develop relationships, create reality, and learn to improvise and evolve theatrically valid scenes as does his adult counterpart.

Harold Hillebrand, in his book *The Child Actors*, propounds the question: "Must we suppose that acting by children is a lost art, like Venetian glass making?" Mr. Hillebrand has obviously seen an average production with child actors. And yet, the uninteresting, precocious, often exhibitionistic level of most children's performances does not stem from inability to understand and learn theater on the part of the child. Rather, it reveals the absence of a method of teaching which presents material to the child that will permit him to utilize his own creative potential within the medium.

There are few places outside of his own play where a child can contribute to the world in which he finds himself. His world: dominated by adults who tell him what to do and when to do it —benevolent tyrants who dispense gifts to their "good" subjects and punishment to their "bad" ones, who are amused at the "cleverness" of children and annoyed by their "stupidities." So often the child is teeter-tottered between dictatorship and license and over-indulgence, and in either case no community responsibility is given the child. He deserves and must get equal freedom, respect, and responsibility (like the adult actor) in the community of the workshop.

The problem of teaching the child is the same as that of teaching the adult. The difference is one of presentation. The need to intellectualize on the part of the teacher-director may well be the cause of resistance in work with the younger age groups. We must recognize a great difference in life-experiences, and the phrasing of questions and introductions to exercises depends on this recognition.

Treating children as peers is not the same as treating them as adults; and this fine delineation must be recognized if the teacher-director is to successfully guide his group. It is suggested that he again read the remarks on approval/disapproval in Chapter I.

The effects of relaxing adult tyranny are sometimes remarkable. A group of boys and girls once did an improvised play in which the children lived in a world where adults no longer existed. These young actors were tenement boys and girls who because of the struggle of their daily lives tended to do much yelling and fighting. The unfolding of the scene was quite a revelation. Never were boys and girls more charming, more courteous to one another. They were gentle and tender, they spoke in soft tones, they were concerned with each other's simplest problems—they loved one another! Watching the scene, one questioned, "Could it be that the adult is the enemy of the child after all?"

If permitted to do so, theater workshop will allow personal freedom and equality to flower. For when an individual of any age knows that what he is doing is a real contribution and service to a project and not imposed authoritarianism pushing him about, he is free to release his humanness and make contact with those about him.

It is a thrilling moment, indeed, when the child accepts us, the adults, as peers within the activity!

The Individual And The Group

The theater experience, like the game, is a group experience allowing students of differing abilities to express themselves simultaneously while developing individual skills and creativity (see Chapter I). The teacher-director should see to it that each individual participates in some facet of the activity at every moment, even if this means nothing more than "standing by for curtain." It is not only the over-aggressive child who is destructive to the group effort; the passive child may be equally harmful, for both refuse to give up their egocentricity. Group-work procedures should be followed at all times when working with the child-actor so as to release spontaneity and thus allow personal freedom of individual expression to emerge.

The Child Actor's Theater Environment

The physical environment for this age group should stimulate, excite, and inspire. There should be at least two areas of work, if possible: a place for games and dance and a place for the theater set-up. In the theater area, it is important to have as many theatrical props as is possible to collect. On a very simple level, this would include a working curtain, a full costume rack, a prop shelf, set pieces, or large blocks, some lighting equipment, a place for sound effects, and of course a section for the audience. This should all be scaled to size, so that the children can do their own back-stage work. With a little effort and ingenuity, almost any room or corner can be fitted up for just such a little theater; and even if the results are not suitable for a public performance, the area will be suitable for workshops. Older children can shape their props and set (Where) out of space as adult actors do.

When working with young children, it is advisable to have one or two assistants who can help the teams organize their improvisations and story-acting, assist in setting up stages, help the children into costumes, and watch for non-participants. These assistants are not to meddle, however, and tell the children what to do; they are simply to assist them in carrying out the group's decisions.

Games

The playing of games should be prominent in the teaching process for children. It is possible for the teacher-director to derive positive insight into each child actor's attitudes, reality, and behavior through this playing.

The competitive, the insecure, the apprehensive, are all quickly revealed, as are those more fortunate ones free of the need to do "right." A young girl responded to the early workshops with such a degree of apathy that she was thought to be of low intelligence. While playing the NUMBERS CHANGE game, however, she showed an extraordinary degree of alertness. Her apathy, then, was easily recognized for what it really was—a protective cover for hidden fear. This early discovery helped the teacher-director to free the child for the creative experience more readily than would have otherwise been possible.

Carefully selected games also serve as a valuable tool in the training for the theater reality for this group. Thorne Rosa is not only a charming version of Sleeping Beauty in song and movement but also has definite "characters" as part of the game. Mulberry Bush, with its daily chores to perform, has the very young child actor doing exactly what the older actors do when working on object involvement and sensory problems. As Neva L. Boyd writes: "Like good drama, the game eliminates irrelevancies and brings events into close sequence in such concentrated and simplified form as to condense in both time and space the essence of a complex and long drawn-out typical life-experience. In this way, and because of the varied content of games, the child gets both more and different experiences from play than is otherwise possible in the process of everyday life." Again, "the vitality of the game lies in the creative process of playing it."

There are sense games and dramatic games, muscle-freeing games and intellectual games, and many other game categories from which to choose (see Game Books). The teacher-director should make a special effort to choose the game pertinent to the problem of the moment and avoid the "gag" game, the game with no other object than to get a laugh at someone's expense.

It is also desirable to give diversified activities to child actors: rhythms, folk dances, extended movement, etc. All are essential in developing self and should be given a definite place in the workshop program. If it is not possible to have specialists in these fields work with actors, then the teacher himself can work with them on the simpler activities in these areas. Any type of group participation with movement, rhythm, and sound is helpful (see Chapter V).

Games can be made up out of many of the sensory exercises: "What am I listening to?" "What am I looking at?" "What am I holding?" "What am I eating?"

The teacher-director can select and use many seemingly complicated acting exercises found throughout the handbook by presenting them in "game" manner. WHO'S KNOCKING? (p. 110) is extremely valuable. Combined with RANDOM WALK (p. 221), games were used as part of public performances by the Playmakers at Childrens Theater and were most successful.

Attention And Energy

There seems to be a definite relationship between the attention-span and the energy level of the very young child. Whether it be the child who evidences an over-abundance of energy, the child with average energy, or the child whose energy level is below par, all—if given interesting problems to solve—will stay with an activity for a long period of time. If we think of attention-span in terms of the energy level of our group, we will know exactly when it is necessary to introduce an activity designed to stimulate child actors to new levels of vitality and perception, experience and learning.

Such stimulation may be provided through the simple expedient of changing areas of activity, having diversified activities, bringing in challenging acting exercises, using scenery and costume parts and props. To further extend the child actor's attention-span in the beginning workshop sessions, it might be advisable to divide each session into three sections: games, creative movement, and theater. Anything that will heighten awareness of the activity, color, music, etc., should be used. In this way, the young actors are re-awakened to the theatrical adventure and can move more easily away from the dramatic play of their early years into the theater experience.

Dramatic Play

Like his adult counterpart, the child spends many hours of the day in subjective dramatic play. While the adult version usually consists of telling stories, day-dreaming, role-playing, wishful thinking, identifying with TV characters, etc., the child has, in addition to these, his pretending and dramatizing of characters and events in his experiences from cowboys to parents and teachers.

In workshops with the younger children, moving from dramatic play (subjective) into the stage reality (objective) goes more slowly than with older students. In most cases, the child actors are not yet mature enough to cope with Evaluation in its fullest sense; and there is a greater dependency upon the teacher —a dependency which cannot be broken abruptly.

By separating dramatic play from, and then bringing it to, the theater reality, the young actor learns to differentiate between pretend (illusion) and reality within the realm of his own world. However, this separation is not implicit in dramatic play. Dramatic play and real life are often confused for the young and, alas, for many adults as well.

A good example of the confusion between illusion and reality was evidenced in a young boy brought into the actor's workshop. Johnny was enrolled in the theater workshop because "he was lying too much." At the beginning sessions, he excited everyone with his "acting." Copious tears poured out of him when his stage sisters would not take him with them. And when they pushed him off stage "out of their room," he was found sobbing uncontrollably in the wings because "they wouldn't let me come along!" If he was banished from a scene, even as the Pirate King, he carried his rejection with him for a long time afterward. In short, Johnny had illusion and reality mixed up. In time, he learned to understand the difference. He became a frequent participant in the big theater shows and reports from home were that he no longer "lied."

All student-actors, young and old alike, must learn that the stage is the stage and not an extension of life. It has its own reality, and the players agree to it and then play it. On the stage we can be witches and sea captains, fairies and elephants. Playing, we can pop up to the moon or live in beautiful castles.

Improvising a situation on stage has, like the game, its own kind of organization. After a group of six- and seven-year-olds experienced the fun of playing house on stage, the following discussion took place.

Were you playing house or doing a play? "We were doing a play."

What is the difference between playing house in your backyard and playing house here? "You have a stage here."

Do you call it playing house here? "No, you call it a play."

What else do you have here besides a stage? "An audience."

Why does an audience come to see a play? "They like to—it's fun."

Did you make the playing house you just did fun for an audience? "No."

Why not? "We didn't share our voices and didn't make it more interesting for them."

What could you do to make it more interesting? "We could be naughty or all want to watch TV at the same time or something."

I'd like to ask you again. Were you playing house just now, or were you doing a play about a house? "We were playing house."

Do you think you could go back on stage and instead of playing house, like in your backyard, do a play about a family in a house and show us Where you are and Who you are and What you are doing there? "Yes."

The scene was done again, retaining all the fun of the first playing while adding the actors' real effort to "make it more interesting for the audience." The spontaneity of the backyard playing was retained along with the added reality achieved in trying to share their experience with their audience.

The child, too, can learn not to pretend but to "make it real." He can learn the theater magic of "pulling a rabbit out of a hat." A group of eight-to-eleven-year-olds were questioned as to why they needed to make things real for the audience and not pretend. "If you pretend, it isn't real, and the audience can't see."

Natural Acting

The problem of bringing forth and then retaining a young actor's naturalness within the art form is a challenging one. The natural child is not necessarily the natural actor; indeed, the generality that "children are natural actors" is equally true or false as it is for the older actor. In either case, personal freedom to move out into the environment and experience it determines the extent of "naturalness" to begin with.

In many instances, unfortunately, whether child or adult, naturalness must be restored. Even young children come to workshop full of already learned mannerisms with physical tensions, held muscles, fear of contact, and natural body-grace distorted;

ego-centricity and exhibitionism have already taken their toll. However, because the child's past life span is of fewer years than that of the adult and because he is, after all, a child, the breakthrough to his "original free state" comes about more quickly.

Again, the actor on stage must create reality. He must have energy, must communicate to an audience, be able to develop character and relate to fellow actors, have a sense of pace and timing, etc.

Although we may be highly successful in restoring and/or keeping the student-actor "natural" we may find that this is not enough. It does not follow that naturalness alone presents an interesting communication from stage to audience. So, we have a twofold problem: first, to release the vitality and beauty of the individual child and, second, to take this naturalness and restructure it to meet the demands of the art form (true for the older actor also).

What must be done, then, is to keep the child in spontaneous play and transform this playing into communicable stage behavior. There must be no intrusion of "techniques." As with his adult counterpart, the acting problems the student-actor is to solve must be presented in such a way that this stage behavior comes by itself "from the very core of the child and appears as if by accident."[1] As we know, whether child or adult, anyone who freely plays, totally involved with solving the workshop problem (Point of Concentration) achieves (or keeps) natural spontaneous behavior at the same time he is making the necessary heightened theater communication.

The Fight For Creativity

If the teacher-director forces set patterns of thinking and behavior (a "right" or "wrong" way of doing things) on his child actors, he is restricting them most severely; and both the individual and the art form will suffer. When the child is forced into molds, taught by formula, or given a diluted, adult concept of theater, his performance can only be static and unpleasant, relieved only by the personal charm that most very young children

---

[1]See Workshop Procedures, Chapter II.

still possess. If we will remember that rote teaching, formulas, and concepts are summaries of another's findings (see the discussion of approval/disapproval in Chapter I), our students can then grow and unfold in a free atmosphere.

Today more than ever before we are faced with the need for developing creative and original thought—in the sciences as well as in the arts. Children, who are our future, are talked at so much that a great many adult formulations are either lost to them entirely or swallowed whole, undigested and unquestioned. Many times one hears a newcomer to the theater (as young as six years old) say "You mustn't turn your back to the audience."[2] Questioning will reveal that an individual in some position of authority in the child's life has told him this. Here, on the very threshold of learning, a door is shut and obviously by one who doesn't have the faintest idea of what he is saying and is simply passing on something he has heard or thinks is so. In how many other areas must this go on, hour after hour, day after day, in a child's life? It is this type of authoritarian teaching that dulls our children and shuts off their centers of inspiration and creativity. Many years are wasted until a child becomes an adult, and then he may or may not rise above the hurdles that were put in his way during his growing years.

Creativity is often thought to be merely a less formal way of presenting or using the same material, in a more ingenious or inventive way perhaps—a different arrangement of the same blocks. Creativity is not just building or making something, not just variations of form. *Creativity is an attitude, a way of looking at something, a way of questioning, perhaps a way of life—it may well be found on paths we have not yet traveled.* Creativity is curiosity, joy, and communion. It is process-transformation-process.[3]

Discipline Is Involvement

We are afraid of leaving the bounds of conventional patterns of thought and action. We feel more comfortable, more in control perhaps, and the thought of a free atmosphere in which free

---

[2] See EXERCISE FOR BACK, p. 150.
[3] See Chapter IV.

students abound conjures up a picture of bedlam in our minds. Is it possible that we confuse license with freedom?

Creative freedom does not mean doing away with discipline. It is implicit in true creativity that a free person, working in an art form, must be highly disciplined.

Let us examine the whole premise of discipline and ask a few questions. Just what do we mean when we speak of this problem with children? Do we mean keeping them quiet? Is it wanting an order given and carried out? Do some think of it as self-control by an individual? Or do we mean conformity? How many hide behind the word when they really mean either imposing their will upon, or suppression of, another? How many children are sent to bed because mother is tired?

A "good" boy or girl may not be a disciplined child at all. He may simply be intent upon getting reward instead of punishment, approval instead of disapproval. He seeks survival by appeasement. The so-called "undisciplined" child is seeking survival also; he, however, is in rebellion against authoritarianism and restrictions he does not understand, and his energy when not channeled into creative action often comes out as delinquent or undisciplined behavior. Again, rebellion often shows itself in a refusal to learn the daily lesson, and so we think many of these children are not quite "bright." It well may be that our "rebellious ones" are the most free, the questioners our most creative children, but they are lost to us if their freedom (because of their bewilderment) becomes a destructive force.

Many years ago around a settlement-house neighborhood, a gang of "bad" boys were bedeviling the neighborhood with their stealing and aggressive acts of all kinds. These boys were invited to an improvised play done by other neighborhood children about keeping alleys clean. After the show, they all promptly ran down the alleys and systematically spilled every garbage can they found, and in the meantime it was discovered that they had also rifled a few purses around the theater.

A meeting was called of the workshop members (ten to fourteen years old) to discuss what had happened. It was from the children that the teacher-director learned two important truths. The essence of what the children said was that the "garbage play" was a "scolding play," for all its theatrical effects. It was only a "costumed lecture" after all and as such had no reality. It did not create audience involvement, without which no insight into the problem was possible. At best it said, "Let's all be 'good' little boys and girls and keep our alleys clean." Since this group of boys were busy being "bad" little boys, they could only act as they did.

The children went on to say: "If we could get them into the theater, not to show them 'crime-doesn't-pay' plays but to have them act in the workshops, then they would find out that workshops are more fun than stealing, and they wouldn't *have* to be bad boys anymore."

Discipline imposed from above simply produces inhibited or rebellious action within the student; it is negative, and nothing is learned. For when the "cage" is lowered, all is as before and sometimes worse. On the other hand, when the problem of discipline is not an emotional tug-of-war for position but is freely chosen for the sake of the activity, it then becomes responsible action—creative action.[4] It takes imagination and dedication to be self-disciplined. As in a game, when the dynamics are understood and not superimposed, the rules are abided by. "It is more fun that way."

If the workshop maintains the game-like structure, the child joyously enters the experience and in trying to solve the problem of the activity will impose these necessary disciplines upon himself. For any child (if he chooses to play) will become involved and abide by the rules (group agreement) and accept the penalties and restrictions that are placed upon him. As he does so, more of his human potential will be released as his social sense and individual talents develop.

Intensity of involvement should be the gauge of children's capacities and potential. Children with the lowest grades in school may be the most creative. Their involvement, unfortunately, is not stimulated by what is at hand. This writer's passion for play was so great that she neglected her school work and got through school by the skin of her teeth. She did not make the high-school drama group, because her grades were too low.

---

[4]See Approval/Disapproval, Chapter I.

The Uncertain Child

The teacher-director will often be confronted with an apprehensive child actor who looks to see what the others are doing and follows their lead instead of working on an acting problem as an individual member of the group. When this occurs, we may wish to stop what the group is doing and have them play the MIRROR GAME (p. 60). This will often help the fearful child to realize that imitation is not wrong but that it belongs only to certain games, not to all. Once the MIRROR GAME has been played, the child will find it much easier to break away from imitation of others during workshop, especially if reminded that "You're playing the mirror game now instead of the game we are playing."

Another habit of the uncertain child is "cheating"—peeking during blindfold games, etc.—because of his drive to be best. For instance, if the game is WHAT AM I KNOCKING ON? (where the children are required to keep their eyes closed while guessing what is being knocked on), this child will open his eyes to peek at the object. When this occurs, the teacher-director need only utter a simple, "If you open your eyes, you are playing a different game. We are playing a *hearing* game, not a *seeing* game." In this way, without lecture or indictment, the child quickly realizes for himself that if he is to "play," it is more fun to play the game the whole group plays. Soon his need to be first, best, right, etc. is replaced by the fun of playing.

XIV. Fundamentals for the Child Actor

Inner Action

The concept behind inner action can easily be made clear to child actors, but it is best not to introduce it until the children have had a good deal of improvisation, story-telling, and even some microphone work (see RADIO-TV, p. 197). Here is an example of handling the concept of inner action when the workshop group is ready.

Do you know what your mother is feeling when you come home from school? If you want to go out and play and you have to ask permission, can you tell if your mother is feeling pleasant? The smallest child nods, remembering.

How can you tell? "By the way she looks . . . the way she acts."

Would someone like to go on stage and be a mother who is in a pleasant mood? Although young children rarely work on stage alone, it is occasionally an excellent experience for them. Choose one of the volunteers.

The young actor chosen goes on stage and becomes the "pleasant mother." When she has finished, either discuss her presentation with the group or have others go up individually and work on this single problem. The student audience will pay close attention to the child on stage.

Now have the children sit quietly and think about seeing their families. *Can you usually tell when someone in your home is worried?* "Yes." Ask them to *show us.*

One child at the Young Actors Company showed her father worrying by placing her head on her knees and putting her hands over her ears in the typical comic-opera worrier position. Later, when her mother came to pick her up, the incident was mentioned to her. She laughed and said: "I know it seems exaggerated, but her father does just that."

When it is clear that the group understands that people tend to *show* what they feel, then explain the acting problem as follows:

We are going to play what-are-you-thinking-about game—and you will show us. Each of you will go on stage by yourself. You are to be somewhere, waiting for someone. While you are waiting, you are thinking about something. When you are through thinking, we in the audience will see whether we can know what you were thinking about. You may be waiting for someone who is late. You may be alone in a strange neighborhood and slightly afraid. You may be waiting for someone who is going to take you to a wonderful party. Everyone will pick his inside thought, and we will see whether you show us.

After they have completed their individual thinking and have communicated to the audience, then put all the children together, in a waiting room of a train station, for example. Here they are to work on thinking the same thing they thought about earlier when they were alone awhile ago.

If this work is presented so that the children are able to understand in terms of their own experience, some interesting inner action will result. Encourage the children to play a game of seeing "how people feel inside" outside of class. They will enjoy watching family and friends and knowing what they are thinking about.

Giving Reality (Substance) To Objects[1]

One afternoon, during an improvisation of a farm, a child actor went to the well to draw water, filled her bucket, and car-

---

[1]See Physicalizing the Object, pp. 73–79.

ried it away as easily as if she had not filled it. After the scene, it was suggested that everybody take a turn filling the bucket and carrying it back. Only one child out of ten showed that the bucket was full.

There was an outside water faucet in the patio of the theater. The children took the bucket out there, and each, in turn, filled it with real water, walked a few feet, and then emptied it out.

After all had had their turns, they were asked: *Was there any difference in the bucket before it was filled with water and after it was filled?* A thoughtful pause filled the air. Then the youngest child, who had stayed on the periphery of the activity until now, spoke up and said, "It's heavier when it's full." This was indeed an exciting observation; and they all agreed immediately.

Why is it necessary for the actor to know that it's heavier when it's full?

Again the same silence. Finally a seven-year-old boy spoke up. "Because there is no real water on stage."

Yes! There's no real water on stage. A well on stage can only be made of wood or paper.

The children then went on stage and played a game called IT'S HEAVIER WHEN IT'S FULL. They set up their Once Upon A Time (Where, Who, and What) and "filled" their baskets and buckets with milk, apples, and treasures and then staggered around the stage under the great weights they had piled up for themselves.

How simply they had learned an important theater truth. How many of us have seen adults—lay actors and professionals alike—who sometimes forget that receptacles are "heavier when they're full"? This awareness of creating reality is easily transferable to other objects.

The Telephone Prop

The telephone is probably one of the most delightful and useful props for child actors. If at all possible, get a real dial phone from the telephone company. If not, have a full-sized (not toy-sized) phone built.

The telephone is particularly useful with the young actor who is slow to respond. The teacher just rings the phone (vocally) from wherever he may be sitting. The most active child will make a bee-line for the prop. When he or she answers, ask for the child who is doing very little.

Mildred: (answering) Hello!

Teacher: May I please speak to Edith (the child who has just been sitting passively in the scene)?

Mildred: Edith, it's for you.

Edith: (walks to stage phone) Hello (soft voice).

Teacher: Hello, hello, is this Edith?

Edith: (faraway voice) Yes.

Teacher: Strange, I can't seem to hear you very well. Perhaps we have a bad connection. Would you mind speaking a little louder?

Edith: (Full voice.) O.K.

To give another example, a mother is sitting in her kitchen, apron right, waiting for her children to come back from their picnic. The children are having their picnic on the full stage. The scene has hit an impasse with both mother and children just sitting. The teacher-director rings the telephone.

Mother: Hello.

Teacher: Why, hello, how are you?

Mother: Fine.

Teacher: What are you doing today?

Mother: I'm waiting for my children. They went on a picnic.

Teacher: My goodness, aren't they home yet?

Mother: No, they're not.

Teacher: It's beginning to get dark, and it's raining outside (the light man goes to work). Don't you think you'd better go look for them and bring them home? It's close to their bedtime.

Mother: I certainly better.

And the mother is immediately spurred into action as she runs to get her children. When they return, ring again (if necessary).

Teacher: Hello. Did you get your children home all right?

Mother: Yes, they're home now.

Terms To Use

Complete Or Incomplete Concentration

Give youngsters the concept of concentration in terms of energy. Send someone on stage to lift an imaginary rock or push a stalled car. This would be the same thing as Point of Concentration or focus with the older actors. If their concentration is to be complete, they quickly see they must put "all their strength" on the stage problem.

Becoming Audience

Becoming audience is a phrase used to reinforce concentration.

The child may watch himself on stage, mirroring himself. He may be a non-participating spectator to the actions of the other actors. He may look out into the house to see whether he has teacher's approval. Handle this problem simply: *We have a special place for the audience, and if you would rather be there than in the play, come down and watch. It's perfectly fine if you want to watch, but then you belong in the audience.*

The children will quickly realize that the stage is the place for actors and that they cannot be actors and audience at the same time. It is important that they understand this separation thoroughly, for this is one of the keys to the stage reality. They may have to be reminded from time to time through side coaching: *The place for the audience is down here! We go where your eyes go! We see what you see!*

Rocking the Boat

"Rocking the boat" encourages self-blocking and is a phrase developed to evaluate the stage picture. It is a visualization which can be grasped by every child. Simply describe the stage as a boat—a rowboat or canoe. Now ask the students to think what would happen to a boat if everyone sat on one side. Just as the boat would become unbalanced and tip, so will the stage picture become unbalanced and upset the scene.

Once this phrase is understood, you have only to call out *You're rocking the boat!* during work on an acting problem to see them spread out into a more interesting stage picture. Without losing concentration, they will recognize the need for sharing voices, actions, and feelings with every member of the audience.

When rocking the boat has been discussed, ask students to go on stage. First, have them deliberately rock the boat. Begin by asking: *Do we ever want to rock the boat? When?* Have them do a scene where they deliberately rock the boat (as in a fire, mob scene, etc.). After discussion, have them do another scene, this time with the Point of Concentration on *avoiding* rocking the boat.

Share With The Audience

This is used in the same way as with the adult group. Have actors play directly with the audience, as in a meeting.

Showing—Not Telling

The problem of showing and not telling can best be introduced to your child-actors in the evaluation following a scene: Did he show us he was playing in the snow, or did he tell us the snow was cold? How could he show us that he was the father? How could he show that he hurt his finger? Did we see the glass in his hand?

Evaluation

There is no one as dogmatic as the six- or seven-year-old who "knows" the answer. He is already reflecting and accepting the

patterns of the world around him. He is right, and they are wrong!
It seems almost impossible at first to eradicate these judgmental
and thus limiting words from the vocabulary of these very young
children.

"He's wrong!" a child will say. *What do you mean by "wrong"?*

"He didn't do it right." *What do you mean by "right"?*

"Like this!" The child then proceeds to demonstrate the "right"
way to jump rope or eat cereal. *But what if Johnny wants to do
it his own way?* "He's wrong."

Did you see Johnny eat his cereal? "Yes." *Why was it wrong?*
"He ate it too fast."

You mean he didn't eat his cereal the way you eat it? "You
have to eat cereal slowly."

Who told you that? "My mother."

*Well, if your mother wants you to eat cereal slowly, that is
the rule in your house. Maybe the rule in Johnny's house is different. Did you see him eat his cereal?* "Yes."

If the teacher keeps at it, individual differences are finally accepted and the words "right" and "wrong" will give way to:

"I couldn't see what he was doing."

"She didn't move like a doll all the time."

"He didn't share his voice with us."

"They had no Once Upon A Time.

"He became audience."

After the work on stage has been completed by a team of
players, Evaluation is handled the same as with the older actors.

To the student audience: was concentration complete or incomplete? Did they solve the problem? Did they have a Once
Upon A Time?

When student-actors are skillfully questioned, after a while
they begin to say: "I walked through a wall"; "I became audience"; "I didn't share my voice." This sort of questioning and response has many more times the value in developing reality,
personal awareness, and perception in children than do the limited and subjective phrases, "They were good," "They were bad."

The fallacy in thinking that there are prescribed ways of behavior came home quite forcibly one day. The student-actors did
a family scene. Mother, father, and grandfather were sitting on a
couch, having a tea party. The player showed us he was the

grandfather by occasionally saying "By cracky!" Then in typical six-year-old fashion, he would climb up and around the couch (made of blocks).

In the Evaluation, Johnny was told that he certainly showed us that he was the grandfather. He was then asked by the teacher-director if he thought older men climb around the couch that way. Johnny was startled to hear that he had. Because of the way the questioning was put, Johnny shaped his thinking to meet the teacher-director's frame of reference and then and there accepted her authority and decided, too, that grandfathers *do not* climb on couches. Suddenly from the audience a young voice spoke up.

"My grandfather does!"

He does?

"Sure, every time he's drunk."

How a teacher-director questions his students during Evaluation must always be carefully watched, so as not to put his ideas or words into the minds and mouths of the students. And while it may be true that only one grandfather out of twenty thousand will climb around couches as does a six-year-old boy, it is a reality that is possible and therefore the student-actor has the right to explore it.

Points To Remember[2]

1. Maintaining the structure of the acting problem and group Evaluation does much of the work for the teacher.
2. Strive constantly to ask the questions during Evaluation that will meet the experience levels of the children and stimulate their learning.
3. Avoid trying to make the children fit subjective concepts of right or wrong stage behavior. Remember, there need not be any set ways of doing anything as long as communication lines are clear.
4. Noise that occurs around the organization and setting up of a scene must be understood as order and not disorder. The teacher can always hear when the sounds are undisciplined.

---

[2]See also the section on directing children, p. 368.

Organizing a scene cannot be done quietly, since the very energy and excitement released can only be expressed noisily. The children will learn to set up quietly when a curtain is used. This discipline will come most naturally to them in time. Do not stifle the spirit of play by concern for "order."

5. Until all the young actors are able to take the initiative in the workshop, place the children who are natural catalysts in positions where they can help spark the activity. Watch that they do not take over, however. In time, each and every child will develop leadership ability.

6. Do not be patronizing to children. Neither expect too much nor allow them to get away with too little.

7. As in a game, theater workshop allows each player to take from it according to his own level of development and encourages individual choice.

8. Self-discipline will develop in students when their involvement in the activity is complete.

9. This age group, too, can learn to create a stage reality out of a group agreement equal to the adults.

10. As with the older actors, we strive for spontaneity, not invention, in our students.

11. Public performance, when children are ready, will raise their whole level of understanding and skills. However, do not hasten this prematurely. Be certain they have integrated their workshop training and will share their play. They must understand that the audience is "part of the game" and not merely exhibit themselves. For this age, too, can learn to handle the tools of the theater with sensitivity and intuitiveness; they can learn to work with a director together with their fellow actors and to perform in public showings, unaffectedly, and be a delight to behold!

In a play where a doll shop had a prominent role, six-year-olds were used as dolls. Some research was done on the characters by the young actors. A couple of dolls were brought to class, and the children found that they moved only at the joints. In movement class, they worked on solving the problem of doing everything as dolls. They played "doll shop" for weeks prior to rehearsing with the full cast of older children (eleven to fifteen). By the time they (the children cast as dolls) were brought to rehearsals, they seemed like veteran actors. The only thing they had to adjust to was working with the older actors.

Stands were built for the dolls on which the children could sit during performance if they so desired. They were told that if a pin was sticking them, they should remove it. They could brush the hair out of their eyes, sneeze if necessary, or cough. There was only one Point of Concentration: *they were to move as dolls no matter what happened.*

Some of the most charming moments of the show thus occurred when they were least expected—when a nose had to be scratched or when a hat fell off. Many adults were amazed at the relaxed quality of the children, at their lack of affectation and their doll-like movements. They were surprised at the "acting" of these "babies."

The important thing was that these children had the full pleasure of performance without anxieties. They kept their complete energies on the physical problem of moving like dolls, and this Point of Concentration gave them sureness and kept them "in character."

After one performance, the little talking doll (six years old) was besieged by children from the audience. Even a few adults clustered around her, crooning: "Isn't she darling! Isn't she the little actress!" The fuss would have been enough to turn the head of many an older person, but the little girl merely thanked the group and, turning to another actor, asked, "Did you think my concentration was complete?"

XV. Workshop for Six-to-Eight-Year-Olds

Planning The Sessions

The exercises set down in this chapter are those which are slanted directly to the six-to-eight year old. By no means should they be considered the only exercises suitable for this age group. They appear here for the sake of emphasis.

As was mentioned earlier, many of the exercises appearing in the middle section of the handbook can easily be adapted for use to the six-to-eight-year olds. For example, the following groups of exercises have been given in six-to-eight-year-old workshops with exciting results: simple involvement exercises (p. 64); simple sensory exercises (p. 78); broadcasting exercises (p. 198); technical effects exercises (p. 203).

The teacher-director must use his own discretion in choosing, altering, and presenting suitable exercises. Once the introductory ONCE UPON A TIME has been given and absorbed, he will have an excellent understanding of students' needs and levels. And armed with this knowledge, he should then be able to plan workshop sessions most profitably from the wealth of exercises presented in the body of this handbook.

First Workshop Session

Six-to-eight-year-olds should not be given the EXPOSURE EX-ERCISE. The formalized Where (see p. 92) is too abstract for this age group, since they should be given real physical props, costumes, etc. as quickly as possible.

Accordingly, the Where for six-to-eight-year-olds is called ONCE UPON A TIME. It may be done with or without an equipped stage. If no real theater is available, just be certain to designate from the start which areas in the room are to be used as the stage, back stage, wings, and audience. If a real stage is available, it is highly desirable to show the child actors around, pointing out various items to them.

The following versions of ONCE UPON A TIME are for beginning the first workshop session with child actors. One version requires no stage facilities. The other allows for stage facilities, and it is to be preferred.

Preliminary Work

Do you enjoy reading or having stories read to you? "Yes!"

What do you do while your mother is reading you a story? "We listen . . . we hear it."

What do you hear? "You hear the story".

What do you mean "you hear the story"? Just what do you hear? "You hear what is happening in the story."

Let's suppose your mother was reading you the story of The Three Bears. *What do you hear in that story?* "You hear about the bears and the porridge. . . ."

How do you know you are hearing about the three bears? "Because the words tell you you are".

Now comes the most important question of all: *How do you know what the words tell you?* "You can see."

What do you see? The words? "No!" With much laughter, they tell you, "You see the three bears, of course!"

Continue the discussion of "seeing" the words. Tell them a story: *Once upon a time, there was a little boy and a little girl and they lived in a bright yellow house on top of a green hill. Every morning a little pink cloud floated by the house and. . . .*

Ask the children what they saw. Keep it a group discussion. Every child will see the story in his own personal terms. Have them describe the color they visualized for the girl's dress, what kind of roof the little house had, etc. Keep up with this discussion as long as the interest level is high, then go on to the next point.

What is the first thing your mother does when she is going to read you a story? "She comes into my bedroom . . . she sits down . . . she says, 'For five minutes, dear'. . . "

Then what does she do? "She reads the story."

How does she do that? "She reads it from the book!" By now the young actors are certain that they have a "silly" teacher who doesn't know the simplest things.

Now, think hard. What is the first thing she does before she starts reading, after she has sat down, after she has come into the bedroom? "She opens the book."

Of course! She opens the book! Would it be possible to read the story if your mother didn't open the book? "Of course not!"

In theater, too, we have a story. And, we too must open the book before we begin. Only, on stage, we open the curtain. (Curtain in this case can be lights. Or it can be the mere calling out of the phrase "Curtain!" to indicate the beginning of a scene if you have no actual curtain.)

How does the story usually begin? "Once upon a time, there was . . . ."

You mean it starts in a place, somewhere? "Yes."

Are there usually people in the story? "Yes, people and animals."

The people in the story of Goldilocks and the Three Bears *are called characters when we take them on stage. Now, just as your mother opens the book and begins with "Once upon a time . . . ," we are going to show the bears and the house. Instead of seeing them in your head as when you are read to, you are going to see them on the stage.*

When your mother reads you a story, does she whisper so you cannot hear her? Does she read from another room in the house? "Of course not! She reads the story so that the children can hear it."

Because if you couldn't hear it, you couldn't enjoy it. Right?

When they have expressed their desire to enjoy the story, go on with the discussion. They will articulate if the questions are clear to them.

The theater has people who are just like you when you're listening to your mother. The theater has an audience. They are our guests. The audience wants to enjoy the story they are seeing and hearing on stage. And, just as your mother shares with you the Once Upon A Time (Where) and the characters (Who) in the book and what is happening to them (What), so the actors must share the story they are playing on stage with the audience. And show them everything: where they are, who they are, and what they are doing.

Does the audience sit and only listen the way you do when you hear a story? "No, an audience looks, like watching TV . . . ."

Yes, an audience looks at what you are doing and sees the characters move around and do things and talk to each other. So, the way to help the audience enjoy themselves is to show them as much as you can and to share with them everything you do on stage.

The foregoing kind of discussion gives the teacher-director an opportunity to bring "share" and "showing" (not telling) into the workshop. However, immediate results will not be achieved by any means. It will take time before learning to share and communicate with an audience becomes organic with this age group.

After completing the initial discussion, go right into:

ONCE UPON A TIME

Once Upon A Time, Minimum Equipment
The first step is to set up the Where, Who, and What.

WHERE

Where would you like to be? Students will suggest many places, one of which will most likely be a schoolroom. If, however, the workshop itself is in a schoolroom program, shift to a living-room scene using the same procedure.

WHO

Who do you want in the schoolroom? For the most part teacher and pupils will be suggested.

WHAT

What is everyone doing there? One of the suggestions will probably be learning arithmetic or reading. *What grade do you want? Kindergarten, first, second, high school?*

When the group has selected their grade, have them set up the stage. Have appropriate props available. As the teacher and perhaps an assistant move the props among them, students should be reminded of the boundaries of the stage area (all props must be within it). Keep reminding them: *You must share your story. Do you think the desk in that position will do it?* Stop for a group conference if necessary. Although at this time the actual audience will only be teacher and assistant, keep the actors aware of their audience responsibility.

When the stage is set up, there will be many things missing from the schoolroom. Ask your students to close their eyes and try to *see* a schoolroom they are familiar with. Quietly coach them to see the floors, the walls, the color of the ceiling. Do not intrude on their visualization; simply give them some direction.

What was in your schoolroom which is missing on stage? "A pencil sharpener." *How many saw a pencil sharpener?* In this way can be compiled a whole list of extra objects which the children should then place on the stage, whether actual or created by the players.

It is best that the teacher-director cast the children during the first few sessions. In later meetings, they will be able to do this themselves.

When all the props are in place, have the children go on stage. Call "Places!" The teacher in the scene will go to her desk and the students to theirs. "Curtain!" is now called.

As this first scene unfolds, voice projection and movement will be at a low level, (this is particularly true of five- and six-year-olds). Most of the children will sit and stare at the few who may be writing on the blackboard. There will be much giggling and looking out front. If the young actress playing teacher asks one of her students a question, she may or may not get an answer.

A few alert children may take over the scene while the others sit as audience for the active ones.

At this point, the teacher-director's assistant has enormous value: send her into the play as a definite character (in a school-room scene, the principal is a logical activiser). The principal comes in to see what is happening. As the principal, she presents activity to all the children and sees that it is followed up: she can quiet the children who are taking over the situation and see that the shyer ones participate. This can all be accomplished through the character of the principal.[1]

Principal: Good morning, Miss X. Isn't it a lovely morning? (She waits for a reply. If the child who plays the teacher responds in a faint, faraway voice, the principal repeats her question.)

I'm sorry, Miss X, but I didn't hear what you said. Don't you think it is a lovely morning? (The chances are that this will produce a projected response. If it still fails, the assistant takes a different tack.)

You know, Miss X, I'm certain the children would like to hear what you are saying. Isn't it a lovely morning? (The third question will bring a more lively tone, if only for that bit of dialogue. Even if the child sinks back into herself for the rest of the "play," whenever the "principal" talks to her, she will answer.)

Good morning, children. How are all of you this morning?

Pupils: Fine . . . oh, we're fine . . . etc.

Principal: (to a little girl) And what subjects are you studying today?

Girl: (faint voice) Reading.

Principal: I'm sorry, Mary, but I seem to have something the matter with my hearing this morning. Would you mind repeating what you just said?

Girl: (firmer voice) Reading.

---

[1]This same technique is useful when inviting children from the audience to work in a scene from SUGGESTIONS BY THE AUDIENCE (p. 222).

Principal: How nice. (Turns to a boy who has sat without moving from the start.) Well, little boy, do you like reading?

Boy: (No answer.)

Girl: (shouting) I like reading!

Principal: (to energetic little girl) That's nice. (Back to boy.) Would you mind nodding yes if you like reading?

Boy: (Nods yes.)

Principal: By the way, what is your name?

Boy: (in a whisper) Johnny.

Principal: What a nice name! Now, which one of you students would like to lead the group in singing?

And so it goes until every child has participated in the "play," even if that participation is as slight as nodding the head. If the assistant can bring forth more action, fine; if not, then be satisfied with any bit of response. After a few sessions, many of the children will be able to play the principal and activise the others similarly. In time, all the children will be on their own, needing nothing but the problem to spur them on.

One six-year-old girl had an amazingly natural theater sense and quickly integrated all she learned. In fact, her energy on stage was so great that it was only with the greatest difficulty that she could be subdued to let the others work. If she was the mother, she rarely allowed her children to slip in a single word. She was told repeatedly: *Let all the characters share in the play.*

The problem was brought up during Evaluation. When her failure to share was mentioned, the girl replied: "But, if I don't do something, everybody just sits, and it isn't interesting."

How can you help the others? She thought she might tell them what to do.

But how can you "tell them" and still be showing us a "play" instead of telling a story? "I could whisper in their ears."

What could you do that would help the others on stage show the audience that they are part of the family? She thought a while and said, "I could give them things to do and ask them questions they could answer."

"Would you please take the papers out of your desk and bring them over to me?" was a question that occurred to her. Previously this child would have gone over and taken the papers herself.

Do not be surprised at the frequency with which this group will repeat a play situation. The schoolroom or the living-room scene may be done a dozen times or more. But with each playing, something new will be added, and the children will switch parts among themselves. Variations on the same scene might include: a new student entering the class, the last day of school, parents' visiting day, and even schoolrooms in other countries. Weather and time can be introduced. Because of students' repeated delight in such "plays," many acting problems can be solved by changing the Point of Concentration within the same familiar Where.

Exercises

ONCE UPON A TIME, FULL EQUIPMENT

This exercise was first created to meet the problem of giving a short-term theater experience to large groups of children such as Brownies, Scouts, etc. Its freshness and the excitement it generates were such that it was then used with six-to-eight-year-old actors with equal success. It was presented as a public performance of the Playmakers, the author's children's theater in Chicago, where it delighted hundreds of children and adults. However, in this case the audience simply called out the props they wanted, and the actors on stage produced them.

The success of this version of ONCE UPON A TIME is completely dependent upon an equipped stage. When done effectively, it transmits the total theater experience so suddenly and with such strong impact that the participating student is pummeled into an active role before he can catch his breath. It would well be worth a teacher-director's time and effort to get a simple stage set-up so as to use this version of ONCE UPON A TIME.

To save time, it is necessary that the teacher have the Where prepared in advance for the first five or six presentations. This preparation should consist of seeing that the prop shelf has been

appropriately stocked, that the costume rack is hung with entic-
ing pieces, that recordings are ready in the sound booth, and that
the lighting board (with dimmers) is working.

Since a living-room setting is usually the most familiar to
the actors and is conducive to a large number of stage effects,
it is excellent for first choice. Because so much will be happening to the stage itself for this first session, it is not necessary to
use costumes. They can be brought in for later sessions.

Starting the session is simple enough. Ask the actors, *What is
the first thing you do when you sit down to read a story?* When
they answer, "Open the book," have an assistant open the curtain.
We see an empty stage.[2]

As they sit looking at the empty stage, ask them to try to visualize their living rooms. Help them along as they concentrate:
*See the walls. Look at the furniture. What's on the floor? Concen-
trate on colors.*

Tell them that each one of them will be asked to place something on stage that is part of a living room. They may choose anything that belongs in the living room they visualize. And, one
by one, ask each student what he would like to put in his room.
When the first actor is asked to go up on stage and get his couch
or whatever, he seems a bit hesitant, since the stage is empty.
Tell him to go back stage and see whether he can find his couch.
All the audience watches with suppressed excitement: what will
he find back there?

Assistance is needed here, since the children must know where
their objects can be found when they go back stage to search for
them. More advanced students are helpful; and to help is most
useful for them, since it heightens their own learning.

If large blocks are among the props, a couch is made quickly;
if not, substitute something else that will suggest a couch. The
assistant and the student come out carrying the couch. *Where do
you want it placed?* He indicates a spot and, with the assistant,
places the couch. The student-actors sitting in the audience are
eager to get into the adventure. The next student might ask for
"a lamp," and so it goes down the line. Each student asks for a
prop, goes back stage to find it, and then places it on the stage.

---

[2]Some of the material used in the preliminary discussion at the beginning of this chapter could be used here.

308

When a piano is asked for, everyone is aghast at so daring a request. This prop is great fun for the scene, and a small spinet piano that weighs but a few pounds can easily be built as part of your equipment (if not a simple stage block will do).[3] Soon a radio, a TV set, a bookcase with painted books, and window frames with neat cottage curtains appear (these can be made so that they can be hung on wires stretched across the stage). A fireplace is a must; pictures, flowers, bric-a-brac, coffee tables, a birdcage—in fact, every conceivable possibility for a living room should be available.

While the students are setting up, the teacher and assistants move around, helping and suggesting placements that will make it a pleasant living room. When it is finished, have the students come back into the audience and close the curtains immediately. For the sake of the first impact, the back- stage crew will now dress the set to help the final effect (such as placing a bulb and gelatin in the fireplace, giving area lighting to the lamps, putting flowers on mantelpiece, etc.). Now call, *"Curtain!"*

As the curtain slowly opens on the living room, with the fire in the fireplace softly glowing, the lamps casting warm lights throughout the room, soft music floating through the air, and the bird chirping merrily away, there will be a tremendous sigh and "oh-h-h-h-h" from the audience. The aesthetic, artistic excitement that rises in the student-actors is thrilling to watch. Here is a stage that they put together, and they are awed by what they see. Each one had a part in creating it! This is the first impact of the reality that can be achieved on stage. This is the magic of theater!

Now the time comes to show how the theater reality is man-made, after all. Go on stage and call for work lights. Immediately the stage is altered: the music stops playing, the fireplace is cold and dead, the lamps are out. Walk to the piano and show that it's nothing but wood and cardboard (or a block of wood); pick up the lampshade and reveal that bulb and cord are missing; the radio is an empty shell; the TV set a piece of cardboard; the fire in the fireplace a bulb and some colored gelatin with a few sticks of wood.

---

[3]When ONCE UPON A TIME was done as part of the performances, a block 2′ x 3′6″ was used as the piano.

How did the magic work? Move to the piano (cue the sound man with a line such as, "I think I'll practice the piano."). As the teacher begins to move his fingers over the keyboard, a lovely nocturne drifts out into the audience. Another line of dialogue, and then the teacher switches on a "lamp," bringing a brighter spot to the stage. And so the teacher moves around the set, lighting lights, turning on the radio to listen to a bit of news, striking a match and lighting the fireplace, and even turning on the TV where a program is already in progress (a couple of enthusiastic young actors from another group might go through a little TV show for your enjoyment). Continue until everything has been made to work, until the stage is restored to the original magic it held when the curtain first opened.

The audience is entranced. How does it happen that so many things that were nothing but cardboard and empty frames worked? Some of the answers will be quite amazing and far from reality. But soon out of the "mystery" will emerge the realization that "somebody" was doing it. Who? The technical crew, of course! The crew is called on stage so the students can meet them.

Now take all the students back stage and show them where the sound comes from, the lighting board, etc. "How does the back-stage crew know when to do all the things they must do?" *We tell them.* "But how?" The students learn that "telling them" is "cuing" and that unless they keep the back-stage crew aware of what they want and when they want it, the props will not work for them.

Have each student go on stage individually and cue his back-stage crew for something. He will learn quickly that dialogue is tied up with back-stage response and that the back-stage crew cannot respond unless they hear what the actor wants. The shyest most timid student, eager to get something to work on stage, will rise above his fear, and within one session, the teacher will have accomplished what might otherwise have taken many weeks to achieve.

During the performance, the actors are always alerted to the effects expected and can meet any crisis. In a production with six-to-fourteen-year-olds, a howling wind was to precede some dialogue relating to the wind. When the time came, no wind.

The actors on stage kept up a clever run of dialogue, still no wind. This continued for a full three to four minutes until the sound effect was finally given. After the show, the cast descended upon the twelve-year-old sound man—What had happened? He had been visiting with the prop man and was not standing by for his cue. You may be sure that he never left his stand after that! And, also important, the audience was never aware that anything had gone awry.

When the students are completely familiar with their stage, it is then time to bring life into the setting: Who.

Who is usually in a living room? This is quickly settled by the group: it's simple to understand that mothers and fathers, children, and sometimes guests populate a living room. It is equally simple to understand that these people are called *characters* on the stage.

What are these characters doing in the living room? brings a rush of story material. A teacher might be coming to talk to the parents, the children might have to practice the piano, etc.

Should the audience know what the characters are doing? "Of course."

Why? "So they can enjoy the play."

Teams are quickly selected. The student audience will watch to see if the actors: (1) let the back-stage crew know what they need; (2) share what they are doing with the audience.

And so the workshop experience begins! Within this short hour or hour-and-a-half, the students learn the necessity for interaction, relationship, and communication if they are to have fun.

When the ONCE UPON A TIME without equipment is used, it is best to keep children six-to-eight as one group. When they are ready and the roles of the audience and actor are more defined, then they can be divided into teams. In ONCE UPON A TIME with equipment, however, note that breaking up into teams can take place from the very first session. As the full group creates the ONCE UPON A TIME together, their interest as an audience is held as they watch each separate team make different uses of the same Where. It is advisable, however, to end every workshop session with full group participation. Just as in the early workshops for the older actor, ORIENTATION GAME and similar group games are used to end each workshop.

When the actors become used to their stage and its conventions and after a few weeks of using different sets for each session, student-actors become capable of setting up their own stages, discussing effects with the back-stage crews, and entering into creative evaluation of each other's work with all the aplomb of veteran actors.

In organizing material for each succeeding session, it is wise to make a breakdown of what will be required in each category:

FOREST SCENE

Lighting	Sound	Set Pieces	Costumes
moonlight	night sounds	cave	bearskin
night	morning	rocks	rabbit's ears
dawn	sounds	stream	butterfly
lightning	thunder	trees	wings
(storm)	crashes		dog's tail and
	animal roars		head
	wind blowing		

Be prepared for anything a student-actor asks for. If the exact prop is not on hand, one can be suggested: a cave from arrangements of blocks or chairs; trees out of curtains wound together at various intervals; bushes from parts of actual bushes, with artificial flowers tied on; a waterfall out of blue lights on silver lamé cloth. As workshop goes along, everyone's ingenuity will be stimulated to meet the needs of the moment, and spontaneous selectivity of appropriate set pieces will take place at a high rate of speed.

STORY-TELLING

There are books on creative theater for those wishing to pursue this form further. The following method follows the structure of improvisation in which the story-teller and the actors work together simultaneously. It is more inventive than spontaneous, for all must stay with the "story" as prescribed by the story and the story-teller. It is of value, however, to the story-teller, and, since each student-actor will have the opportunity to participate as story-teller during the workshop program, many benefits are to be derived. It gives the embryonic director even as young as six to eight the total view of the medium and an understanding of the problems of integrating a scene. (See the remarks on spontaneity in Chapter I.)

Unless the group is unusually large, one story-teller a period is usually sufficient. The scene should not take more than half an hour. Sometimes, after a story-telling period, it is valuable to pick out a few points to work on and chose some specific exercises for the actors to do.

If the story-teller has organized his material away from the workshop, his casting and other preparation should not take too long. Moreover, the teacher-director and his assistant will be there to keep the activity moving.

The story-teller relates the story to the actors on stage, and they follow his direction. He either picks out a story or makes one up. It is wise to assign this task a week in advance. He might also draw pictures of his characters, sets, costumes, and props. While these, in all probability, coming from six- and eight-year-olds, will be most primitive and not too useful for visual reference by the actors, the drawing will stimulate the story-teller in organizing his material.

Once the story is chosen, the story-teller casts his show and shows the drawing to the cast. He picks the stage crew as well and assigns back-stage duties (stage manager, sound, lights, etc.). He also costumes his show. The stage is set as the story-teller wishes, and he directs the stage manager to call "Places!"

The story-teller takes his place at the side of the stage (or at the microphone if there is a sound booth) and begins his Once Upon A Time. The actors act out the story as he tells it. Watch to see that the story-teller allows freedom of lines and action for the cast.

To avoid having the players merely stand around and parrot the story-teller, caution the story-teller not to give the actors set lines or tell them exactly what to do.

Saying "Then the mother scolded the little boy" will allow the actors (mother and son) to say and do what they wish within the frame of the story. This may be difficult to impart at first, but constant hammering at the point will eventually make story-telling classes much more exciting.

During a story-telling of Jack and the Beanstalk, the giant was a boy of six who sat by most passively while Jack stole all his things. The story-teller, wishing to get some activity out of the giant, said, "The giant was very angry when he woke up and found his eggs gone." The little boy on stage merely opened his eyes wider and looked blandly about. This did not satisfy the story-teller, so she tried again. "And the giant was very angry, and he jumped up and down." Our giant tried to do this but without pleasing the narrator, for she continued, "The giant was real angry. He was never so mad before, and he jumped and hollered and said all kinds of nasty things."

Then, to the satisfaction of all present, the six-year-old giant roared out, "Goddamnit, who stole my eggs!"

It is important that during classes the teacher-director or assistant sit close to the story-teller to aid in keeping the whole cast and back-stage crew working. The story-teller can be reminded that so-and-so is not doing anything or that the light man has not pulled his switch for some time.

If a somewhat flexible technical stage is available, delightful effects will come from the "technical" department. One story-teller said, "It was night, and the wind began to blow and frightened the little children." The light man (all of seven) promptly dimmed down the stage and made a howling sound through the microphone, while the actors huddled in fright.

Story-telling is equally useful for older children and adults. With them, actors and story-teller may improvise together (GIVE AND TAKE). The story-teller becomes the "guide," relieving the players of concern as to where the story is going, helping the players explore the emerging beats (EXPLORE AND HEIGHTEN).

CREATING SCENES WITH COSTUMES

Two methods may be suggested for creating scenes with costumes. Either players agree on Where, Who, and What and then pick costume pieces to fit scene; or players pick costume pieces at random and then choose Where, Who, and What based on their costumes.

At first, the student-actors will love the idea of costumes and will put them on indiscriminately, whether a scene requires them or not, odd piece by odd piece. After a few months, however, this attitude has gradually changed, and they are choosing only costumes that fit their specific scene.

A typical scene built around costume pieces was done in the following manner. The children looked over the rack filled with colorful costumes (if costumes are too large, pins and ties will make them fit).[4] One boy picked out a high silk hat and a feathered cap and hood which had been used for a bird costume in a play. Three girls took fancy dresses and crowns from the hat box. Another lad took a beard and a tropical helmet. A girl took a modern dress, hat, and veil. Another girl put on a dog's tail and ears.

After they had put on their costumes, they were asked whether they wished to choose their own characters or to have the group choose for them. They elected to choose their own. Each stood before the mirror to see what he looked like.

In this case, the first boy decided quite logically to be a bird, and with the silk hat on, he further decided to be a rich bird. The three girls became a queen, a princess, and a friend of the princess. The beard and helmet naturally created an explorer, and the dog ears and tail made a dog. But the last girl, in the modern dress, had a problem. What should she be? The boy playing the rich bird who had been quite enamored of her had a suggestion: she could be a "bird-lover." The girl very coyly agreed.

Here, then, was the cast for their scene:

Rich Bird	Princess
Bird-Lover	Friend
Explorer	Dog
	Queen

The scene went as follows:

The Explorer was in the jungle with his Dog, hunting for rare birds. He was in the employ of a lady Bird-Lover who was building a collection. The Explorer caught a rare specimen of a Rich Bird, brought it back, and the Bird-Lover decided to take it to show the Queen, the Princess, and her Friend. The Dog came along, too.

---

[4] Old neckties can be used as belts and make it possible to use any size dress or coat by simply pulling up extra length etc. to be held by belt. Wire coathangers can quickly be bent to form many costume effects.

Was something missing from this situation? Perhaps. But both the children on stage and the audience loved it. And this sort of scene can be done with only partial costumes and small props, all of which can be readily collected.

Formal Theater and
Improvisational Theater

XVI. Preparation

The Director

This chapter is primarily for the community-theater director of the formal play. The director of improvisational theater will find that by the time he has passed through the handbook, putting on a performance will grow out of the exercises. However, there are some pointers in this chapter on directing which might prove useful to him.

The director is the eye and the ear of the audience to come. His energies must, at all times, be concentrated on finding deeper insights, perspectives for his actors and technical crew which will further enrich the theater communication. He must dip into and extract from each and everyone, including himself, the last drop of juice.

If he is fortunate enough to have highly gifted and experienced actors and technicians, his work will be greatly implemented. However, from the first choice of the play (or selection of scene material for improvisational theater) to the approval of its lighting plot, what is finally selected is the result of the sensitivity, awareness level, and good taste of the director himself. He is the catalytic agent, seeking to channel the energies of many people into one unified action.

For the improvisational theater, his part in the theater action is to see and select the scene or story as it emerges out of the actors' playing (while solving a problem). The director must always see the process going on (or set it in motion when the players have lost their way) out of which a scene can possibly evolve.

The Director's Point Of Concentration

When directing production for performance (formal or improvised play) the teacher-director takes on a role different from his role in the workshop. As teacher, he focuses on the individual student-actor and what problems to give to help him in experiencing. As director, he focuses on the play and what problems to use to bring it to life. (An additional point for the director of improvisational theater is what problems to give the actors to find scene material.) Sometimes the roles are totally separate; sometimes and when necessary, whether in workshops or in rehearsals, they work together.

Rehearsals (playing) require an environment in which both actor's and director's intuitions can emerge and work in union, for it is only in this way that life can be brought to the director, the actor, the play, and the stage. This is why problem-solving techniques are used for rehearsing the play. They have been experimented with over the years, especially with children and lay actors, and, as in workshop, if the intent of the problem is understood by the director when presented to the players and if solved by them, a vitality and a high level of response both in acting and development of scene material is the result. It works!

This chapter suggests ways and means to help the director keep his Point of Concentration constantly focused on finding the play's *reality*. He must know what problems to give his players so as to have the play grow into a meaningful harmonious, unified production.

Long before casting, the director will have read the play through many, many times. He will have digested it and be familiar with it and the playwright. He may even have seen it done somewhere.

Then, he must discard his "dream" play and as much of the remembered one as possible. (The director of improvisational theater will not have this problem in quite the same way, although he may have selected scenes that have come up in workshop which he wants to explore more fully. This would bring him to about this same point with the director of formal plays.)

The problem of bridging one's ideal of the play to its actual production on the boards is no small task. But, since a production is nourished by the skills, creativity, and energies of many, it is necessary that the director realize that he cannot push actors, and technicans into preconceived patterns and still hope to have and alive performance. No solo flights for director or actors.

If, for instance, the actors are hung up on words, with little if any blocking or stage business appearing, the director may decide to use GIBBERISH or perhaps EXTENDED MOVEMENT or games to set the scene in action. His selection would be dependent upon his diagnosis as to what is causing the problem to begin with. If the intent of a scene is not clear, BEGIN AND END will sharpen the meaning for actor and director alike. For improvisational theater needing scene material, PREOCCUPATION, WHAT'S BEYOND? D, EX-PLORE AND HEIGHTEN, and other special exercises in this area can be selected.

Out of this playing, then, the play itself, its story, its life, will emerge for the director to see. Working this way continues group agreement and finding the solution to the stage problems through group solving of problems. Nor is the single actor negated, for if for any reason work on individual character development must take place or more understanding of relation to an individual role is necessary, there are many exercises to use.

For the improvisational director, this is the only way he can work. The substance of the scene itself must be evolved along with everything else, and this is the way it will come about.

Theme

The theme is the moving thread that weaves itself into every beat of the play or scene. It intertwines and shows itself within the simplest gesture of the actor and in the last bit of trimming on his costume. It is both the bridge from scene (beat) to scene (beat) and the scene (beat) itself.

In the theater as in all art forms, it is difficult exactly to define theme. Look for it to grow out of the parts of the very play that is being done, for within a well-built play or scene the theme awaits. As a comet is static unless shot out by the energy that propels it, so is the play until it is moved forward by the energy extracted from each second of its progression. The source of this energy must be found in the objective reality of each scene. This will give the play its momentum as each scene is fused into life. Paradoxically, the theme gives the play its life and finds its life from the play itself.

The improvisational theater is so structured that its energy source is reached at the same time that the scenes evolve, for every scene grows from an objective reality (agreement). This is why in the improvisational theater a theme can be stated and the scenes built around it.

In simple terms, then, the director should think of theme as the thread that links all the separate parts together—a means for keeping costumes, set design, play, technicians, director and actors together, working under one banner. Sometimes, watching, listening, it is a single word or phrase that sparks us; sometimes it is simply a non-verbal "feeling" that develops. The director may find the theme before rehearsals begin, or he may be well into rehearsals before it appears. In some cases it never shows itself. The director must be careful, however, not to be rigid about finding a theme and in desperation impose one upon the play. Such rigidity can produce a dead end rather than an open path for all.

Choosing The Play

It is difficult to set down a blueprint for choosing a play. However, there are a few specific questions which the director should ask himself before making his final decision:
1. Who will my audience be?
2. How skillful are my actors?
3. Do I have a technical staff that can handle the effects the play will need?
4. Is it a play *I* can handle?
5. Is this merely a costumed lecture (moralizing)?[1]

---

[1]See the remarks on involvement as discipline, p. 286.

6. Will the play respond to my work on it?
7. Is the play worth doing?
8. Is the play theatrical?
9. Will it be a creative experience for all?
10. Can I and the actors add touches?
11. Will it be fun to do? Will it play?
12. Does it have life (reality)? or is it psycho-drama?
13. Is it in good taste?
14. Will it give a fresh experience, provoke individual thought for the audience and thereby insight?
15. Are the parts (beats and/or scenes) within the play constructed so they can be brought back to life?

In considering a play, the director should think about whether each rehearsal period could be organized around an acting problem which when solved would stimulate a worthwhile performance. Break the play (or selected improvised scene) into many minute scenes or beats, small parts of the whole, and thoroughly absorb them (never losing sight of the *whole* play). Throughout rehearsal periods, observe each beat in action. Constantly question.

For the formal play:
1. How can the playwright's intent be clarified?
2. Are individual mannerisms getting in the way?
3. Should the scene be heightened visually with more meaningful blocking and business, unusual prop or effects?
4. Are crowd or party scenes handled ineffectually?
5. Should we play more?

For the improvised scene or play:
1. How can the intent of the scene be clarified?
2. Can richer content be given the scene?
3. Is the scene contrived? Are the actors ad-libbing, making jokes, etc., instead of improvising?
4. Is it in good taste?
5. Should we play more?

From this referral point, then, the director prepares problems for the actors to solve. He gives them the problem to play with and then takes from the players what they have to give while solving it. The players take what the director has to give back to them in the way of bits and pieces, additions of his own which he has spontaneously selected while watching the actors work on the problem, in order to enrich the scene.

It is exactly this organic way, this spontaneous selection, between people, this give and take from the points of view of both the players and the director, that is used during the development of scenes for improvisational theater and that is equally useful for the written play. It keeps the integrity of both director and actor and gives each his part in sharing the experience. It brings out scene material in the improvisational theater. For the formal theater it develops total action out of which the meaning of the play arrives.

Seeking The Scene

One word to the director of improvisational theater in his search for scene material for performance. Unless a group has been working together for a very long time and understands the difference between ad-lib and improvisation, avoid going directly for a scene. This will invariably become a "story conference" while moving around stage instead of an improvisation. If the group is clever, such material may be very topical, ingenious, imaginative, even funny and certainly usable for performances; if the group is not too clever, the material that will come out of their "story conference" will be uninteresting. In either case there will not be the rich textured fabric of both character and scene which comes out of true improvisation.

If the director is engaged in a community project specifically to dramatize a particular topical or local theme, he should give actors a problem and suggest the situation or structure or have them work around the theme. Just be certain they do not work on the *story*. For instance, if a community wishes to poke a bit of fun and decides to use suburbia as the theme, simply have players (when setting up a problem) place their Where, Who, and What in a situation that might bring a usable scene out, such as trying to get baby-sitters, or fighting off door-to-door salesmen, or the election of the local alderman. With this, use an acting problem that is particularly useful for scene-making as suggested in Chapter IX.

If the director decides, for example, to bring the problem OBSTACLE WHERE to the cast and they decide to use a door-to-door salesman, a very amusing scene of a housewife trying to get something done may easily arrive out of the obstacle problem. Keeping the same situation of the salesman, the cast can run it through a variety of problems, or they can do the reverse, which would be keeping one problem and running it through a variety of situations. In either case, players will be working on the problem and not the story. It will be in process, not static. The actor who works with the set story is forced to ad-lib and cannot improvise; that is exactly why the director is always needed. His role, his part in this most democratic of groupings is to select material (whether fragment or play) which emerges from the playing, relieving the actors' concern about getting a scene. He further helps the players to "keep playing."

It is the sharing (union), this give and take, of each and everyone's excitement, experience, and intuitive energy that produces the improvised scene. This is why, after improvisational training, even people with little stage experience can produce stage-worthy scenes and are *never* at a loss for appropriate material.[2]

Casting

The method of casting depends on the particular formation of the group of people who have come together for the play. Are they coming for the first time? Are they experienced or inexperienced? Children or adults?

---

[2]"As does all improvisational theater, Playmakers requires a special breed of actors. In this instance they are all students in. . .acting workshops, guided by Viola Spolin. It is often amazing to outsiders that these actors develop such skills and spontaneity despite the fact that they are not professionals. Their talents at improvisation result directly from workshop training. . . .Lawyers, lab technicians, secretaries, writers, salesmen, housewives and children all come to learn about improvisational theater. . . .The workshops teach more than just acting techniques. They teach the more vital part of improvisation which is the art of selecting and developing scene material." – *Chicago Scene*, March 15, 1962, following a Playmakers production.

If a play is done paralleling the workshop, it is simple to cast directly from the classes. Posing situations that will utilize the characters and the problems well in advance of the announcement of the play is easy on all concerned; and the student-actors, having no idea they are being cast, will give the director a clear picture for observation.

The try-out is, of course, the more common way of casting. It is fiercely competitive, however, and the severe tension does not always show people in a good light. Some actors are clever at first reading but never move much beyond that, while a poor first reader may be discarded although he may be potentially superior to the actor chosen. The director must have infinite insight; for he is, after all, looking not for a finished piece of work when he casts but for a tone of voice, a sense of reality, a bodily quality—that indefinable "something" which is only sensed initially. He must consider the amount of work each person will take to develop fully. He may see someone who has the character qualities he wants but has so little background or so many set patterns and mannerisms that it may not be possible to get what is needed during the rehearsal period.

Another method of casting is to utilize a combination of the try-out and the improvisation. This can be done quite successfully with new people. It tends to relax the actors; and, in a tension-free atmosphere, the director is more likely to see everyone's possibilities clearly. Give those trying out a quick verbal resumé of the scene: the Where, the problem, and a quick run-down of the kind of character. Then let them improvise it. Or, give a scene around a problem which is similar to, but not the same as, the play. After the improvised scene, they can then read for the play.

A fourth method—if the group has been together for a time—is to run through GIBBERISH (see p. 123).

In some cases, the director reads the full play to the assembled group prior to casting. If this is done, the director should take care to read with as little character quality as possible, to avoid subsequent imitation by the actors. Sometimes scenes are read. More often, actors are simply given "sides" to read with little if any comment by the director.

Whatever procedure is chosen, it is best that the director's anxieties be well concealed. Casting is a tense period for him, for much depends on his choice. It is certain that the seed of the character must exist within his actor when he finally casts a role.

Casting for improvisational theater is quite different. Many of the scenes the group will be doing have evolved out of the group playing, for the most part the actors, as in workshop, *cast themselves*.

The Acting Side

Now the play is cast and ready for rehearsals. What about scripts? Some directors use full scripts; others prefer "sides," which consist of one or two words of the cue and the subsequent full speech of the individual actor, usually with stage directions typed in. The side can be creatively stimulating and is to be preferred.

It should be typed on 8½ x 11 paper and folded horizontally so that it may be held easily. The addition of the action cue along with the word cue will eliminate much of the problem of slow pickups. The action cue is the word or combination of words which sets the next actor in motion or alerts him to answer.

> *Cue: quiet* .... *hear me?*
>
> Line: All right, if you feel that way.
>
> *Cue: Get out* .... *Get out!*
>
> Line: I will, and don't expect me back! (Exit)

In the first cue and speech, "quiet" is the action cue, and "hear me" (coming some words later) is the word cue. In the second cue and speech, the first "get out" is the action cue, and the second is the word cue. The inner action (bodily response) of the actor hearing the lines begins at the action cue; and he is ready for action and response when he hears the word cue.

If "action cue" is not clear to the actors, an explanation should be given at the time the sides are introduced:

Do we begin to answer another person while he is still speaking, or do we start thinking about our answer after he has finished? "While he is speaking."

The director should carry on a conversation with the actors to point up the problem:

327

Do we always wait until the other person has stopped speaking . . . action—the actors are already answering . . . *or do we sometimes break into their conversation?* Some have already broken into the above speech and have answered, "We don't always wait."

The director should point out how they were able to anticipate the outcome of the discussion. He should suggest that they observe people as they converse, to determine which are the action cues and which are the word cues. Sometimes, of course, both cues will be identical (as in a cry for help).

The acting side prevents an actor from reading the others' lines sub-vocally and eliminates any mouthing. Mouthing is a common failing in unseasoned actors. They follow the other actors' lines by reading them rather than listening to them; and very often their lips actually move as the other actors speak. This mouthing is a serious mechanical reading habit and is often difficult to eradicate.

Sides prevent sub-vocal readings or mouthing, since the lack of a complete script involves the actor from the first moment and forces him to be part of what is going on. He must *listen* and *watch* his fellow actors in order to follow the action and know when to come in. Since he is unable to memorize the other actors' lines, he is forced to act upon the spoken word.

Sides are small and can easily be held in one hand. This frees the actor to pick up props, make contact, etc. Sides also help eliminate some of the problems of mechanical reading, particularly in children. It is possible this is true because the sides cannot be clutched in both hands, a position which may be associated with schoolroom reading.

Only stage directions which lead to action or dialogue (entrances, exits, etc.) should be included on the sides. Even if the director feels a security in keeping them, it is best to avoid many of the playwright's directions (such as "speaks happily," "heaves a heart-rending sigh," or "winks knowingly"). The director should let the physical actions and facial expressions come from the actors' own inner action and from the dialogue itself. There will be plenty of opportunity in the second section of rehearsal, when actors are free of all restrictions, for the director to bring in the playwright's stage directions to further the action.

XVII. Rehearsal and Performance

Organizing The Rehearsal Time

The over-all rehearsal schedule can be broken down into three sections. Briefly, the first section is for warming up the actors and the director, for laying the groundwork in relationships and attitudes to the play and to each other. The second section is the spontaneous, creative period—the digging sessions, where all energies are channeled toward full artistic potential. The third section is for polishing and integrating all production facets into a unity.

The amount of time spent in rehearsal depends upon the actors' availability. Professional actors, of course, have no other commitments. But with lay actors in community theater groups, the opposite is true; and the number of hours they have free to rehearse is limited.

To rehearse a show within these limited hours becomes a real problem. But by utilizing the three rehearsal sections and by extending the over-all rehearsal schedule over a two- or three-month period, the director will have a good picture of where he is going. When the daily hours of rehearsal are limited, this long time-span between casting and showtime is uniquely valuable; for it is in this period that seasoning takes place.

Not one minute of rehearsal should be wasted. The schedule should be carefully planned to be certain that every actor present is working at every possible moment. It is advisable to think in terms of two kinds of time: clock-time and energy-time. Energy-time is the more valuable, for the director can get as much from his actors in two hours of inspired, excited rehearsal as he can in six hours of boredom and fatigue.

While it is unavoidable that all actors be present at run-throughs, it is wise not to keep them around at other times just on the chance that they may be needed. Some directors are more secure having the actors at their beck and call, and some feel that the actors should be around to see where the play is going; but proper organization of rehearsals will give the director a very good picture of where he is at every moment without inconveniencing his actors. The psychological as well as the obvious benefits of such careful scheduling are considerable. The actors are always fresh, always excited and eager to work. They are pleased by the consideration shown them and respond, in return, with maximum results.

Whether it is a vignette, a one-act play, or a three-act play—whether the clock-time is eight hours or sixty—the rehearsal time can be figured by noting what must be covered in each session. If the group meets only three times a week and each session can have only a maximum of two hours, the director must schedule himself accordingly. When the time arrives for costume parades, dress rehearsal, etc., he will, of course, have to find extra hours for these time-consuming activities.

Atmosphere During Rehearsals

If the rehearsal period is one of tensions, anxieties, competitiveness, and bad temper, this will be absorbed by the actors along with their parts and will be a shadow over the finished work. If, on the other hand, the atmosphere is relaxed, social, and joyous with the excitement of the work at hand and the anticipation of the show to come, this too will be evident in the final production. A nuance, perhaps, but an important one; for when actors are free and enjoying their roles, then the audience is relaxed, and an extra note of pleasure is added to their viewing.

Lay actors often come to rehearsals at a point where energy levels are low: after school, tired from a day's work or from putting the children to bed, etc. Outside problems may be carried into the rehearsal, whether they be a child's poor report card or an adult's quarrel with the boss. In either case, making their transition from one place to another a pleasant one is well worth the trouble. A refreshment break will often enhance the social aspect of rehearsal and also relieve fatigue.

The Director's Ability To Inspire

"Inspiration" is often a vague term. We know, however, that behind it something exists and that, in the case of a director, its presence or absence can be readily noted by observing those around him.

The most apparent characteristic of inspiration could probably be termed "reaching beyond one's self" or deeper "into one's self." People who are inspired may pace the floor or talk animatedly. Eyes sparkle, ideas pour forth, and the body releases its holds. If many people are inspired simultaneously, then the very air around them seems to sparkle and dance with excitement.

Inspiration in the theater situation can best be described as energy. "Energy" does not mean leaping wildly about the stage (although this might help at times). It is the intensity of the director's attention to what the actors are doing, plus the use of every skill he can call up, which subsequently prods the actors into extending themselves, into "reaching beyond." Sometimes the director must literally *pour* this energy into his cast as he might pour water into a glass; and, in most instances, the cast will respond and will be able to pour it right back into him. An actor once made the comment that "playing to you is like playing to a full house at the Opera!" This is the kind of energy the director must give his actors.

Never for one moment should the director show tiredness or boredom, for a director who loses his energy is doing more harm to his play than can be imagined. If this tiredness should occur, it is far better to stop rehearsals completely and have the stage manager take over for a sit-down line rehearsal, or go into voice exercises or an improvisation, than it is to continue with a lifeless rehearsal.

An actor without energy is worthless, for he is without contact with what he is doing. The same holds true for the director. The director must not make "inspiring the actors" a mere phrase. Indeed, when a lag in rehearsals does occur, he would do well to look to himself.

Am I giving enough energy? Am I staying overlong on mechanics? Which actors need individual attention? Do they need more improvisations? Are rehearsals too drawn out? Am I nagging at the actors? Am I attacking the actors? Are the actors working at odds with me? Is the problem physical or psychological? Am I just being a traffic manager? Is it necessary to stimulate more spontaneity? Am I using the actors as puppets? Am I over-anxious? Am I asking them for more than they can give me at this time?

If the director searches for and handles his problem honestly, he will solve it. The only initiative he needs is the knowledge that when necessary his ingenuity, spontaneity, and energy can give the inspiration to his actors.

Blocking The Show

Natural-looking blocking is possible with any age group or experience level. Neither the child actor nor the lay actor need move around the stage awkwardly, clinging to props and furniture, spreading fear and discomfort through the audience. Exercises in non-directional blocking should be given the cast if they have not had workshop training (see Chapter VI).

As long as the lay actor is constantly directed in the mechanics of stage movement and does not understand that stage movement can only grow out of involvement and relationships, he can, at best, only remember the conventions and will therefore be unable to move naturally.

To test this theory, the following experiment was carried out by actors with little or no theater experience and only minimal workshop training. They were given two different scenes.

For the first scene, the actors were given full scripts which contained the lines for all the characters plus the stage business and blocking as set down by the playwright. During the first rehearsal, they were constantly stopped for blocking by the director. Then they were asked to take their lines home and memorize them.

For the second scene, the same actors were given acting sides only. The action cues and word cues of the other actors were all they had to work with. There were no stage directions given. During the first rehearsal, they were occasionally coached by the director to share the stage picture. They did not take their lines home to memorize.

At the next rehearsal, the difference was remarkable. During the first scene, set rigidly from the outside, the actors neither saw their stage nor heard their fellow actors as they struggled to remember cues, lines, and stage directions. Their concentration was so intent upon remembering, and their fears of not performing well produced such physical tensions, that they were rigid. Their bodies could not move freely. The stage movements of these unskilled actors under such imposed conditions could only be stiff and awkward—what is commonly called "amateurish."

The second scene, though more complicated in its demands, did not trouble the actors; for, intent upon each other and with nothing to remember (no performing) other than "sharing," they were free to solve the problems that came up during the actual rehearsal. This experience was similar to the improvisation, where the problem must be solved during the playing of the scene and not away from it. It is in this way that actors achieve spontaneity.

In another experiment, lay actors with many months of workshop training behind them were given the full script (as in the first scene with the new actors). In their case, they were able to take the directions given by the playwright and the director and translate them into the necessary stage relationships. But the lay actor who in play after play is directed rigidly, step by step, with every movement plotted for him, cannot hope to discover for himself the natural stage movements (blocking) required. The fear and tensions that were part of the first rehearsals and all subsequent plays have been memorized along with his lines and stage directions and have become a part of his work and keeps him in the past (memorization) other than the present (process).

The director who wraps his actors up in yards of imposed movement and inflections until they cannot walk is the same director who places the burden of "stupidity" or "no talent" on them when he finds they cannot function on their own. He bemoans their inability to loose the ties that bind them, but it is he, in reality, who has secured the knots. Rigid actors are often the product of a rigid director.

Integration In Blocking

Integration is being present to the moment that is present. Integration is an organic response to the stage life. While it is sometimes necessary for an instruction to be given to the actor, he must translate it into an organic or integrated experience. The following dialogue was with a ten-year-old player.

Why did you go upstage just then? "Because you told me to."
Isn't that mechanical? "Yes."

Why do you think you were directed to go upstage? "I went upstage to wait for Tom to enter."

Why couldn't you wait for him where you were? "I wasn't part of the scene going on at the moment. I have to be out of the scene, but I can't leave the stage."

What can you do standing where you are, out of the scene, and still be part of the stage picture? "I'll put my Point of Concentration on listening for Tom to come in."

Stage Business

It must be realized that the most skilled director or actor cannot always intellectually find interesting stage business. The director himself must often stimulate stage business when neither the actor nor the script are helpful. There are many ways to accomplish this. Sometimes the director will receive inspiration from his actors at the moment it becomes necessary and will then spontaneously select from this what is appropriate for the actor and scene. Using the acting exercises (see Time Chart, p. 364) will bring up more business than the director or actor could find in many hours of work on the script.

Both the director and the actor must understand that stage business is not just a random activity to keep actors occupied. Like blocking, it should be interesting and non-obtrusive and should appear spontaneous.

General Improvisations Around The Play

In the first rehearsal section, keep all improvisations close to the Where and the problem of the actual play; but in the second section, when it becomes necessary to provoke the actor beyond the exact lines and to bring a greater reality to relationships, general improvisation is most helpful. General improvisations will seem to have no direct relation to the written play. They are presented, however, to give the actor insight into the character he is playing.

In a production of *The Emperor's New Clothes,* establishing the relationship between the minister (who was the villain, browbeating and cheating the weavers) and the weavers became a problem. It was solved by stopping rehearsals and doing an improvisation around Nazis coming to a village during the war. The weavers took the parts of villagers; and the minister and his entourage played the Nazi soldiers. The Nazis marched in, billeted themselves, herded people together, established authority, and used physical violence against those who protested. The villagers wept, fought, and shouted. All the emotional conflicts necessary for the play they were working on came forth and were heightened. It was never necessary to rehearse these relationships again in this play by Charlotte Chorpenning.

Once the quality needed for a scene is captured, it remains (with rare exceptions). In the foregoing example, the reality of the Nazi scene had to be shaped into the structure of the play; but the intensity was never lost. Audiences were moved by the strength of these scenes and were astonished that "mere children" (who were playing the roles) could give such amazing portrayals.

General improvisations often give actors an insight beyond their words by helping them to "see the word" and achieve a reality for the scene. In effect, they resemble WHAT'S BEYOND for improvisational theater. Sometimes improvisations are not necessary; but when used, they will invariably enrich the work.

The Non-Stop Run-Through

The non-stop run-through is especially valuable to the director with a limited amount of rehearsal time. It is, simply, a complete run-through of the play *without stops of any kind*. It should be held sacred; under no circumstances should a director break in for any reason. Notes for spot rehearsals, pointers for individual actors, and places in the individual acts that need more work can all be jotted down by the director and cleaned up at a later rehearsal.

These non-stop run-throughs strengthen the whole basic structure of the production, for the flow and continuity that they generate gives the actors a sense of the movement and rhythm of the total play which can only help them with the details of their scenes.

The mechanical problems which the director has in getting his cast and play together during the first rehearsal section are so time consuming that a non-stop run-through would be impossible during this time. Indeed, setting just one act of a three-act play usually takes most of the daily rehearsal period at this early stage. But in the second rehearsal section, when blocking, relationships, character, motivation, etc., have already been roughed in, the non-stop run-through should be scheduled as often as possible.

The Relaxed Rehearsal[1]

The Relaxed Rehearsal, falling within the second rehearsal section, gives perspective to the actors. By this time, they should be off their lines. The actors lie on the floor, shut their eyes, and breathe slowly with strong accent on the exhale. The director walks around from time to time, lifting a foot or a hand to make sure muscular release is complete.

The actors then go through the lines of the play as they lie there with their eyes closed. They are to concentrate on visualizing the stage, the persons with them, and themselves in the scenes.

The director should continue to insist on complete release. The actors' voices should be quiet and almost sleepy. In spite of the past work, old reading patterns and anxieties will often show up in rehearsal, particularly on a first play. Actors might be tense

---

[1]VERBALIZING THE WHERE, p. 128, could be combined with Relaxed Rehearsal.

and worried about the mechanics of their action, memorization, cues, movement, etc. This relaxed rehearsal, coupled with the visualization of the stage, usually dissipates that sort of fear.

During the relaxed rehearsal, the director should quietly remind the actors that they are not to mouth the other actors' words but must try to hear them. They must concentrate intensely on seeing the stage in their own minds. The director quietly asks them what colors they are seeing and how far away the other actors seem. Perhaps he can even give them the image of a stereoscopic camera. They should try to see the stage in full dimension, color, and movement, to be hyper-conscious of everything that takes place.

If properly handled and prepared for, this time will be enjoyable to all. The actors will be able to extract bits and pieces from their former work and add them to their conceptions of their roles. The last vestiges of anxiety will usually disappear; and this still weeks before the opening!

Spot Rehearsals

As a rule, it is best to schedule spot rehearsals in the third section, when the play has definite shape and flow. The spot rehearsal is utilized to give special time to working over a scene which has been troubling the director and/or the actors and which has not developed within the general rehearsals. It might be a simple entrance or an involved emotional scene. It might be a problem of achieving a more effective mob scene or helping a single actor to underline and heighten a long speech. In improvisational theater, playing a problem is often the way to evolve a scene.

This type of rehearsal will often intensify a scene which has previously been weak. Spot rehearsals pull the actor and the director away from the generality of the over-all play and focus on the minute details of a scene. They create quiet concentration and an intimacy between the actor and director which result in deeper insights for both. While the director may find himself spending hours on a scene that takes but a few moments on stage, such intensive work on these selected bits and pieces enriches the actor's role and brings added depth to the total play.

Seasoning The Actor

We speak of an actor as being "seasoned" when he stands in good relationship to his part, the play, and the other actors; when he has ease of movement and flow of speech; and, above all, when he is aware of his audience responsibility.

One of the most common weaknesses of the lay theater is the awkward, rough level of performance given by most of its actors. While much of this roughness can be attributed to inadequate experience and training, other factors are also involved.

How often are most lay actors on stage? Their work, for the most part, is directed toward one date— one production—and when that moment has passed, the experience ends. This abrupt breakdown in group expression thwarts creativity just when it should be blossoming forth. It stops the growth, the seasoning process.

For the group interested in developing a repertory company, the seasoning that takes place during performance is especially valuable. But, between the problems of rehearsal time and the technical and mechanical difficulties which most community theaters face, there is little opportunity for gaining insights into the play and accomplishing the desired seasoning.

No director can expect to get fully seasoned actors in a short period of time. However, the following suggestions, if carried out, will round off many of the rough, uneven edges:

1. Plan a long time-span for rehearsing.
2. Use acting exercises during rehearsals.
3. Do not allow actors to take their lines home too early.
4. Use non-directional blocking whenever possible.
5. Create a tension-free pleasurable atmosphere during rehearsals.
6. Bring in costume pieces and props early in the rehearsals to assure ease and comfort at the time of performance.
7. Work to have actors meet every crisis and adjust to sudden changes.
8. Break dependency upon words.
9. Have a weekly run-through of the full show throughout the second rehearsal section.
10. Schedule as many performances as possible; show to

many different audiences; show in other places, if possible.

Memorization

In community theater, memorizing lines is usually considered the most important single factor in working on a role in a play. In truth, it is only one of many factors in rehearsing a play and must be handled carefully to keep it from becoming a serious stumbling block to the actor. For those trained in improvisational techniques, memorization is not a boogey-man!

The director should not allow his actors to take their sides home after rehearsal. This may be confusing to them, for many feel that line-memorization should be done immediately and gotten out of the way so that the actual direction can begin. However, it is important to realize that dialogue should grow out of the involvement and relationships between players; and premature memorization creates rigid patterns of speech and manner which are often very difficult (and sometimes impossible) to change.

The director should stop to think just who may be waiting in the home to "help." What well-meaning friend or relative who fancies himself a good judge of talent and cannot resist the chance to find the "right" way for the actor? And how many mirrors reflect the image of the actor busily emoting in front of them as he learns his lines? The time between rehearsals should be a fallow period as far as the play is concerned—it should lie quietly.

Memorizing the lines too early brings many anxieties; for the fear of forgetting them is great. These anxieties remain as a shadow over every performance. If for some reason early memorization is unavoidable, the director should show his actors how to accomplish it in a relaxed manner.[2]

Actors may feel a bit concerned when they are not allowed to take their scripts or sides home during the early rehearsals; for even the youngest actor has tied up working on a part with learning words (memorization). Because of this, they are often

---

[2]See p. 370, points 5 and 6 in Removing Amateur Qualities, Chapter XVIII.

quite fearful that they may not be able to memorize in time. It is the director's job to reassure them.

All the elements of production should be organically memorized simultaneously. It is only during rehearsals with the cast that relationships are worked out and understood. It is during rehearsals that the actor frees himself from words he is seeking to memorize. When this freedom becomes evident, then it is safe to let him take his lines home. For when the director sees that his actors are integrated and relating to all the aspects of the theater communication, then are they ready to memorize—in fact, for most of them the job has already been done. They will find that they need only to go over a difficult speech here and there. In fact, sometimes all that is needed is to take the sides from their hands during rehearsals; and, much to their surprise, they will know their lines!

If the groundwork has been laid and the Time Chart (p. 364) has been followed, the director will probably find all his actors off their lines before the start of the second rehearsal section. This method of working is particularly valuable for child actors, where the fear of reading and of not being able to memorize lines becomes a serious obstacle in their work and keeps many of them from developing as actors.

A director from a community theater once visited the Young Actors Company at a dress rehearsal. She was surprised to see the director down at the mouth because of the usual "dress rehearsal." "You should feel elated," she said. "Your young actors are all off their lines!" This is indeed a sad state of affairs when the bogey of knowing the lines determines the whole quality of the performance.

Reading Lines Naturally

The student-actor is often quite fearful around words—particularly the child actor, whose anxiety grows out of his past experiences with reading. As he struggles to pronounce the words "correctly," his discomfort is continuously in the foreground. In the unseasoned actor, the inability to read lines naturally is often evident. Lines become words "in place of" dialogue—a substitute for action and relationship between players.

The first step in helping student-actors to lose this preoccupation with the lines is to preoccupy them elsewhere. Avoid any direct reference to the cause of their anxiety. Give them an acting problem that will remove focus from the words and solve the matter for them.

Gibberish, extended movement, dance movement, singing dialogue, contact, and postponement of memorizing words are all designed to help the actors in this way. If they are to lose their fear of line-reading, actors must come to sense that lines grow out of dynamic action and involvement. For those who read haltingly, give gibberish or ad-lib lines until relationships form. It works. Try it!

Another way to "lose" words is to focus on the shape of the words—the vowels and consonants—independent of meaning, concentrating on the visual appearance of the vowels and consonants, their physical shape and design as written or printed. In a sit-down reading, have the cast concentrate first on only the vowels, then on only the consonants. In reading, they are to heighten these *vowels and consonants* in any way they wish— sound, body movement, etc. Try to keep the reading at a normal pace. Stop at an appropriate time and resume the normal reading of the lines. Have cast think of words as sound which they shape or design into word patterns.

Timing[3]

As much as he would like to, the actor cannot develop timing intellectually. Such skill can only be learned through experiencing. That is why rigid blocking and the mechanical following of directions must be done away with. The actor's sense of timing must come from his innermost self.

Timing is generally believed to exist in only the most seasoned actors. However, if "seasoned" is understood to mean that actor who has both self-awareness and the ability to attune to the needs of the scene, the other actors, and his responsibility to the audience, then every student-actor can develop timing to some degree.

If problems are solved, the cumulative effect of all the acting

---

[3]See also Timing, Chapter II.

exercises in the workshops will develop timing in the actor; for each problem insists on really playing, and in this rests selectivity and attunement to multiple stimuli. When the actor has developed his timing, he will then know when a play is dragging, when cues are dropped, and when stage action is not alive—in short, when his "guests" are not enjoying themselves.

If actors are without workshop training, try to find the Point of Concentration in each separate scene within the written script. Then have actors focus on problems exactly as they would in workshop. This will send them out into the stage environment and help objectify their work, which is the essence of timing.

Picking Up Cues

Slow cues cause a serious lag in a scene. If the director is still having trouble with slow cue pickups in the third rehearsal section, his actors have not completely solved the problem of involvement and relationship. Other devices must then be used.

The director might snap his fingers simultaneously with the cues. Shadowing might be used to encourage quicker uptake. Or tossing a ball back and forth between actors; the moment the ball hits him, the actor must begin speaking. Or, the director might have the slower actor deliberately top the other's lines, cutting off the last few words.

The actors should be cautioned that picking up cues does not mean faster speech. If a speech has a slow tempo, then tempo remains slow, even though the cue itself is picked up rapidly.

Laughter In Rehearsals

During the second rehearsal section, actors are usually quite free from early tensions, social aspects are high, movements are fairly sure, and the actors can begin to have more fun. Fun, however, must be understood as the pleasure of working within the play and with the other actors. Uncontrolled laughter and wisecracking during rehearsals should be seen by the director for what it is.

When laughter is moderate and enjoyable, it is useful. It most often denotes a breakthrough. It will help, not impede the work. When it has elements of hysteria in it, however, it will prove destructive and must be carefully handled by the director. In time, the director will listen to laughter and know what it means, much as a mother is able to tell what each separate cry of her child means.

Although actors will assure the director that they "will never laugh on stage," he might be permitted a moment of doubt. It might help to tell them the Soup Story:

A wife tried to get her husband to stop making noises when he drank soup, since they were soon to have company for dinner. "Don't worry," he said. "As long as we're by ourselves, I can make all the noise I want. But when company comes, I will drink my soup quietly."

The next time they had company for dinner, the man was very careful not to make noise; and for the first few spoonfuls all went well. He did so well, in fact, that he completely relaxed. The longer the soup course went on, the more he enjoyed himself; and the more he enjoyed himself, the louder he slurped. To the embarrassment of the guests, he ended up making more noise than he had before his wife warned him.

Sometimes, when laughter breaks out among the cast in rehearsal, the director can let them release it by actually helping them to laugh and joining in on the joke. However, if the laughter is uncontrollable, he should recognize the danger sign, stop the scene, and go on to another.

Young actors and older lay actors will often say, "He makes me laugh!" But it is important to point out to them that "he" never makes them laugh. It is their own lack of focus, for whatever reason, that causes the trouble. Laughter sometimes is a means of pulling away from the stage environment and becoming a judging audience. They are playing a role and suddenly see their friends instead of the other characters. Or they see themselves doing something, expressing some emotion out of the ordinary.

Laughter is energy; and players can learn that its physical impact on the body can be re-channeled into another emotion. As in workshop, student-actors learn to "use their laughter." Laughter can readily be turned to tears, tantrums, "play" laughter, physical action, etc.

Growing Stale

There are two points at which actors may grow stale: one is during rehearsals, the other is during a run of performances. When this happens, it is a sign of grave danger, for when actors become mechanical and lifeless, something has gone wrong.

Sometimes this is because of a serious weakness in the basic structure of the production; at other times, it may be just a temporary setback. Sometimes the choice of material is poor, and the director finds himself working with such superficiality that it responds only slightly to his work. Sometimes actors have ceased to "play," and spontaneity and creativity have been replaced by the actors simply repeating themselves. Or the actors may have lost focus and begun to generalize their environment, their relationship (Who), and their settings (Where), so that no reality exists for them. Rehearsals, like the play itself, should have a growing developmental theme and climax. Staleness may be a sign that the director has neglected to carefully plan his rehearsal time to build maximum inspiration and excitement for his actors (see the Time Chart, p. 364 ff.).

Several factors may account for the cast going stale during rehearsals:

1. Director has set his play too definitely from the outside, giving every movement, every piece of business, every voice inflection to his actors.

2. Actors have memorized lines and business too early. Characters, blocking, etc., were set before relationship and involvement developed.

3. Actors have been isolated too long from the other aspects of production and need a "lift." The director should bring in a handsome set piece, a costume part, or a prop and space this so maximum effect will be derived. He should heighten the theatrical atmosphere as he moves to the third rehearsal section. This opens up new vistas for the actors and builds greater vitality for the production.

4. Actors need more fun or play. This can be handled through re-channeling the director's attitude or by using games. This is particularly true of children and lay actors, where it may take months of workshop before their involvement with the theater

problems generates enough energy to hold their interest without outside stimuli. Carefully selected games are excellent for any rehearsing group.

5. Actors with limited backgrounds are certain they have reached their goal and achieved characters—they want the performance to begin. Sometimes only one or two actors may be having difficulties. It may be that they do not like their parts, or they may feel they should have had larger ones.

Other faults that usually lead to staleness during performance:

1. Imitating previous performances.
2. Seduced by audience reaction.
3. Never varied performance. (Actors can vary performances endlessly, respecting the limitations of the play's structure.)
4. Giving "solo performances."
5. Actors getting lazy and sloppy.
6. Actors losing detail and generalizing objects and stage relationships (Use VERBALIZING THE WHERE, p. 128, when this occurs.)
7. Actors need director's guardianship.
8. Play needs pickup rehearsals.

An interesting problem arose with an actor who was playing in his first performance. It was at a settlement house; and he was a neighborhood man who did a brilliant piece of work when he stood up to the villain of the play. After the first performance he received a thunderous applause. The next performance there was *no* applause. He was perplexed and wanted to know what had happened.

The first time you played, you were really angry, and we all knew it. The second show, you were only remembering the applause. He thought for a moment, nodded his head, and as he rolled up his sleeves and flexed his arms, he said: "Wait till I get him tonight!"

Acting Exercises During Rehearsals

Interjecting an acting exercise in a rehearsal that is going nowhere brings refreshment to both the actors and the director. For the most part, the director should select the exercises that help solve the problems of the play, as mentioned earlier in this chapter. Sometimes, however, exercises independent of the play are useful for generating energy in the actors and are an aid in the maturing or seasoning process.

Every early rehearsal should make use of at least one acting exercise. The Time Chart (p. 364) suggests many methods for doing this; but at best it is only a general plan, and each director will learn to add or subtract from it as his individual problems appear.

Gibberish (see p. 120)

Because gibberish requires total body response to make a communication, it provides excellent exercises to use throughout the three sections of rehearsal. Gibberish quickly opens up the actors and helps the director to see the individual potentials of the group. Because it physicalizes the relationships and involvements, it has extraordinary value in developing spontaneous business and blocking and gives many clues for procedure to the director.

If employed early in rehearsals, gibberish produces remarkable acceleration in every aspect of production. In an experiment with a one-act play that had only eight hours of rehearsal time (using actors with limited backgrounds), gibberish was used four times, consuming two and one-half hours, or one-fourth of the rehearsals. The resulting performance had unusual vitality; and the cast handled their play with the ease of experienced actors.

When using gibberish during rehearsals, take the actors who have not had workshop training through GIBBERISH EXERCISES 1 through 4. After that, work on the problem of the play using gibberish. A scene that will not "play" in gibberish is a scene without reality, therefore without life. Theater communication cannot be made through words; the actor must truly *show*.

Where (see p. 89)

Where exercises can be used at the very beginning of rehearsals. During the second sit-down reading of the play, draw a floorplan of the set (if it is too early for specifics, approximate it) and place this in front of the group so that they can refer to it. As they are reading, have them think themselves around the stage within the set. Ask them to concentrate on colors, on the weather, on the style of clothing. (This should only be used by actors who have had workshop Where.)

Divide the cast into small groups and have them solve Where (making physical contact with all the objects on stage). This is to be done on an empty stage with only the blackboard for referral. The playing may or may not relate to the problem in the scene; but the floorplan on the blackboard will be for the play they will be doing.

The SPECIALIZED WHERE (see p. 138), with real props, is very valuable and should be given after a few walk-throughs. If the play calls for a window to a fire escape, a door to a closet, a door to a bathroom, a pull-down bed, a telephone, and a wall safe, have the cast (separated into small teams) use exactly these set pieces for improvisation. They are to do a scene around them independent of the action of the play, although they must take similar characters (the old man in the play can be the old man in the improvisation, etc.). In specialized Where exercises, they must let the set pieces suggest the situation.

If all or some of the foregoing Where suggestions are used, the first walk-around rehearsals with lines will find the actors moving quite easily about the stage area.

Contact (see p. 184)

We sometimes see plays where actors stay in their own little areas, afraid to touch, look directly at, or listen to each other. Strong contact between actors, where a hand really holds another's arm or an eye looks into an eye, makes productions more alive, more solid. An audience is able to sense when a real contact has been made. And the director should remind his actors of this throughout rehearsals.

Contact may be made either through direct physical touch, the passing of props, or eye focus. A cast that has not had workshop training can gain much by taking time out to do a scene from the play as a contact exercise.

Objects To Show Inner Action (see p. 244)

Exercises in using objects to show inner action are *continuously* useful during rehearsal and should be used whenever physicalization is needed.

Space Or Extended Movement (see p. 81)

Using space or extended movement during rehearsals helps to integrate the total stage movement. Such exercises break the static isolation many actors still cling to in spite of work on other acting problems. While especially useful for fantasy, movement exercises also do much for realistic drawing-room plays. Then try the opposite NO MOTION. Exercises in using space substance (p. 81) parallel the use of dance or extended movement and can be applied during rehearsals with satisfactory results.

This type of rehearsal helps players, young and old alike, to realize that, like a dancer, an actor is never merely to "wait his turn" while working on stage. His whole body, even when still, must always be ready to spring into stage action. This gives an interesting energy to the stage, and often a choreographed quality appears.

Blind (see p. 171)

As it did in workshop, the exercise called BLIND will force listening and help actors to move firmly within the stage environment, as they feel the space around them and develop a sense of "each other." During rehearsals, BLIND is best given to actors after they are off lines and are quite familiar with their stage.

Working on a darkened stage can contribute to rehearsals although of course the director cannot see his actors. It does, however, help a director hear his actors and the actors to hear one another. This is similar to the technique of "listening to your actors" discussed next. If it is impractical to move your actors about, similar to the relaxed rehearsal, have them just sit on a darkened stage reading lines to one another.

Listening to The Actors

At various intervals during rehearsal the director should turn his back on his actors and listen to them. This listening without seeing them in action often points up weaknesses in relationship, uncovers lack of "seeing the word," reveals falseness of characterization, and shows up "acting."

In the improvisational theater useless dialogue is quickly recognized.

Seeing The Word (see p. 232)

Exercises in visualizing words as shapes come in handy for spot rehearsals. They help to underline and enrich many lines and moods. Add inner action to an exercise if sensory awareness alone does not work.

For instance, a student-actor who had a serious problem of monotone speech was given the special exercise of describing a flood he had witnessed. Coaching him to see color, concentrate on motion, sound, etc., had little effect on his speech. But, when asked how he felt "inside" when he saw the water, he replied that he had a funny feeling in his stomach. The "funny feeling" then became the basis for side coaching during his talk, and the changes were immediate. As he concentrated on fear of drowning, animation came into his speech.

In the case of this young boy, he would have been unable to recognize the fact that he had "fear." Asking him for an "emotion" would have provoked no response. But asking him how he felt "inside" (physically) enabled him to concentrate on his physical feeling and made it understandable to him.

Shadowing (see p. 177)

Shadowing should not be used until the third, or polishing, section. Then the director should get on the stage with his actors and follow them around. Prior to doing this, the director should explain that they are not to lose their concentration no matter what he might do; for if they are amused or disturbed by his shadowing, then the point of the action will be lost.

Shadowing will help the actors to understand their own inner action, to visualize, to make contact, to move. It will also give the director his actors' point of view and may clarify a few things for him. He should talk to the actor he is shadowing (since he stays very close to him, he can speak quietly without disturbing the others) and should pick up the reactions of that actor as well as the others:

Why does he look at you like that? . . . Doesn't that irritate you? . . . What right has he to do that? . . . Do you think he's going to talk to you? . . . What makes him look out the window that way? . . . Why don't you force him to look at you? . . . .

This gives the actors an extra burst of energy from the director; in a sense, it exposes them, some weeks before the opening, to the most scrutinizing of audience reactions, for shadowing is like the closeup of a camera. If they get rattled when being shadowed, they are not secure in their parts and need more work on spots.

This particular technique should not be used until the actors have been with their roles long enough for some seasoning to have taken place.

Use Of Games

Like dance or space exercises, games release spontaneity and create flow as they remove static body movements and bring the actors together physically. Games are especially valuable in cleaning up scenes requiring sharp timing.

A difficult problem arose in a cocktail-party scene where six or seven players had to mill around and socialize while surreptitiously watching for the high-sign from their leader to break loose and create bedlam. When the scene was rehearsed, the results were static and unspontaneous. The problem was finally solved through the game WHO STARTED THE MOTION? (p. 67).

After WHO STARTED THE MOTION? was played four or five times, the cocktail-party scene came off, and the needed "looking without looking" quality emerged very sharply. The excitement released by the game was retained by the players throughout their performances.

A park scene with passersby crossing and recrossing the stage (requiring continuous entering and exiting) created a serious problem of timing for the actors. It was impossible to "set" the crosses through cues, since there had to be random crossing but never too many at one time. The game OBJECT RELAY solved this problem for the actors.

OBJECT RELAY[4]

Two teams.

Teams line up side by side. The first player on the team has an object in his hand (a rolled-up newspaper, a stick, etc.). The first player from each team must run to a goal agreed upon, touch it, run back, and hand the object to the next player on his team who must, in turn, run, touch the goal, run back, give the object to the third player on the team, and so forth until all players have finished and a team has won.

After OBJECT RELAY had been played once, it was repeated, but this time the actors walked instead of running to the goal and back. This solved the problem on stage for the actors from then on; and as one or two exited, the others entered with no lag or static.

The director would do well to have a few good game books on hand at all times and to be familiar with their contents for that moment when he might be called upon to solve a stage problem through the game situation.

Biographies

Toward the end of the second period of rehearsal, ask the actors for biographies of their characters. It is a device for getting them to think of character in dimension and occasionally brings some insights. Within this material the director, too, may find something that is usable to help the actor when he seems to be getting nowhere with his part.

The biography is everything about the character being played.

---

[4]Adapted from Neva L. Boyd, *Handbook of Games* (Chicago: H. T. FitzSimons Co., 1945).

Write out as fully as possible: schooling, parents, grandparents, favorite foods, main ambitions, loves, hates, what entertains him, how he spends his evenings, etc. Add the reasons which brought this character to the immediate stage situation.

This should not be done until the character is settling into the actor. Done too early, it is harmful and creates quite the opposite effect, for it keeps the character in "the head" of the player.[5] Some biographies may be sketchy, irrelevant, and superficial. There should be no discussion about them. Simply accept them as they are and use them for reference material if and when the need arises. In a well-written play, an actor need only do the scene, for the character we meet holds his past within him.

A biography written by a fourteen-year-old girl who was playing in a fantasy stated that she and the villain had gone to school together as children and that she had loved him very much. While logically this would have been impossible in the social structure of the play, it gave her relationship with the villain another dimension. She was able to give a sense of former love for the character she now detested. The audience, of course, was never aware of this "story," but it brought much greater depth to her work. (When these two players grew up, they married each other.)

Suggestions For The First Rehearsal Section

1. The director must trust his casting. Great fear will sometimes arise in the early rehearsals that he has erred in his choice of actors. If this is really so, he should re-cast quickly, for his attitude will affect everyone.

2. Without telling the cast, select two actors for barometers: one whose response is high and one whose response is low. This way you will always know if you are giving too much or too little in your rehearsals.

3. Do not allow actors to keep their eyes glued to sides when other actors are reading. Watch for this even at sit-down

---

[5]Because of this, it is avoided in training for improvisational theater, and exercises on character agility are used instead.

readings and remind them to watch the other players and to listen to them whenever necessary.

4. Avoid artificial reading habits from the first moment. Use special exercises if necessary.

5. Handle cue pickups naturally by having the actors work on action cues. *Do not handle this mechanically.* If it becomes necessary to work on word cues, wait until the latter part of the second or early part of the third rehearsal section.

6. Avoid setting character, lines, business, or blocking too early. A "rough-in" is all that is necessary. There is plenty of time.

7. Details are unimportant in the first period. *Do not nag the actors.* Once the character and relationships are set, it will be simple to bring in details. So, the life of each scene within the play must be found.

Suggestions For The Second Rehearsal Section

This is the digging period. The actor is now ready for fuller utilization of his own creativity. As he brings up actions through the exercises or in the reading of the script, the director picks them up, enlarges them, and adds something of his own, if necessary. The play is more or less blocked; and almost everyone is completely off lines. Relationships are clear.

1. The beginning of self-discipline. No chitchat in the wings or in the theater. At this time, stage attitudes and stage behavior off the stage as well as on are to be established.

2. If the groundwork has been well laid, the director can move directly to stage action with no danger of intruding on the actor's creativity or a static quality appearing. He can cajole, shout, plead, and give exact steps without developing anxieties or stopping spontaneity. There will be no danger of his hampering the stage work.

3. Some first-section exercises can be continued here if necessary. Gibberish exercises are particularly good for digging up more stage business.

4. Director's energy must be high and apparent to the actors.

5. Watch for signs of growing stale and correct them quickly.

6. Work for more heightened characterization. Nuances of blocking and business are important to note also.

7. Spot rehearsals, when done, must be thoroughly pursued, going over a scene again and again until full realization, full climax, is achieved.

8. Use acting problems from workshop in spot rehearsals when needed.

9. If the full cast can meet only three times weekly, the director should be working *daily* in spot rehearsals.

10. Director should begin to build scenes one upon the other. Each scene has its own beginning and ending and its own climax. Every subsequent scene must be above the one before it—like a series of steps, each a bit higher than the last—as they build to the play's climax.

11. After the big climax, the subsequent scenes gentle off into the end of the play.

12. Work outdoors whenever possible during this period. The need to rise above the outdoor distractions seasons the actors.

13. Have actors rehearse barefooted and in shorts (climate permitting). You can then watch full body actions and tell quickly whether an actor is mouthing words or physicalizing the stage situation.

14. Listen to the actors as well as watching them. Turn away from the stage and concentrate on dialogue alone. Superficial readings, sloppy speech, etc., will then appear very quickly to the director's ear.

15. The director should not allow a sense of urgency to cause him to stop run-throughs. Just keep notes on action that can be gone over again when the single act or spots are done. Remember, there is plenty of time.

16. If actors seem to be working at odds with the director, he would do well to check the over-all theme. Is there one? Are the cast and director treading the same path?

17. Third acts have a way of taking care of themselves. Give most of the work and spot rehearsals to the first and second. If relationships and characters are well established, the third act will need only the resolving of the play.

18. Some scenes may have to be gone over dozens of times

to move them smoothly. Others may need very little work other than the regular rehearsals. Any scene that has special effects must not appear awkward in performance, even if it means hours of work.

Suggestions For The Third Rehearsal Section

This is the polishing period. The jewel has been cut and evaluated, and now it must be put into its setting. Discipline must be at its highest. Lateness to rehearsals and failure to read the call-board or check in with the stage manager must be sternly dealt with. The director is preparing his actors for a performance in which a late actor or a misplaced prop could throw the whole show.

The organization of back-stage work must begin as early as work on the stage; and the rules must be observed. In most little theaters, the technical crews are also composed of lay people. Prop men, sound men, and lighting men must all be just as attentive to time and responsibility as the actors; and their responsibility must be built up rehearsal after rehearsal. Any ten-year-old child can handle the light cues efficiently if respect is given to him and to the job at hand.

Spot Rehearsals

In the third rehearsal section, the director will find many fine points which have to be covered. By this time, the run-throughs should have a certain smoothness; the seasoning process has borne fruit; the characterizations exist. Can the director go further than this with non-professional actors? Are the problems of pace and timing and the finer distinctions of character beyond reach? Pace, timing, and finer character detail develop out of the essential life of a scene.

This is where the spot rehearsal is of inestimable value, for finding this reality often happens here. The director should schedule as many spot rehearsals as possible during this period. If his actors can only come individually three times a week, he can still schedule daily spot rehearsals.

The Director's Re-Evaluation

The director should now re-read his play in a quiet place, free from the tensions of the theater. By now the play will be more than a projection of his own ideal. He will be meeting the playwright again; and, like a doctor observing his patients' symptoms, he will probably see very clearly what has been a problem within his own show—and this while he still has time to work on it.

Re-reading will aid the director in holding the reality and theme, observing the action of the play, and discovering where it is going. He will see his actors in motion; and he will be able to see extra nuances of character that can be added, bits of business here and there, ways of strengthening the mood, building climax, etc. All of this will come rushing out of the script.

For the first time, perhaps, the director will be able to coordinate the confused images of rehearsal into a definite picture. He will visualize the stage in dimension and color and action. This will tend to relieve his own anxiety in much the same way that the Relaxed Rehearsal freed his actors. He will, in all probability, *see his show*.

Seeing The Show

"Seeing the show" is simply the director's insight into his production—the moment when he suddenly sees all the aspects integrated. There will suddenly be rhythm, pace, characterization, fluidity, and a definite unity to all of it. Many scenes will be rough, sets will be far from finished, costumes will still be in the "talking" stages, and a few actors will be moping around; but it will seem, on the whole, a unified piece of work.

The director may see this unified show for an instant and then not see it again for a number of rehearsals. But this is no cause for concern—it was there, and it will come again. He must now clean up rough spots, strengthen relationships, intensify involvement, and make alterations here and there.

Once the director has "seen his show," he must accept it even if he feels it should have been different. This is most important. There are few directors who are completely satisfied with their productions. To work with young people and unseasoned adults, the director must be aware of their capacities. If he is not satisfied with his production because of the limitation of his actors, he must nevertheless realize that at this stage of growth it is all he can expect from them. If there is integrity, playing, life, and joy in performance, it will be well worth viewing.

Stage Fright In The Director

If the director does not accept his show at this late date, he will intrude his own emotional problems on the actors. By now, he is getting stage fright. He is concerned with whether the audience will accept and like "his" presentation. This feeling must be hidden from his actors. The very process of doing a show has a great deal of natural excitement. If he adds his own feeling of hysteria to this, the actors will catch it from him. During this period, he may be short-tempered; and he should explain this to his actors, warning them that he may be gruff during the integration of the technical aspects. They will respond to him most sympathetically.

A director who worries his actors until the last minute, hoping to squeeze a little more out of them, will not help the play in any way. One way to prevent this stage fright is to give the production over to the technical aspects of the play in the last hours of rehearsal.

Makeup And The Actor

This is a good time to have character makeup sessions, especially if the play is fantasy which requires unusual makeup. Time spent on applying makeup and allowing actors to experiment with their own characters will aid their work on stage. Just as lines must come as a part of the actor himself, so must his makeup. It is far better that each actor develop his own makeup, with an assist from more experienced people, than to have it applied for him.

Whenever possible, encourage research on characters. During rehearsals for *The Clown Who Ran Away*, Bobby Kay, a clown from the Clyde Beatty Circus, came to the Young Actors Company to tell the cast about clowns and clown makeup. He so entranced the young actors with his stories of the traditions behind clown performances and the dignity with which each clown puts his mark upon his face that when the time came for them to create their own clown characters, not one of them made just a "funny face." Each struggled to place his "mark" upon his face with all the individuality of a real clown creating his own character.

It is advisable, after a session or two, to have each actor make a chart of his own makeup and keep it for reference. If makeup is handled as a developing factor in the total fabric of the theater experience, children as young as six can learn. (It was not an unusual sight at the Young Actors Company to see a seven-year-old helping a five-year-old to apply his makeup; although it was our guess that, at home, the seven-year-old couldn't even comb her hair properly.) Makeup, like a costume, must be worn easily and with conviction. It should not be used for the first time on the day of the opening performance.

Makeup should not totally mask the player, giving him a facade to hide behind. It should be recognized for what it is— an extension of his character, not the basis for it. Eliminating makeup, particularly with young actors playing older roles, can often provide a valuable experience for both actors and audience. This, of course, is particularly true for improvisational theater, where a hat or a scarf or a beard on a string is all the costume or makeup an actor ever wears as he changes from role to role.

This keeps the actors as "players." As such, they personally are always visible to the audience and so help create the "artistic detachment" essential to objective viewing and thus keep the audience "part of the game."

The Costume Parade

It is advisable to run the costume parade together with a make-up rehearsal. Briefly, the parade is just that: a grouping of the actors, completely dressed and made up, so that the director can see how they look under the lights. Changes can be made quickly, if necessary; and everything will be looked at for fit, comfort, etc. If there is no time for a costume parade alone, it may be combined with a rehearsal.

A costume parade can be tedious or fun, depending upon its organization. If possible, the director should schedule it at a time when his actors will be fresh and free from other commitments. It can help to make the last week a joyous, relaxed time, instead of an anxiety-ridden one. This time should not be squeezed in. The director may need a good number of hours to complete the dress parade, depending upon the type of play and the number in the cast.

The First Dress Rehearsal

There is an old theater superstition that "a bad dress rehearsal means a good performance." This is nothing more than an obvious attempt to keep everyone from becoming discouraged. A first dress rehearsal should be kept as free from tension and hysteria as possible, despite all the confusion which it will bring. It may, indeed, seem a bit lifeless; but this partial letdown is far better than a rehearsal in which chaos is come again.

Under no circumstances should the first dress rehearsal be stopped once the curtain has gone up. As with the run-throughs, the director should take notes as the acts progress and should have a meeting with the cast after each act to cover sight-lines, roughness, etc. He should only bring up those things which can be altered without disturbing past work.

If the director does not "have a show" at the first dress, he will not get one by overworking his actors during the last hours. He must have faith in himself and in his actors. The first dress rehearsal for any play is usually discouraging; but a second dress will follow—as well as the preview before an invited audience— to pull the show together.

The Special Run-Through

There are no "mistakes" on stage as far as the audience is concerned, for they do not know the script or the action of the play. And so, an actor need never let his audience know when he has gone astray. *The audience knows only what the actors show them.*

The special run-through puts the cast completely on their own. Developed for child actors, it works equally well with adults. It goes as follows:

At a regularly scheduled run-through of the play (just prior to dress rehearsal), tell the cast that in the event of a break of any kind (laughter, lost lines, etc.) by one of the actors, all— the *full cast*—must cover up and keep the scene going. If they fail to do so, they will have to go back to the beginning of the act. For instance, if an actor breaks at the very end of the second act and no one has covered for him, the director quietly calls: "Begin the second act, please!"; and the actors must go back over the ground they have just covered.

After a few "begin again's," the director will find his cast descending upon the culprit who made the break. If this should occur, remind them that all of them are equally responsible for keeping the play going and they must cover for their fellow actors in case of trouble.[6]

This is the fullest expression of the group experience at work.[7] It puts a severe discipline upon the individual player, since he is now directly responsible to the group (the play). At the same time, it gives him a deep sense of security; for he knows that no matter what happens on stage, and in whatever crises or danger he finds himself, the group will come to his aid for the sake of the play.[8]

The special run-through is very exciting for the actors and keeps them all on their toes, alerted for that moment when it may become necessary for them to cover up for a fellow player. After one or two such rehearsals, the show will go on even if the very roof should fall in.

---

[6]See also the remarks on self-blocking, p. 156.

[7]The intent of the director is not to harass or punish. He is simply functioning as part of the group. This is the last salient point—the special run-through cuts the actors *away* from the director, and they are in truth "on their own."

[8]Constant adaptability and resourcefulness are of course basic to improvisational theater, and so the special run-through is never needed prior to performance.

The Performance

The audience is the last spoke which completes the wheel, and its relation not only to the play but to the playing is most important. The performance is certainly not the end of the line. It brings the whole creative process of doing a play to its fruition; and the audience must be involved in this process.

No one can use an audience for self-glorification or exhibitionistic reasons. If this is done, everything the director and actors have worked for will be destroyed. If, on the other hand, the whole concept of sharing with the audience is understood, the actors will have exciting performances. They will get the feel and rhythm of the audience, just as the audience gets the feel and the rhythm of the actors and the production. The mark of the fine actor is this response to audience. That is why it is desirable to give as many performances as possible—to allow this response to be developed in the actors.

Freedom and creativity must never go beyond the limitations imposed by the play itself. Laughter from the audience often causes an actor to lose his head (and his focus). This distorts his relation to the whole, as he works each performance for himself to achieve the laughter again. He is the actor working only for applause, for personal gratification; and if this persists, then the director has somehow failed with him.

It is difficult to state all the problems which will arise during performance. Often the director is forced to work with insufficiently trained actors or with people who hold fast to preconceived ideas of what an actor's role should be. The director's own experience and temperament will have to be allowed for. He must remember to strive for audience appreciation of the play as a whole and not of just one or two of the actors or the set or the lighting. The audience's response to the production can help the director to evaluate his work.

Random Pointers

1. Stay away from the back-stage area during the show. Everything should be so well organized that it will run smoothly. Messages can always be sent back stage, if necessary.

2. Be certain that costumes are always well buttoned and sitting right. A runner who is worried about whether his shorts will hold up is not free to run.

3. Be easy and pleasant around the cast if you should drop into the dressing rooms.

4. Have one run-through between performances if possible—unless they are nightly. If this is not possible, a short talk after each performance will help to eliminate the few bits of roughness or sloppiness that may be appearing here and there.

5. A short pickup talk prior to performances may be necessary from time to time.

6. Rehearsals during the run of the show help actors keep focus on the problems in the play and keep them from getting lazy and generalizing. They also bring greater clarification of random flaws and more intensification of what already exists.

7. Actors should learn to allow the audience full laughter. Begin to train early with the simple rule of allowing laughter to reach its peak and then quieting it by a movement before beginning the next speech.

8. Back-stage discipline must be observed strictly at all times.

9. The actors will grow in stature during the performances if all factors allow them to do so. The stage is the X-ray picture, where everything structural shows up. If the play is presented shabbily, if its "bones" are weak, this will be seen, just as any alien objects show up in the X-ray. False and dishonest characterizations and relationships come through. This can be understood and stressed for the actors whenever necessary.[9]

10. Working through the rehearsal plan outlined in this chapter may not produce a fully seasoned actor in his first show, but he will be well on his way.

11. If, toward the end of the run, the actors decide to "cut up," remind them that their last performance is the audience's first. Enjoyment must come from the performing itself, not from cheap tricks on fellow actors.

---

[9]In improvisational theater this point would relate to scene structure as well. If a scene is structured simply for making jokes and imposing cleverness upon an audience, this would be clearly X-rayed.

XVIII. Post-Mortem and Special Problems

Every play and every group is different and has individual problems peculiar to it; but the need for growth and creative expression must be recognized in all. Remember that the techniques needed to rehearse the play have grown out of the acting workshops.

Recognize *growth* as against forcing, *organic* direction as against mechanical direction. Remember that mechanics are mere devices and that while snapping the finger to achieve a fast cue may work, using shadowing, tossing a ball, etc., will give organic response to picking up cues.

The Time Chart For Rehearsals

The following chart outlines the plan that was followed most successfully by the author over her career in working with unseasoned actors. It has produced remarkable results, but of course it may be modified as the individual director sees fit.

Time Chart for First Rehearsal Section

DIRECTION	PURPOSE
Children begin here. Tell story of play. Gibberish. Give stage set in mind.	Helps cast. Orients actor to stage locale. Early work on relationships.
Reading of play aloud by director, then casting. Or casting and then reading play aloud.	
More gibberish. Add Where with blackboards of stage locale. Characters as cast.	Familiarizes actors with stage space.
Adults begin here after casting.	Thinking on cluttered stage pictures started.
Sit-down reading, stopping for pronunciation, typographical errors on sides.	Eases into use of sides and familiarizes with content.
Second sit-down reading.	
(a) Reading POC on seeing the word: vowels, consonants.	(a) Brings words into dimension.
(b) Concentrate on color, other actors, weather.	(b) Helps understanding of words.
(c) Concentrate on visualizing stage set.	(c) Relates spoken words to stage environment.
Walk-through with sides, first act. General stage-plan given.	Non-directional blocking—general blocking may be added if necessary, setting reality.
(a) SPECIALIZED WHERE	(a) Gives flexibility in use of set, especially in fantasy.
(b) Walk-through with sides, second and third acts.	(b) Non-directional blocking—director keeps notes of business which emerges.
(a) EXTENDED MOVEMENT following movement neces-	(a) For business, ease of movement (unusual blocking

sary to play. Singing dialogue, use of games.

comes up). Develops char-
acter, pace, timing, and total
group action.

(b) Walk-through with sides
(actors almost off lines)

(b) Keep as much of the new
action that comes up as
possible.

(a) Walk-through three acts.

(b) Stop to clarify relationship,
when necessary.

The first step in giving the
player a sense of the unity of
the full performance.

CONTACT

Sides now taken home for *difficult* readings only.

Forces player to see another
and strengthens relationships,
and extra stage business
emerges.

Shows how to use the techniques of the Relaxed Re-
hearsal while reading at home.

(a) BLIND (actors off lines)

(a) Develops "sixth" sense, timing, strengthens stage environment and places actor
solidly within it by giving
space substance.

(b) Sit-down reading. Concentrate on the words.

(b) Cleans up speech with no
danger of rigidity.

(c) Concentrate on action cues.

(c) Picks up cues.

(d) Extended sound.

(d) Develops organic voice projection.

(a) Calling over long
(Where) distances

(b) Rehearse outdoors if
possible

(c) Director moves a far
distance from stage,
calling "share voices!"
when necessary.

(d) Singing dialogue.

EXPLORE AND HEIGHTEN (transformation of the beat) should be used throughout all rehearsal sections. It fosters exploration of content and relationship.

Time Chart For Second Rehearsal Section

DIRECTION	PURPOSE
Relaxed Rehearsal	Removes anxieties. Helps actors visualize the total stage movement and environment, (including himself).
	Shows dialogue to be an organic part of play.
Complete non-stop run-through once a week from here on. Wear different costume parts. No interruptions (keep notes).	Continuity of play established. Speeds seasoning process.
(a) Rehearsals of individual acts. Stop and start.	(a) Heightens all facets of play.
(b) Stage movement—*did you integrate that?*	(b) Gives direction for action.
(a) Improvisations around problems (conflict) in play.	Strengthens individual characterization and group relationships; helpful in mass scenes.
(b) Improvisations away from the play. WHAT'S BEYOND?	Bring life and group agreement to on stage scenes.
Gibberish Spot rehearsals	Freshens meaning of, and action behind, words. Creates new stage business.
NO MOTION.	Excites new energy from deeper sources.
Wearing costume parts, handling difficult props; check biographies. Barefoot rehearsals.	Gives further clues to help actor with character.

Acting problems based on situations in the play—reverse parts.	Helps develop insight into characters, play as a whole.
Spot rehearsals on business. Whenever show has difficult scenes, try them in a different way; play games, use space exercises.	Removes awkwardness, smoothes way for complex business. Gives new insights.

Time Chart For Third Rehearsal Section

DIRECTION	PURPOSE
Director re-reads play. Complete non-stop run-throughs more often. Makeup rehearsals.	Implements seasoning and learning process. Gives flow to play.
(a) Stop and start rehearsals of individual acts. Bring in interesting set-pieces.	(a) Heightens all aspects of play.
(b) SHADOWING. EXITS AND ENTRANCES. BEGIN AND END.	(b) Helps physicalizing, gives extra inspiration, creates extra stage business and heightens stage energy.
(c) Work on picking up cues, heightening speech and reactions.	(c) Pace and timing strengthened.
Spot rehearsals. Stage movement.	Gives actor insight into his role. Heightens moments in playing. Supportive.
Special run-through.	Group functions as one unit; Actors will meet every crisis during performances—will be able to assist each other.
Last week of rehearsal. Technical run-through, costume parade, makeup rehearsal.	Integrates technical aspects of production.

First Dress Rehearsal.	Integrates complete show.
Second Dress Rehearsal.	
Preview Performance.	Working for response with sympathetic audience.
Day of rest.	Relieves tensions of final week.
First Public Performance.	Full creative expression.

Directing The Child Actor[1]

Most of the non-authoritarian techniques for training the actor and directing him for performance used in this handbook were originally developed for the sole purpose of retaining the joy of playing for children from six to sixteen at the moment of dedicating them to service in a great art form. Our boys and girls can learn to be players on stage and not exhibitionists. A great and overwhelming love for the theater can be instilled in them so that their performances have reality, exuberance, and a vitality that is exciting and refreshing to behold.

Children can and should be players in plays for children. The average viewer, unfortunately, has a deplorably low standard for child performers, and a clever imitation of adult clichés, blatant exhibitionism, or cuteness is often called talent. There is no need or excuse for distorting the child by imitation of the adult, nor, in trying to avoid this problem, is it necessary to limit his theater experience to dressed up dramatic-play.

A twelve-year-old may not be able to play a villain with the same psychological insight of an adult, nor would it be in good taste for him to do so. However, he can keep the rhythm and line of his character and give it his full energy. Like the adult, he can develop the ability to select a few physical characteristics which he heightens in his role and brings sharply to the attention of the audience (see Chapter XII).[2]

Naturally there are plays with adult characters that are inap-

---

[1]See also Chapters XIII–XV.
[2]By changing the word "child" to "non-professional actor" and the word "adult" to "professional actor" in the context of the foregoing paragraphs, we can see that this same problem exists for the older lay actor as well.

propriate for child actors, and such roles could well be distorting to the child. But, this same child can play adult characters that many fanciful plays call for.

As far as back-stage work is concerned, an eleven-year-old prop man can check his list like an adult. A twelve-year-old can follow a cue sheet and handle as many light cues as the play demands. The assistant stage manager (the stage manager should be an adult) can perform duties and exact discipline from actors who will respect his role.

For ten years, the Young Actors Company in Los Angeles, using no one but child actors from six to sixteen, played to city-wide audiences and received constant review on the drama pages of the metropolitan newspapers. The young actors were respected for the quality of their work and for the refreshment received by the audience from their plays. As actors, children can be as exciting and refreshing to view as adults, and they can learn to meet every crisis as it arises. At the Young Actors Company, and later at the Playmakers in Chicago, the ability to step into anothers's role (as a result of improvisational training) with little or no rehearsal was such that rarely indeed were there understudies for any part. Any message sent back stage, whether it was to get something off stage or to end a scene (improvisational theater), was handled effortlessly and ingeniously by the young actors within the action of the play.

One of the most difficult problems in rehearsing a show with children is adult regulation of his life. A child cannot give all his time and attention to the activity. He can rarely, for instance, say *definitely* that he will be at rehearsal, since his mother may decide he must be somewhere else. He cannot be kept overtime, since the average child has an extremely active program of school, homework, sports, music lessons, and home chores.

A few extra reminders when working on a play with children up to fifteen years old:

1. Do not be the "teacher" in the theater-situation. There is only the director and the actors.

2. Always have an adult back stage to be in charge; this is usually an assistant or stage manager. Neither parents nor the director himself are ever allowed back stage during performance.

At the Young Actors Company, there were always the strictest orders to keep the director out of back stage during the show. And the boys and girls knew they were allowed to enforce it.

3. For the children as well as the adults, have a call-board which they are to use.

4. All back-stage organization mentioned in this chapter is suitable for children.

5. All recommended rehearsal suggestions are to be followed by children as well as adults.

6. If children come to the theater after school, be certain there is some food for them. An energy drop often results just from being hungry.

7. Remind children repeatedly that "an audience does not know what the play is about" and thus that any mishaps can be turned into part of the play.

Removing Amateur Qualities

Many of us have sat through shows cast with children or non-professional adults where, aside from an occasional glimmering of natural charm or a moment of spontaneity, there was little or nothing to redeem the performance. The actors might, indeed, have been "expressing themselves," but they were doing so at the expense of the audience and the theater reality.

This section sets down some of the so-called "amateurish" qualities in young and inexperienced actors. It does so not only to aid the director in recognizing them but also to show him their causes and refer him to the exercises which will help free his actors from crippling limitations.

The Amateur Actor

1. Has intense stage fright.
2. Does not know what to do with his hands.
3. Has awkward stage movement—shifts back and forth, moves aimlessly about stage.
4. Feels he must sit down on stage.
5. Reads lines stiffly, mechanically; forgets lines.

6. Has poor enunciation, rushes his speeches.
7. Usually repeats a line he has misread.
8. Mouthes the words of his fellow actors as they are playing.
9. Creates no theater "business."
10. Has no sense of timing.
11. Drops cues, is insensitive to pace.
12. Wears his costume awkwardly; makeup has a stuck-on look.
13. "Emotes" his lines rather than talks to his fellow actors.
14. Is exhibitionistic.
15. Has no feeling for characterization.
16. "Breaks" on stage.
17. Has a fear of touching others.
18. Does not project his voice or his emotions.
19. Cannot take direction.
20. Has slight relationships to other actors or the play.
21. Hangs on to furniture or props.
22. Becomes his own audience.
23. Never listens to other actors.
24. Has no relationship to the audience.
25. Casts eyes downward (does not look at fellow players).

This is a horrendous list, but the majority of child and adult lay actors possess at least ten, if not more, of these characteristics.

Causes and Cures

1. Stage fright is fear of judgment. The actor is afraid of criticism, of being ridiculous, of forgetting his lines, etc. When it occurs in a trained actor, it is usually the result of rigid authoritarian training. It can be overcome by a dynamic understanding of the phrases "share with the audience" and "showing, not telling."

2. Most immature actors use only the mouth and hands. When students learn to act with the whole body (physicalize) the problem of what to do with the hands disappears. In fact, it will never arise after student-actors understand the idea of the Point of Concentration, for they will always have a strong objective focus while on stage.

3. Awkward stage movement is usually the result of imposed stage direction. When the actor is trying to remember instead of allowing stage movement to evolve out of the stage reality, he cannot help but move awkwardly. Any object-involvement exercise will help here.

4. The immature actor feels he must sit down on stage, or he shifts from foot to foot because he is trying to "hide" from the audience. He lacks focus and therefore motivation for being where he is. WHERE WITH OBSTACLES will help here (p. 104).

5. Mechanical reading is the result of not creating reality. Recitation of the words has become more important to the actor than an understanding of their meaning and relationships. They have remained "words" instead of "dialogue." See dialogue (p. 378); seeing the word (p. 232); gibberish (p. 120); Relaxed Rehearsal (p. 336); and VERBALIZING THE WHERE (p. 128).

6. Poor enunciation and rushed speeches usually result from a lack of understanding on the actor's part that the audience is an integral element of theater. Poor enunciation also stems from the same source as mechanical reading. In the event that a real physical defect exists in the actor's speech, therapeutic exercises may be necessary. Otherwise see the exercises in Chapter VIII.

7. Lines misread and then repeated word for word are examples of rote memorization taking its deadly toll of spontaneity. Training by rote is also the cause of many other amateurish qualities. Meeting a crisis on stage should become second nature to even the youngest actor. Through training, he can learn to improvise through any problem of lost or misread dialogue (see Chapter I).

8. Mouthing of each other's words is caused by premature memorization and often by allowing young actors to take scripts home, where they memorize everything on the page.

9. The ability to create interesting stage business and blocking can come only from a real understanding of group relationships and involvement (see Chapter VI).

10. The sense of theater timing can be taught. Timing is recognition of others in the theater reality.

11. Dropped cues and failure to sense pace (like timing) occur when an actor is insensitive to his audience and fellow actors. *All exercises are geared to develop this sensitivity.*

12. The awkward appearance of an actor in his costume and makeup may result from his failure to comprehend all the elements of the play (set theme, fellow actors, relationships, etc.) as an integral whole. Or he may have been given difficult costuming too late in the rehearsal period.

13. Declamatory acting or "emoting" results from isolation and using stage subjectively. It is egocentric and exhibitionistic, for the actor is unable to relate the words to his fellow actors and thus to the inner feelings which have caused them (see Chapter XI).

14. The exhibitionist, the "cute" child, the "ham"—these types result from approval/disapproval orientation and thus lack a sense of self. (See Chapter I).

15. Everyone has a natural feeling for characterization in varying degrees (see Chapter XII).

16. When actors "break" or fall out of character on stage, they have lost sight of the internal relationships of the play and their Point of Concentration as well.

17. This is resistance and fear of involvement. CONTACT and GIVE AND TAKE exercises do specifically what growing security in the training will do naturally (see pp. 184, 230).

18. Inadequate projection is caused by fear or neglect of the audience as fellow players.

19. The inability to take direction often stems from a lack of objectivity or inadequate communication between actor and director. The actor may not be free enough yet to meet his responsibility to the group. TELEVISION EXERCISE (p. 202) gives the student a look-in at the director's problems.

20. The actor with little or no relationship to his fellow actors and the play stands on the ground floor of theater training. Playing games and using all the acting exercises of group involvement should help.

21. When the actor moves hesitantly about his stage, clinging from chair to chair, or moves aimlessly about the stage, he is showing fear of being exposed to the audience, the central problem of non-professional theater. Stressing exercises of group interaction and sharing with the audience will help.

22. When actors move outside the play and become audience,

they are seeking approval. Their Point of Concentration is on themselves.

23. Failure to listen to other actors is a vital problem. It means the whole skein of stage relationships has been broken or never understood. BLIND (p. 171) is an especially valuable exercise specifically devoted to eliminating non-listening.

24. An audience's response comes to the seasoned actor (see p. 158). Be aware that the phrase "share with the audience" is the first and most important step.

25. The actor pulls everything into his immediate environment and makes his world the size of a postage stamp. The exercises WHAT'S BEYOND? (p. 102), SPACE SUBSTANCE (p. 81), CALLING FROM A LONG DISTANCE (p. 194), and EXTENDED MOVEMENT should help break his fear of moving out into the larger environment. CONTACT and EYE CONTACT will alleviate fear of looking at another player (p. 171).

The exercises in this book are not uniformly scaled to eliminate *single* problems. The exercises are cumulative and if used *simultaneously* will solve the above problems almost before they arise. In a short while students will all function organically, and when this occurs, the skills, techniques, and spontaneity needed in the theater will fast and forever *become their own.*

Definition of Terms

Definition of Terms

Teaching is necessarily repetitious, so as to make the material the students' own. The following terms are defined with this in mind in the hope that they will act as a further teaching tool. If they seem over-defined, it is because they attempt to fit as many readers' frames of reference as possible, so as to spark insights and thus clarify the intent of theater games.

ACT: To make something happen; to move out into the environment; to act upon.

ACTING: Avoiding (resisting) POC by hiding behind a character; subjective manipulation of the art form; using character or emotion to avoid contact with the theater reality; mirroring one's self; a wall between players.

ACTING PROBLEM: Solving the POC; a problem when solved results in an organic knowledge of the theater technique; a problem which prefigures a result; developing theater techniques; theater games.

ACTION: The energy released in working a problem; the play between actors; playing.

ACTIVITY: Movement on stage.

AD-LIB: Not to be confused with improvisation; ad-lib is individual cleverness, not evolved dialogue.

ADVANCED STUDENT: A player who involves himself in the POC and lets it work for him; a player who accepts the rules of the game and works to solve the problem; a player who keeps the agreed reality alive; one who plays.

ASSUMPTION: Not communicating; letting fellow actors or audience detail a generality; letting others do actor's work; filling in for another player; *Show what you mean! Say what you mean!*

AUDIENCE (INDIVIDUALS): Our guests; the most revered members of the theater; part of the game, not the "lonely looker-inners"; a most important part of theater.

AUTHORITARIANISM: Imposing one's own experiences, frames of reference, and behavior patterns upon another; denial of self-experience to another.

AWARENESS: Sensory involvement with the environment; moving out into the environment.

BEAT: A measure; the time between crises; a series of scenes within a scene; can be one moment or ten minutes; "begin and end."

BECOMING AUDIENCE: Tendency of an actor to lose his objective reality and begin to judge himself as he plays a scene; looking out to audience to see if they "like" his work; watching fellow actors instead of participating in scene; watching one's self.

BELIEVING: Something personal to the actor and not necessary to creating stage reality.

BIOGRAPHIES: Information, statistics, background, etc. written about a character in a play so as to place him in given categories to assist the actor in playing a role; sometimes useful in formal theater to help the director to gain insight into his actors; should be avoided in improvisational theater, for it prevents spontaneous selection of material and keeps players from an intuitive experience; "No biographies!"

BLOCKING: Integration of the players, set pieces, sound and light for the stage picture; clarity of movement for the communication; emphasizing character relationship; physicalizing stage life.

BREAKTHROUGH: The point at which a student's spontaneity arises to meet a crisis on stage; the moment of "letting go" resistances and static frames of reference; a moment of seeing things from a different point of view; a moment of insight into the POC; trusting the scheme; the moment of growth.

BODILY AWARENESS: Total physical attentiveness to what is happening on stage and in the audience; skill in using all parts of the body (doors can be shut with feet, and a hip can move an object); physicalizing.

BODY MEMORY: Memory retained in the body at the point of past experiences; physical memory as opposed to mind or intellectual retention of past experience; sensory retention of past experiences; muscular attitudes; "Let your body remember!"

CHARACTER: People; human beings; real people; the physical expression of a person; speaks for himself.

CHARACTER AGILITY: The ability to spontaneously select physical qualities of a chosen character while improvising; ability to use image, color, sound, mood, etc. to locate character qualities.

CHARACTERIZATION: Selecting certain physical mannerisms, tones of voice, rhythm, etc. in order to play a specific character or type of character; giving life to the character through the stage reality.

COMMUNICATION: Experiencing; the skill of the player in sharing his stage reality so the audience can understand; direct experience as opposed to interpretation or assumption.

CONFLICT: A tug-of-war with one's self or between players calling for some decision; persuasion or goal to be reached; lack of agreement; a device for generating stage energy; an imposed tension and release as opposed to problem (organic).

CONTACT: Sensory impact; physical and visual involvement with the theater environment (Where, Who, audience, etc.);

to touch, see, smell, hear, and look; to know what you touch; communication.

COSTUME PIECES: Partial costume bits which can be used in creating character; character costume suggestions as opposed to full-dress costumes (a box full of hats).

CREATION: Create (limited) plus intuit (unlimited) equals creation.

CRISIS: A heightened moment ready to change form; theater (playing) is a series of crises; alternative; the peak or breaking point of a static moment or situation where many eventualities are possible; a moment of tension in which the outcome is unknown; the player must be primed to meet any change, simple or extraordinary, the crisis may bring.

DETAIL: Every object, minute or massive, animate or inanimate, that exists within the stage environment.

DETACHMENT: Necessary for the stage to prevent "acting"; ability to relate objectively to avoid "emoting"; relationship free of emotional involvement; artistic detachment makes "playing" for both actors and audience possible; keeps everyone "part of the game"; to become aware of the life of the object; ability to become aware of the life in the environment; functioning within the group without being swallowed up by it; for the sake of greater stage involvement; "Get lost!"

DIAGNOSIS: The teacher-director's skill in finding out what problems are needed to solve problems.

DIALOGUE: Words actors use in talking to one another to implement and build the reality they have created on stage; a vocalization of the physical expression of the scene; verbal extension of the involvement and relationship between players; verbalization growing organically out of the life of a scene.

DIGNITY: Being one's self at any age; the acceptance of a person without trying to alter him; sense of self not to be violated by "acting."

DRAMATIC PLAY: Acting out and/or living through old (or

someone else's) real life situations to find out how to fit within them; common play among nursery school children attempting to become that which they fear, or admire, or don't understand; Dramatic play continued into adult life results in daydreams, wishful thinking, identifying with characters in film, stage and literature; acting out old material as opposed to a fresh experience; living the character; can be used as a simplified form of psycho-drama; not usable for the stage.

EGOCENTRIC: Fear of no support from others or from the environment; mistaken self-protection.

EMOTE: Imposing self on audience; role-playing instead of playing a role.

EMOTION: Organic motion created by the playing; subjective emotion carried to the stage is not communication.

ENERGY: Level of intensity with which one approaches the problem; the inspiration released when a problem is solved; the power held bound in resistance to solving a problem; the power released in "explosion" (spontaneity); diagnostic action; the result of process (playing); contact.

ENVIRONMENT: The conditioned stage life agreed upon by members of the group; all the animate and inanimate objects within the theater, including self and the audience; an explorable place.

EQUALITY: Not to be confused with sameness; the right of everyone of any age or background to become part of the theater community, enter into its activities, view its problems, work on them; the right to gain knowledge; the right to knock on any door.

EVALUATION: Method of criticism through involvement with the problem rather than each other.

EXPOSURE: Seeing or being seen directly, not as others would like you or themselves to be.

FEELING: Private to the actor; not for public viewing; feeling between players on stage must become the object between them; belongs to sensory equipment.

FLOORPLAN: A drawing or a plan (on paper or on a black-board) of the structure for an acting-problem Where (the objects), Who (the actors), What (the activity), POC (the problem; a layout of the Where agreed upon and drawn up by a group of players; the "field" upon which the "game" will be played; a map of the territory the players must enter into and explore; groundplan.

FOCUS: Directing and concentrating attention on a specific person, object, or event within the stage reality; to frame a person, object, or event on stage; it is the anchor (the static) which makes movement possible.

FRAME OF REFERENCE: A referral point on which judgments are made; a referral point from which one views the world; a reference conditioned (framed) by cultural, familial, and educational patterns.

GAME: An accepted group activity which is limited by rules and group agreement; fun, spontaneity, enthusiasm, and joy accompany games; parallels the theater experience; a set of rules that keeps a player playing.

GENERALIZATION: An assumption which keeps the actor from detailed selectivity; lumping many things together under one heading or description; putting everything in the same basket; occluded sensory perception; refusal to give "life to the object"; assuming others know what you are trying to communicate; the cliché comes out of a generalization.

GIBBERISH: Meaningless sounds substituted for recognizable words so as to force the players to communicate by physical-izing (showing); an acting exercise.

GOOD TASTE: Allowing something its own character without imposing anything alien upon it; adding nothing to detract from itself; a sense of the inherent nature of an object, scene, or character; it is one's recognition of the nature of something; good taste can never be aped; good taste will never offend, but "not being offensive" does not necessarily mean that one has good taste.

GROUP: A community of interests; individuals freely gathering around a project to explore, build, use, or alter it.

GROUP AGREEMENT: Group decision; agreed reality between players; agreed reality between players and audience; acceptance of the rules of the game; group agreement on POC; cannot "play" without group agreement; breaks tie to teacher-director.

HEIGHTENING: Intensifying a relationship, a character, or a scene on stage; creating a high level of reality; giving a greater dimension to life reality; underlining life; enlargement of character or event for clarity in communicating to audience; to make a point through heightening; using anything or everything (acting, technical, or verbal) to make an impact.

HOW: Pre-planning How keeps the intuitive from working by plotting of a situation as opposed to meeting whatever comes up at the moment of playing; preparing one's self for every move as opposed to waiting to see what will happen; fear of venturing out into the unknown; giving examples of ways of solving the problem; performing.

ILLUSION: The theater is not illusion, it is a reality agreed upon by the group and understood by the audience; subjective projection.

IMAGINATION: Subjective; inventive; creating one's own ideas of how things should be; playing in the theater requires *group* creation as opposed to individually creating one's own idea of how things should be; belonging to the intellect as opposed to coming from the intuitive.

IMPROVISATION: Playing the game; setting out to solve a problem with no preconception as to how you will do it; permitting everything in the environment (animate or inanimate) to work for you in solving the problem; it is not the scene, it is the way to the scene; a predominate function of the intuitive; playing the game brings opportunity to learn theater to a cross-section of people; "playing it by ear"; process as opposed to result; not ad-lib or "originality" or "making it up by yourself"; a form, if understood, possible to any age group;

setting object in motion between players as in a game; solving of problems together; the ability to allow the acting problem to evolve the scene; a moment in the lives of people without needing a plot or story line for the communication; an art form; transformation; brings forth details and relationships as organic whole; living process.

IMPROVISED PLAY: A scene or play developed from improvisation used for performance; group-created material; a scene or play developed from situation or scenario; play or scene evolving out of the group playing; not a "story conference."

INNER ACTION: Recognizing an emotion through sensory response; use of inner action allows player the privacy of his personal feelings (emotion); using emotion as an object; "Physicalize that feeling!"

INSIGHT: A moment of revelation; seeing that which was there all the time; knowing:
> The tree was a tree
> Before you could see
> The tree.

INSPIRATION: Energy fortified with intuitive knowledge.

INTELLECT: The computer, collector of information, facts statistics, data of all kinds; should not function separately; part of an organic whole.

INTERPRETATION: Giving one's frame of reference as opposed to directly relating to events; adding or subtracting from a direct communication; might cause inability to meet a fresh moment of experience.

INTRUDING: Telling how to solve the problem; showing actors how to walk, talk, emote, feel, and read lines; meddling; inability to "play."

INTUITIVE: An area to be prodded and investigated by everyone; unhampered knowledge beyond the sensory equipment (physical and mental); the area of revelation.

INVENT: Rearrangement of known phenomena limited by personal reality; from the intellect; solo playing.

INVOLVEMENT: Complete absorption with the agreed object (not the other actors) as determined by the POC; earnestly entering into the game or exercise; playing; involvement is discipline; involvement with object creates release and freedom to relate; reflection and absorption.

JUDGMENT: Subjective placement of good/bad, right/wrong based on old frames of reference, cultural or family patterns (personal) rather than a fresh response to a moment of experiencing; imposition.

LABELS: Terms which tend to obscure their origin and block organic knowledge; the use of labels limits one to "things" and categories and neglects relationships.

LEARNED RESPONSE: A reaction rather than an action; keeps players from moving out into the environment; keeps players from exploration and self-discovery; "That's no way to do it!" "Why?" "My teacher said so!"; a shut door.

LEARNING: The capacity for experiencing.

MANIPULATION: Using problem, fellow actors, etc. for egocentric purposes; being opportunistic; manifests itself by resisting relating to fellow players.

MIND: Flows through the physical brain.

MULTIPLE STIMULI: The many things coming out of the environment at the player which he must be aware of and act upon; many-handedness; the Where, scene development, sharing with the audience, etc., that the player must act upon simultaneously as a juggler.

NO MOTION: A series of stills (steps) that create movement; an exercise in which movement is broken down into held parts and then reassembled back into movement; an exercise which shows students that since present movement includes past time, they need not dwell on the past; can be used to heighten time; gives insight into compulsive action; helps student to see his present (on stage) environment and make contact with himself within it.

NON-ACTING: Involving one's self with the POC; detachment; a workmanlike approach to the problems of the theater; keeping one's personal feelings private; learning to act through "non-acting"; showing not telling; "Stop acting!"

NON-DIRECTIONAL BLOCKING: Sharing the stage picture; self-blocking without outside direction; developing the skill to see the stage (outward) picture while inside it; group assistance from fellow players in blocking; necessary technique for the actor in improvisational theater; player's skill in evolving stage movement from the progressing scene; a way to self-identity; helps break dependency on teacher-director.

NON-VERBAL: Teaching without lectures on techniques for the actor; language used only to present and clarify or evaluate a problem; not telling the student How to solve a problem; not "spelling it out"; breaks dependency on the teacher-director; non-verbal system of teaching as used in this handbook; another form of communication between players.

OBJECT: Object and POC may be used interchangeably; sets the actor in motion; used for playing, as a ball, between players; involvement with object makes relationship between players possible; mutual focus on an outside reality (the rope between players); a technique to keep actors from subjective response; meditation; a mutual problem allowing freedom of personal expression in solving it; the springboard into the intuitive; the physicalization of an agreed object, feeling, or event out of which a scene evolves.

OBJECTIVE: Anything outside a person; to be objective; the ability to allow an outside phenomenon its own character and life; not changing what is to suit subjective assumptions; being objective is basic to improvisational theater.

OBJECTIVE REALITY: That which can be seen and used between players; created by group agreement; a means of sharing our humanness; a changing theater reality that springs from group agreement.

OCCUPATION: The stage activity; that which is created by the actors and visible to the audience; that which the audience shares with the audience; the What.

ORGANIC: A head-to-foot response where mind (intellect), body, and intuition function as one unit; in one piece; part of everything, of itself; out of itself; functioning out of total humanness.

PANTOMIME: An art form related to the dance; not to be confused with "silent scenes" or a "scene without words."

PERCEPTION: Knowing without use of the intellect alone; osmosis; awareness of outside phenomena; ability to reach out into the environment; to become the object; intuition; X-area.

PERFORMANCE: Not to be confused with exhibitionism; letting go; a moment of surrender creating harmony and refreshment; a moment of personal freedom with no ties to the past or future.

PERSONAL FREEDOM: One's own nature; not mirroring others; an expression of self free of authoritarian (approval/disapproval) needs; freedom to accept or reject rules of the game; recognition of limitation and freedom to reject or accept it; not to be confused with license; freedom from emotionalism; a moment of reality in which one has a part in the construction; freedom from survival clothes; a private matter.

PERSPECTIVE: Looking into; an objective view; detachment; the long view.

PHYSICALIZATION: Showing and not telling; a physical manifestation of a communication; a physical expression of an attitude; using self to put an object in motion; giving life to the object; "Physicalize that feeling! Physicalize that relationship! Physicalize that pinball machine, kite, fish, object, taste, etc.!" "acting out" is telling, while physicalizing is showing; a visible means of making a subjective communication.

PLAYER: One who plays; person skilled in creating the theatrical reality; pulling rabbits out of a hat; one who plays objects as opposed to playing self; an actor; a non-acting actor.

PLAYING: Fun, enjoyment, enthusiasm, trust; heightening the object; moving relations with fellow players; involvement with the POC; playing generates energy from out-going (objective); the physical expression of the life force; a term usable instead of rehearsal in improvisational theater. "Let's play!"

PLAYING A ROLE: Playing as in a game; playing a role and not subjective playing of self; sharing a characterization and not using a character for emotional outbursts; keeping self-identity.

PLAYWRITING: Manipulation of situation and fellow actors; an unwillingness to believe that a scene will evolve out of the group playing; not understanding the POC; deliberately using old action, dialogue, information, and facts (ad-libbing) instead of spontaneous selection during improvisation; not usable in improvisational theater; "Stop playwriting!"

POINT OF CONCENTRATION: A chosen agreed object (or event) on which to focus; a technique to achieve detachment; the object around which the players gather; involvement with the POC brings relationships; "trust the POC!" a vehicle that transports the player; it opens the student-audience to receive the communication; preoccupation.

PREOCCUPATION: The energy source; that which is not visible to the audience; by creating two-way problems, eliminates "watcher" and thus makes playing possible.

PRE-PLANNING: Planning how to work a scene as opposed to "just letting it happen"; related to "playwriting"; a mental rehearsal; "the uncertain child"; pre-planning is to be used only for structure.

PRETEND: Substitution for reality; subjective as opposed to real (objective); "If you pretend, it isn't real"; imposing self on a problem as opposed to creating reality; thinking about an object's reality instead of giving it reality; improvisational theater grows out of objective reality; not accepting *any* reality.

PROBLEM: Not to be confused with conflict (an imposed tension and release); a natural tension and release resulting in organic (dramatic) action.

PROBLEM-SOLVING: A system of teaching acting techniques

through solving of problems as opposed to intellectualizing and verbalizing use of material; puts student-actor into action (physicalizes); problem prefigures a result; teacher-director and student-actor can establish relationship through problem as opposed to involvement with each other; within solving the problem is How to play; does away with pre-planning; presents a simple operational structure (as in a game), so that anyone of any age or background can play.

PROCESS: The doing; process is goal, and goal is endless process; there can be no final statement on a character, relationship, scene, system of work.

PSYCHO-DRAMA: Putting one's own emotion into play to create action; living story instead of "in process."

REACT: Withdrawal; self-protection; response to another's act as opposed to self-acting; attacking to avoid changing position; making thrust into the environment instead of moving out into it; fear of acting; fear of taking responsibility for an action.

RECALL: Subjective memory (dead); deliberately bringing back a personal, private, past life experience to get an emotional or character quality; confused by many with acting; to use past experience, deliberately evoked for a present-time problem, is clinical and can be destructive to the theater reality and artistic detachment; in spontaneous selection, the intuitive gives us past experiences organically as part of a total life process; can be used by a director as a *device* (when nothing else works) for getting a mood or quality; bringing back a past memory through manipulation; related to psycho-drama.

RELATIONSHIP: Contact with fellow players; playing; a mutual involvement with an object; relationship grows out of object-involvement; allows players the privacy of personal feeling while playing together; prevents intrusion or meddling.

RESISTANCE: Manipulation of Where, Who, What; unwillingness to understand and/or explore the POC; indicated by jokes, playwriting, clowning, withdrawal, "acting"; fear of changing in any way; resistance is held or bottled-up energy; when resistance is broken, a new experience takes place.

RESPECT: Recognition of another; to *know* one another.

RIGIDITY: Held in; inability to alter one's point of view; inability to see another's point of view; armored against contact with others; armored against ideas other than on.'s own; fear of contact.

ROCKING THE BOAT: Unbalanced stage; refers to self-blocking; "You're rocking the boat!"; a term for very young actors in teaching them self-blocking.

ROLE-PLAYING: As opposed to playing a role; imposing a character as opposed to creating a role out of the problem; psycho-drama; dramatic play; artificial imposition of character on self as opposed to allowing natural growth to evolve out of relationship; subjective response to "what is a character"; using a character to hide behind; a mask keeping one from exposure; withdrawal; solo performance.

RULES OF THE GAME: Includes the structure (Where, Who and What) and the object (POC) plus group agreement.

SCENE: An event that grows out of the POC; the results of playing; a fragment; a moment in the lives of people needing no beginning, middle, or end; biography or statistics; the scene is the game coming out of the rules; playing is the process out of which the scene evolves by involvement with an object (POC) and relationship with fellow players.

SEASONING THE ACTOR: Integrating all parts of the whole (theater techniques, playing, showing, etc.); releasing ability to meet all crises with certainty; making one's self comfortable in the stage environment.

SECOND CITY: A theater-club with professional actors doing performances based on improvisation.

SEEING: Seeing (objective) as opposed to believing (subjective); a term used as opposed to imagining or pretending; "See it!"; part of the sensory equipment; to see so you can show; to let the audience see a play as in a game; skillful playing; to look; seeing the phenomenal world and *seeing* it; seeing as opposed to staring; looking and seeing as opposed to pretending to look and thus staring; "If you see it, we (the audience) see it!"

SEEING THE WORD: The physical reality of consonants and vowels; the visualization brought up by a word; a sensory contact with words; the design and shape of sounds.

SELF: Refers to the natural part of ourselves; free of crippling mores, prejudices, rote information, and static frames of reference; that part of us capable of direct contact with the environment; that which is our own nature; the part of ourselves that functions free of the need for approval/disapproval; cutting through make-up, costume, rags, mannerisms, character, junk jewelry, etc., that make up the covering (survival clothes) of self; self must be found before one can play; playing helps find self. Right brain; X-area.

SELF-IDENTITY: Having one's own place and allowing others theirs; securely placed within an environment; where you are is where *you* are.

SENSORY: Body and mind; to see, taste, hear, feel, think, perceive; to know through the physical as opposed to the intuitive.

SET PIECES: Random furniture, blocks, props used to make the Where.

SHARE WITH YOUR AUDIENCE: Brings harmony and relationship betwen players and audience; making audience "part of the game"; used in side coaching to develop self-blocking; the same as rocking the boat used for very young actors; "Share your voice! Share the stage picture! Share yourself!"; used from the first workshop to accomplish self-blocking and voice projection; removes need for labels; develops ability to see the outside view of the stage while inside of it.

SHOWING: Physicalizing objects, involvements, and relationships as opposed to verbalizing (telling); spontaneous experience; the actor brings his creation or invention into the phenomenal world by showing it; physicalizing.

SIDE COACHING: An assist given by teacher-director as fellow player to the student-actor during the solving of a problem to help him keep focus; a means of giving a student-actor himself within the theater environment; a message to the total organism; a support in helping players to explore the emerging plays.

SIGHT-LINES: The clarity of vision of an *individual* in the audience to every single *individual* at work on stage.

SITUATION: A Where, Who, What, and Why which becomes the structure for a scene; the framework (skeleton play) in which problem is placed; the situation is not the problem; if not understood, situation will fall into "playing the story."

SKELETON PLAY: A set form from which improvisation is used; a scenario; a way of building an improvised play; a series of beats/scenes which must be filled in by the players; a situation or series of situations.

SPACE: Something about which we know very little; the stage area where a reality can be placed; space can be used to shape the realities we create; an area of no boundaries; without limits; the player uses space to bring reality into the phenomenal world; to make space for the object; the larger environment; the space beyond; a place to perceive or receive a communication.

SPONTANEITY: A moment of explosion; a free moment of self-expression.

SPONTANEOUS SELECTION: Selecting that which is appropriate to the problem without calculation; a spontaneous choice of alternatives at a moment of crisis; since theater is a series of crises, spontaneous selection should be working all the time; selecting out of the "explosion" that which is *immediately* useful; balanced working of the intuitive and the intellect; insight.

STAGE BUSINESS: A stage activity used to implement, accent, intensify, or heighten; the manner in which one plays the objects in the environment; the way the "ball" is kept bouncing; stage business grows out of involvement with objects and relationship with fellow actors; GIBBERISH is a special exercise useful to this point.

STAGE FRIGHT: The fear of disapproval or indifference; separation of audience and actors, placing audience as viewers or judges; fear of exposure; when audience is "part of the game," stage fright leaves.

STARING: A curtain in front of the eyes to prevent contact with others; playing for one's self only; a self-protective wall; "See us!"

STATIC: A held moment having what has happened and what will and/or may happen within it; crises.

STATISTICS: Giving audience and fellow players facts, information, and/or biographies about each other; telling, not showing; expressing a character verbally; using facts, past information, etc., instead of improvising and letting the character come forth; "No facts, no information, no biographies. Show us!"

STORY: A story is an epitaph; the ashes of the fire; story is the result (residue) of a process; improvisational theater is process; for story (play) to live, it must be broken down into its separate parts or beats (disassembled) to become process again; a well-written play is process.

STRUCTURE: The Where, Who, and What; the field on which the game is played.

STUDENT'S PROGRESS: Any distance a person has traveled from his starting point.

SUBJECTIVE: Self-involved; inability to contact the environment and let it show itself; difficulty in playing with others; defensiveness which makes it difficult to understand how to play the game.

SUGGESTIONS BY THE AUDIENCE: A primitive audience involvement; overtly making audience part of the game.

SURVIVAL CLOTHES: Behaviorisms, mannerisms, dress, I.Q., affectations, makeup, personality traits, frames of reference, prejudices, body distortions, opportunism used to protect ourselves in living; must be seen for what they are to be freed for the learning process; status.

TEACHER-DIRECTOR: Teacher works for the students (unblocking etc.), director works for the over-all stage; presents problems for both the individual experience and the stage experience.

TELLING: Verbalizing the involvements, Where, etc. of a situation rather than creating a reality and showing or allowing the scene to emerge through physical attitudes, relationships, etc.; inaction; non-playing; results of telling are ad-libbing, playwriting, manipulation; imposing self on object, not letting object move self; "acting."

THEATER REALITY: Agreed reality; any reality the players choose to create; total freedom in creating a reality; giving life to a created reality; allowing space for a created reality.

THEME: The moving thread (life) that weaves itself into every beat of the play and unifies all the elements in the production.

TIMING: Ability to handle the multiple stimuli going on within the theater activity.

TRANSFORMATION: Creation; momentarily breaks through isolation, and actors and audience alike receive (ahhh!) the appearance of a new reality (theater magic); improvisation.

TRUSTING THE SCHEME: Letting go and giving one's self to playing.

TWO-WAY PROBLEM: Gives focus to the intellect and thus preoccupies the actor so as to remove any inhibiting or censoring mechanisms that keep him from playing; blanks the mind; "I didn't know what I was saying"; preoccupation/occupation; releases intuitive levels of new energy.

VERBALIZATION: Players telling the audience about the Where and the character relationships rather than showing;

teacher-director giving *his* knowledge to the students; excessive verbalization of subject matter; suggests egocentricity and/or exhibitionism; excessive verbalization on the part of student-actor is mistrust of self-ability to show; a cover-up; teaching through words as opposed to allowing student-actor to experience; teaching swimming verbally without allowing anyone in the water.

VISUALIZATION (IMAGE): The deliberate use of an existing form (animate or inanimate) to aid in creating a character or a dramatic moment; evoking stimuli for a character or feeling through a device outside of the scene involvement. Not recommended.

WATCHER: A constant "eye" upon us; a restrictive control; one who judges; approval/disapproval; fear of the "eye" keeps self hidden from fresh experience and brings forth a "dummy" self through posturing, delinquency, apathy, stupidity, wordiness; "a watched pot never boils."

WHAT: A mutual activity between actors, existing within the Where; a reason for being somewhere: "What are you doing there?"; part of the structure.

WHERE: Physical objects existing within the environment of a scene or activity; the immediate environment; the general environment; the larger environment (beyond); part of the structure.

WHO: The people within the Where; "Who are you?"; "What is your relationship?"; part of the structure.

WORDS: Gibberish, chatter; verbalizing for lack of action; "Just words!"; playwriting; words as opposed to dialogue; words "in place of"; keeps self hidden.

Recommended Game Books

All the following books are published by the H. T. FitzSimons Co. of Chicago. The second, third, and fourth volumes are especially useful in working with children up to the age of eleven or so. The simple folk games and songs can easily be learned by any teacher, and the material is packed with dramatic stories in song and dance. These books have been listed because they are drawn from folk material and presented in such a way as to preserve the spirit of play.

Neva L. Boyd and Anna Spacek. *Folk Dances of Bohemia and Moravia.*

Neva L. Boyd and Dagny Pederson. *Folk Games of Denmark and Sweden.*

———. *Folk Games and Gymnastic Play.*

Neva L. Boyd. *Handbook of Games.*

———. *Hospital and Bedside Games.*